Flannery O'Connor and Cold War Culture offers a radically new reading of O'Connor, who is known primarily as the creator of "universal" religious dramas. By recovering the historical context in which O'Connor wrote her fiction, Jon Lance Bacon reveals an artist deeply concerned with the issues that engaged other producers of American culture from the 1940s to the 1960s: national identity, political anxiety, and intellectual freedom. Bacon takes an interdisciplinary approach, relating the stories and novels to political texts and sociological studies, as well as films, television programs, paintings, advertisements, editorial cartoons, and comic books. At a time when national paranoia ran high, O'Connor joined in the public discussion regarding a way of life that seemed threatened from outside – the American way of life. The discussion tended toward celebration, but O'Connor raised doubts about the quality of life within the United States. Specifically, she attacked the consumerism that cold warriors cited as evidence of American cultural superiority. The role of dissenter appealed greatly to O'Connor, and her identity as a Southern, Catholic writer – the very identity that has discouraged critics from considering her as an American writer – furnished a position from which to criticize the Cold War consensus.

D1203377

CAMBRIDGE STUDIES IN AMERICAN LITERATURE AND CULTURE

Flannery O'Connor and Cold War Culture

CAMBRIDGE STUDIES IN AMERICAN LITERATURE AND CULTURE

Books in the series

Continued on pages following the Index

Flannery O'Connor
and Cold War Culture

JON LANCE BACON

CAMBRIDGE
UNIVERSITY PRESS

PUBLISHED BY THE PRESS SYNDICATE OF THE UNIVERSITY OF CAMBRIDGE
The Pitt Building, Trumpington Street, Cambridge, United Kingdom

CAMBRIDGE UNIVERSITY PRESS
The Edinburgh Building, Cambridge CB2 2RU, UK
40 West 20th Street, New York NY 10011–4211, USA
477 Williamstown Road, Port Melbourne, VIC 3207, Australia
Ruiz de Alarcón 13, 28014 Madrid, Spain
Dock House, The Waterfront, Cape Town 8001, South Africa

http://www.cambridge.org

First published 1993
First paperback edition 2005

A catalogue record for this book is available from the British Library

Library of Congress Cataloguing-in-Publication Data
Bacon, Jon Lance.
Flannery O'Connor and Cold War culture / Jon Lance Bacon.
p.   cm. – (Cambridge studies in American literature and
culture ; 72)
Includes index.
ISBN 0 521 44529 9 (hardback)
1. O'Connor, Flannery – Political and social views.   2. Literature
and society – United States – History – 20th century.   3. Social
problems in literature.   4. Cold War in literature.   I. Title.
II.   Series.
PS3565.C57Z57   1994
813′.54 – dc20   93-18947
                                                                    CIP

ISBN 0 521 44529 9 hardback
ISBN 0 521 61980 7 paperback

Contents

Acknowledgments

Of the many people who contributed to this study, Cecelia Tichi merits a special expression of gratitude. As a teacher, as a dissertation director, as a colleague, she has influenced my scholarship enormously. I thank her for the assistance, advice, and encouragement she has given me – and for the example her own scholarly work has provided.

I also thank the other members of my dissertation committee: Jay Clayton, who helped me define my critical approach and alerted me to works that proved crucial; Sam Girgus and Michael Bess, both of whom offered valuable comments regarding the focus of my argument; and Michael Kreyling, whose observations during my doctoral examination inspired the fourth chapter.

I am grateful to Vivien Fryd for her thoughtful critique of those passages dealing with visual art. Fred Ashe, David Bartlett, Ken Cooper, and Lee Meier also shared their expertise in their various fields, and Nancy Blomgren provided a sounding board for my ideas. I thank them all.

My study has benefited greatly from the suggestions offered by Eric Sundquist. For guiding me through my first encounter with the publishing world, Julie Greenblatt and Clare Payton at Cambridge University Press have my deepest gratitude. I also consider myself fortunate to have worked with Mary Racine, whose enthusiasm buoyed me through the production process.

For their assistance with the illustrations, I am indebted to Jamie Adams, Lynn Schrader Anderson, Ken Beck, Cecil Bentley, Wendy Gaines Bucci, Kimberly Cody, Jan Constantine, Wanda Corn, Mary Doherty, Angela Dyson, John Fitzpatrick, James W. Goodrich, Thomas D. Grischkowsky, Debra Gust, David R. Haarz, Jill Johnston, Melissa Kroning, Ellen Kutcher, Kathy Lendech, Elise McMillan, Julie Mendoza, Larry K. Mensching, Jim Peele, Steven C. Pettinga, Lieschen Potuznik, Marian Powers, Ed Renfro, Jean J. Rickard, Annemarie Robins, Christine Schiller, Vanessa Simmons, Craig Smith, Fae Sotham, Daisy

vii

Stroud, Rob Walker, Suzanne Warner, Leslie Werner, and Cécile Whiting. I am particularly grateful to Dale Manning and the staff of the Jean and Alexander Heard Library.

For his generous assistance at the eleventh hour, I thank Stephen Cox.

The completion of this project makes me think of beginnings. In this regard, Larry Frank deserves recognition as my first mentor in literary studies. And, above all, my thanks go to my parents, Keith and Mary Bacon, for the support they have shown over the years. My debt to them, and to Connie, Kent, and Brenda Bacon, is immeasurable.

Abbreviations

C   *The Correspondence of Flannery O'Connor and the Brainard Cheneys*, ed. C. Ralph Stephens (Jackson: University Press of Mississippi, 1986)

CS   Flannery O'Connor, *The Complete Stories* (New York: Farrar, Straus & Giroux, 1971)

CW   Flannery O'Connor, *Collected Works,* ed. Sally Fitzgerald (New York: Library of America, 1988)

HB   Flannery O'Connor, *The Habit of Being,* ed. Sally Fitzgerald (New York: Farrar, Straus & Giroux, 1979)

MM   Flannery O'Connor, *Mystery and Manners,* ed. Sally Fitzgerald and Robert Fitzgerald (New York: Farrar, Straus & Giroux, 1969)

PG   *The Presence of Grace and Other Book Reviews by Flannery O'Connor,* comp. Leo J. Zuber, ed. Carter W. Martin (Athens: University of Georgia Press, 1983)

VBA   Flannery O'Connor, *The Violent Bear It Away* (New York: Farrar, Straus & Giroux, 1960)

WB   Flannery O'Connor, *Wise Blood,* 2d ed. (New York: Farrar, Straus & Giroux, 1962)

Introduction

In September 1960 the small town of Milledgeville, Georgia, offered
visiting reporters a choice of celebrities. One reporter came to interview
Flannery O'Connor, whom he ranked among "the most highly regarded
of younger American writers." As her visitor noted, O'Connor had
already received major literary honors, including the O. Henry Award,
by 1960. The other reporters came to interview Barbara Powers, who
had gained a different sort of fame that year. Her husband, the pilot
Francis Gary Powers, had been shot down over the Soviet Union in May.
His capture gave Soviet premier Nikita Khrushchev an opportunity to
denounce "American militarists" and to refute their "clumsy inventions"
regarding the U-2 flown by Powers. After Khrushchev revealed that
Powers had survived the crash, U.S. president Dwight Eisenhower admitted that the U-2 was not a weather observation plane, as the government had originally claimed, but a spy plane. The incident doomed a
May summit conference to failure; for Powers himself, it led to an espionage conviction in August. Barbara Powers had just returned from his
trial in Moscow when reporters sought her out at her mother's home in
Milledgeville.[1]

I start with this odd conjunction – between a literary figure known for
staging "universal dramas" in rural Georgia[2] and an accidental celebrity
who came to public attention because of international political events –
to suggest a radically new context in which to consider the work of
Flannery O'Connor. That context is the Cold War. By treating Milledgeville as a site with meaning for historians of the Cold War, I stress
the historical contingency of O'Connor's fiction. She completed a preliminary draft of her first novel in 1950, the year that President Harry S.
Truman sent U.S. troops to Korea; the week in which she died, while
preparing her second collection of short stories, was the week in which
President Lyndon Johnson began ordering air strikes against North Viet-

I

nam. These military actions, like the U-2 incident, grew out of the diplomatic rivalry between the United States and the Soviet Union.

Among scholars, the term "Cold War" refers primarily to this rivalry – which came to mean a bipolar division of the world, as the superpowers established their spheres of influence and their nuclear arsenals. In a long-standing debate, historians have tried to assign responsibility for the course of diplomatic relations after World War II.[3] Political scientists have also concerned themselves with the rivalry between the superpowers, addressing the stability or instability of a bipolar system founded on nuclear deterrence.

But students of the Cold War do not necessarily emphasize diplomatic and military events. Focusing on the perceptions shared by policymakers and the U.S. public, many treat the Cold War as an ideological construct that has explained and guided such events. To media scholars, for instance, "it has been largely a communications phenomenon wherein the 'war' was carried out in activities variously called public information, propaganda, or disinformation."[4] As a framework in which specific incidents "made sense," the Cold War affected subsequent decision making and helped to determine the course of the geopolitical rivalry. This is the framework identified by Todd Gitlin – whose scholarship brings together cultural history and media studies – when he refers to "the entire cycle of action and reaction which is the Cold War, the dominating narrative of our epoch."[5]

The concept of "narrative" opens up the Cold War to those scholars whose chief concern is the literary text. The symbolic order imposed on international relations by a clearly defined, morally charged conflict lends itself to literary study. To demonstrate the imaginative power of this ordering, I read the Cold War as a text in relation to other texts.[6] Such an approach does not diminish the gravity of actual events. I do not deny the reality of the conflict in which pilots were shot down and defectors were shot. I simply maintain that politics and war can be described as Alton Becker, a comparative linguist, describes them: as "areas of knowledge in which text-building . . . is a central activity."[7] I suggest, in other words, that many of the actions essential to the construction of the Cold War narrative were *expressive* acts.

As a narrative, the Cold War not only influenced foreign policy, but also informed the thinking of Americans remote from the policy-making process. The Cold War served as a point of reference for writers on issues that were unrelated, or related only tangentially, to the conflict between the superpowers. Not surprisingly, the narrative employed by the U.S. government to justify military buildup and political orthodoxy entered into discussions of national identity. At the same time, however, the

Cold War figured in discussions of regional and religious identity, consumerist values, even literary standards.

If an intertextual approach shows the pervasiveness of the Cold War narrative in American culture, it also sheds new light on the literary narratives that O'Connor created. Through her fiction, O'Connor expressed her misgivings about a culture so dominated by one political worldview. She concerned herself, as a writer, with the cultural effects of the political narrative – not with the actual conflict between the United States and the Soviet Union. She offered no commentary on the course of their diplomatic and military rivalry. Her correspondence, to be sure, includes scattered references to major participants and incidents in the geopolitical conflict, such as "Uncle Joe" Stalin and the launching of *Sputnik*, the "Russian moon," in 1957 (*HB* 46, 246). Her fiction, however, focuses on the cultural climate promoted by the anxiety that Stalin and *Sputnik* could elicit.

O'Connor dramatized "the combination of fright and self-righteousness" that sociologist David Riesman attributed to many Americans during the Cold War.[8] Her works reveal her familiarity with the imaginative structures by which fiction writers, among others, gave form to the national anxiety over Soviet aggression. One such structure was the invasion scenario, which helped to shape her treatment of two privileged settings in American culture, the pastoral and the domestic. O'Connor joined in the public discussion regarding a way of life that seemed threatened from outside – the American way of life, as embodied by these settings. The discussion tended, for the most part, toward celebration; O'Connor was one of the few to break with the consensus and criticize U.S. society. She called attention to the discrepancy between an idealized "American way," which politicians cited frequently as evidence of U.S. cultural superiority, and the social realities produced by this merger of politics and culture.[9]

From her perspective, the celebration of the American way had a detrimental effect on intellectual activity. In a propaganda war over rival ways of life – American versus Soviet – the personal intentions behind creative and critical expression could easily be subordinated to political ends. O'Connor knew she could be drafted, as a writer, by either side. For this reason, she refused to allow the sale of her work to Polish and Czech publishers in 1956 (*CW* 1249). "I've written them to drop the matter of publication . . . in any Russian-occupied country," she told her editor at Harcourt, Brace and Company. "They would probably use The Misfit to represent the Typical American Business Man" (*HB* 151).

Although she worried about the integrity of American intellectual life during the Cold War era, O'Connor was no friend of the radical Left.

She raised no objections when she learned in 1949 that the Federal Bureau of Investigation had been scrutinizing Yaddo, the artists' colony where she was in residence, because a Marxist journalist had enjoyed a lengthy stay there. Indeed, O'Connor felt that the executive director had threatened the reputation of the colony by giving the journalist special treatment. "I definitely won't be coming back to Yaddo," she wrote at the time, "unless certain measures go into effect here" (*HB* 11).

Her commitment to political dissent stopped short of tolerance for Americans who openly supported Communist causes,[10] but it sufficed to make O'Connor vulnerable to the charge of political subversiveness. After all, she criticized the American way at a time when the only alternative seemed to be Russian totalitarianism. The mere suggestion that such a dichotomy was false could be politically risky. O'Connor took that risk. Despite her aversion to Communism, O'Connor refused to ignore problems at home. "The Communist world," she wrote in 1961, "sprouts from our sins of omission" (*HB* 450). The need for dissent, which American "sins" demonstrated, outweighed the risk that a dissenter would have to take.

As an analyst of the cultural climate in the United States, O'Connor was also attentive to a fear more basic than the fear of political censure: the dread occasioned by the mixture of "nuclear fission and the Cold War" (*HB* 87). In 1961 she and her mother considered building a fallout shelter on their property; "at night," she wrote, "I dream of radiated bulls and peacocks and swans" (*HB* 449). In a 1949 letter, O'Connor expressed curiosity about Los Alamos, New Mexico, where scientists had produced the first atomic device. "Was Los Alamos a place before the bomb?" she asked her correspondent, who had taken a job there. "I should think you would have definite sensations about living in a place completely Post Bomb" (*HB* 18). O'Connor lived in a nation that was "Post Bomb" in its thinking. Ihab Hassan suggested as much in 1961 when he described the culture that had produced the contemporary American novel. *Radical Innocence,* one of the first book-length studies to include O'Connor among major new writers, opened with a sketch of the cultural drama in which these writers participated, "the melodrama of fission and fusion, of grim threats and endless lamentation."

Hassan said nothing more specific about this link between the collective experience of Americans, apprehending "a war we dare not call by any name,"[11] and the fiction of O'Connor. He concentrated, instead, on the religious themes in her work. And most of her interpreters since the 1960s have agreed with the idea, articulated by Miles Orvell, that it is a mistake "to read Flannery O'Connor on a chiefly political or social level."[12] A political context did seem appropriate to a critic writing on O'Connor in 1971, at the height of the Vietnam War – the conflict described by Gitlin as "a real war fought in the name of the rock-bottom principles of Cold War liberalism."[13] The critic, Marion Montgomery, likened her concerns to those of the New Left, or, more precisely, the "new revolutionaries" who opposed war in Vietnam as well as consumerism at home. Instead of politicizing O'Connor, however, this comparison allowed Montgomery to spiritualize the leftist protesters: "While refusing to be cannon fodder physically in an Asian war, they sacrifice themselves on the intellectual battleground of a larger war which has raged over man's proper role in the world since our first fall from grace."[14] To Montgomery, a political context merely supplied evidence of an eternal, unchanging truth.

This has been the general tendency in O'Connor criticism: assigning priority to the "universal" religious themes with which her stories of the Bible Belt resonate. Although some critics have discussed her work in different terms – feminist, Lacanian, Bakhtinian – theological issues continue to dominate O'Connor studies.[15] Even the debate initiated by John Hawkes, the debate over her membership in "the Devil's party" (HB 449), has reinforced this tendency.[16] Wherever they stand on the question of her orthodoxy, critics tend to emulate what O'Connor called "my other-worldly attitude" (C 26).

My interest lies elsewhere – in the process by which a particular historical moment could shape the expression of perennial human concerns. By recovering the political dimensions of O'Connor's work, I am able to show the centrality of her writings in the literary history of postwar America. More than any other writer, O'Connor needs to be repositioned in that history. The theological approach has deepened our understanding of O'Connor, but it has also excluded her from most analyses of American fiction that turn on social and political issues.[17] Even as they have praised her imaginative power, her admirers have marginalized O'Connor.

There is no disputing her prominence in postwar literary history. Her works, anthologized soon after their initial publication, have gained canonical status quickly. Her application of New Critical precepts, the precepts that governed most American literary criticism during her career in the two decades after World War II, brought O'Connor such influential patrons as Cleanth Brooks and Robert Penn Warren. The 1959 edition of Understanding Fiction, the Brooks and Warren anthology from which O'Connor learned New Critical technique, reprinted one of her short stories, "A Good Man Is Hard to Find." In 1988 her works joined those of Hawthorne, Melville, and James in the Library of America series. Frederick Crews has described her inclusion in the series as "the closest thing to a formal canonization that our dispersed and eclectic culture can now bestow."[18]

Still, in his essay on the publication of O'Connor's *Collected Works,*
Crews called for a reevaluation of her literary stature. Crews had good
reason to reopen the question. The O'Connor who appears in the an-
thologies, and in the syllabi of American survey courses, remains something of a local "character." Her prominence is that of a talented misfit, a
literary curiosity. The traditional emphasis on the Catholic aspects of her
work has shaped her image as a writer oblivious to issues other than
spiritual salvation or the religious nature of the South, the "Christ-
haunted" region in which she lived (*MM* 44). Granted, critics are fully
justified in addressing what O'Connor identified as the "two circumstances that have given character to my own writing . . . being Southern
and being Catholic" (*MM* 196). For too long, however, critics have
disregarded her admonitions against critical efforts that truncate the cultural context in which a literary work is produced. "Catholic discussions
of novels by Catholics are frequently ridiculous," she wrote in 1963,
"because every given circumstance of the writer is ignored except his
Faith" (*MM* 195). It is time to recover her historical circumstances.

Critics have usually equated her Church with its "catholic" system of
belief, treating Catholicism as a body of doctrine that transcends time
and place. I argue, by contrast, that an American Catholic writing for
publication during the Cold War participated in a history both political
and religious. O'Connor would object, no doubt, to the fact that I stress
politics over theology. "If you're a Catholic," she told a correspondent in
1955, "you believe what the Church teaches and the climate makes no
difference" (*HB* 103). My readings in the social history of Christianity
have convinced me otherwise.[19] One of the fundamental assumptions of
my study is the conviction that any attempt to separate religious ideals
from political realities is misguided, suggesting not so much the tran-
scendental purity of Christian faith as its irrelevance to contemporary
life. O'Connor herself acknowledged the worldly considerations of those
who ran the Catholic Church. In a 1959 letter, O'Connor discussed the
Church as a political entity: "She seems always to be either on the wrong
side politically or simply a couple of hundred years behind the world in
her political thinking. She tries to get along with any form of government that does not set itself up as a religion" (*HB* 347). In the United
States, O'Connor well knew, Church leaders like Francis Cardinal Spellman allied themselves publicly with anti-Communist politicians (*HB*
262). Moreover, the secular goals of the Church weighed heavily on the
minds of many political commentators during the 1940s and 1950s. Like
them, O'Connor deliberated the institutional role of the Church in U.S.
society. When the subject of this role arises in her fiction, the beliefs
shared by American Catholics collide with non-Catholic perceptions of
the Church.

Reconsidering O'Connor as a Catholic writer also means reconsidering her as a Southern writer. The national political concerns evident in
her fiction impinge on regional concerns. During the Cold War era, the
question of Southern regional identity was more than a question of
"mocking-birds and beaten biscuits and white columns" (*MM* 57). The
assertion of that identity, in the repeated attempts to resist federally
mandated integration, worked against national goals at a time when
national unity seemed essential. In a letter from October 1957, O'Connor noted that events within the region had distracted Southerners from a
turning point in the space race. She described the launching of *Sputnik* as
"light diversion" for those who seemed ready to "secede from the
Union" over efforts to integrate the races (*HB* 246).

My study will contribute to the reconception of Southern studies
going on today.[20] Part of that reconception is a new view of the relation
between history and literature. Although history has always been a key
term in Southern studies, it has traditionally been viewed as the privileged content of Southern literary works. Instead of treating literature as
a form of reflection on past historical events, I treat literary works as
events in themselves. I agree with Louis A. Montrose, who maintains
that literary works "make things happen by shaping the subjectivities of
social beings."[21] Because other cultural products contribute to this process, I relate the fiction of O'Connor to films, paintings, political speeches, Supreme Court decisions, sociological studies, advertising copy, television programs, and the illustrated narratives of comic books. In short,
my focus is interdisciplinary as well as intertextual.

Insofar as it unearths the connections between the popular culture of
the era and the literary art of a writer trained in New Criticism, my study
would hardly surprise O'Connor. She admired Marshall McLuhan, a
writer whose cross-cultural approach anticipates the cultural anthropol-
ogy of Clifford Geertz and the new historicist studies indebted to Geertz.
When a friend returned her copy of *The Mechanical Bride* (1951) after a
"quick perusal" in 1956, O'Connor advised her friend to read McLuhan's
book "completely and slowly" (*HB* 173).[22] One goal of *The Mechanical
Bride*, McLuhan wrote, was to show the interdependence of all those
who produce culture. McLuhan found in industrial culture "not just a
filtering down from high-brow to low-brow arts but equally a nourish-
ing of the esoteric by the popular. The few must depend on the many as
much as the many stand to gain from the few." He further contended,
"The great artist necessarily has his roots very deep in his own time –
roots which embrace the most vulgar and commonplace fantasies and
aspirations."[23] O'Connor is just such an artist, dramatizing the vulgar
and the commonplace; her greatness lies in the alternatives she proposes.

1

The Invaded Pastoral

When O'Connor depicts farm life in her short stories, one narrative pattern predominates. Someone or something enters the pastoral setting and disrupts or destroys the lives of its residents.[1] Her first collection, *A Good Man Is Hard to Find* (1955), includes four stories of invasion set on a farm. The role of invader goes to a confidence man in "Good Country People" and "The Life You Save May Be Your Own." In both stories, the intruder makes off with the daughter of the woman who owns the farm. "A Circle in the Fire" assigns the role to three juvenile delinquents from Atlanta. O'Connor develops the invasion motif more fully in "A Circle," where the significance of her trademark device, the dark "fortress wall" of trees, first becomes clear: it protects the internal status quo from the external threat (*CS* 176). At least, it is supposed to protect the way of life within its boundaries. In the farm stories, the wall is always penetrated; an alien reality always breaks through. "The Displaced Person" underscores the suggestion of an alien reality by making the invader a foreigner, a European who barely speaks English. In the second collection, *Everything That Rises Must Converge* (1965), the invaders are not even human. They range from the mechanical, the steam shovel in "A View of the Woods," to the animal, the bull in "Greenleaf." The setting of these stories is quite literally pastoral. The shovel destroys a cow pasture, while the intrusive bull threatens to ruin the breeding schedule devised for a herd of dairy cattle.

Of course, the pastoral setting in O'Connor's fiction owes a great deal to the landscape at Andalusia, the family farm near Milledgeville, Georgia. The reporter who visited the dairy farm in September 1960 noted "an extensive stand of timber" bordering "pasture-land for a herd of a hundred cattle."[2] But the fictional treatment of the pastoral involves far more than scenic description. In dramatizing the invasion of this setting, O'Connor adapted a scenario that pervaded American culture during her literary career. Its prototype was the Cold War narrative – the overarching conflict between the United States, the democratic nation that led the free world, and the Soviet Union, the totalitarian power that plotted to subvert ideologically the nation it could not conquer militarily.[3] The U.S. response to the threat of Soviet expansionism encouraged Americans to think in terms of invasion and subversion. Rejecting the isolationism that had characterized U.S. diplomacy before World War II, the federal government committed itself to the interventionist policy of "containment" in the late 1940s; the United States would take action abroad, whenever necessary, to prevent the spread of Communism. The idea of containment dominated not only foreign affairs, but also domestic politics.[4] The possibility that Communism was spreading at home as well as abroad generated much of the anxiety experienced by Americans during the period of the Cold War. The House Committee on Un-American Activities and the Senate Internal Security Subcommittee, under the direction of Joseph R. McCarthy, played on this anxiety. They were fighting Communist infiltration, they claimed, by exposing party members and sympathizers in public life.

The American Legion, one of several powerful organizations supporting McCarthy, informed its members in 1955 that Communism was making inroads into the agricultural setting via *The Southern Farm and Home,* which published "party line editorials."[5] The notion that the Communists had specifically targeted U.S. farmers for political indoctrination never gained much credence. Nonetheless, the agrarian setting had tremendous symbolic value during the Cold War: it functioned as a synecdoche for the United States. Rural life, in other words, was identified with the American way of life. In this respect, the scenario of the invaded pastoral represented a subspecies of the Cold War narrative – one that gained symbolic weight from nostalgia as well as anxiety. With their government committed to the containment of Soviet expansion, Americans could find the security of national isolation only in the past – when it seemed possible for the United States to resist involvement in the affairs of other countries and remain impregnable to outside forces, whether military or ideological. In postwar culture, the pastoral setting symbolized this lost isolation.

The invaded pastoral appeared in a variety of texts, exemplifying various forms of discourse. O'Connor described in literary narratives what others sensationalized in visual narratives, including films and comic books, or analyzed in scholarly studies. The fiction writer with a graduate degree from the University of Iowa would be less surprised to discover herself in the company of academic scholars than to find herself grouped with the producers of popular culture – especially those who aimed their works at adolescent readers. But the simplistic dialogue and garish artwork of the comic books should not distract us from the story

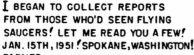

In the comic-book version of alien invasion, a farmer usually served as one of the first witnesses. "Down to Earth," *Weird Science,* vol. 1, no. 16. Copyright © 1952 by Fables Publishing Company, Inc. Copyright © renewed 1980 by William M. Gaines. Illustrator: Wallace Wood.

lines that incorporate the scenario of the invaded pastoral. The pastoral setting rivaled Washington, D.C., as the favored site of alien invasion in two of the most popular science fiction comics, *Weird Science* and *Weird Fantasy.* The invader in "The Green Thing!" attacks a farm, for example, after its spaceship crash-lands "over the crest of the south pasture."[6]

The story by O'Connor that features an intrusive bull, "Greenleaf" (1956), bears a remarkable number of structural similarities to a story published in *Weird Science.* "It Was the Monster from the Fourth Dimension" (1951) also concerns the invasion of a dairy farm. The first panel of the comic-book narrative shows the invader at the boundary of the property, coming over a wooden fence. The invader is nonhuman, a hovering blob, "an oozing, quivering, raw, flesh-colored mass," which consumes its first victim, a cow, wholly and instantly.[7] "Greenleaf" likewise connects the invasion from outside with the consumption of those living inside. Mrs. May, sleeping in her farmhouse while the scrub bull chews the shrubbery under her bedroom window, dreams of being devoured by "something" unspecified:

> She had been aware that whatever it was had been eating as long as she had had the place and had eaten everything from the beginning of her fence line up to the house and now was eating the house and calmly with the same steady rhythm would continue through the house, eating her and the boys. (*CS* 311–12)

HANK, THE HIRED HAND, SPED ACROSS THE FARM-
YARD TOWARD THE HOUSE! THE SILVERY OBJECT DIS-
APPEARED OVER THE CREST OF THE SOUTH PASTURE AND
SANK FROM VIEW! SUDDENLY, THE GREY SKY WAS RUP-
TURED BY A FLAMING ORANGE GLOW...

"The Green Thing!" *Weird Fantasy*, vol. 1, no. 16. Copyright © 1952 by I. C. Publishing Company, Inc. Copyright © renewed 1980 by William M. Gaines. Illustrator: Joe Orlando.

"It Was the Monster from the Fourth Dimension," *Weird Science*, vol. 1, no. 7. Copyright © 1951 by Fables Publishing Company, Inc. Copyright © renewed 1979 by William M. Gaines. Illustrator: Al Feldstein.

As the house fails to protect Mrs. May from the threat in her dream, so the barn provides no adequate shelter for Hank, the narrator of "It Was the Monster." Hank slips out the back just before the blob breaks down the front door and leaves the barn "all battered and smashed."[8]

The works differ thematically, of course. Mrs. May's anxieties, as manifested in her dream, concern the potential subversion of the social hierarchy on which she has based her identity. The "scrub-human" Greenleafs, whose rise into "*Society*" she predicts with disgust, are identified with the dream threat; they alone survive the general destruction of the May farm (CS 312, 317, 318). While O'Connor addresses social issues, using them as a springboard for religious themes, "It Was the Monster" explores questions of physics, or pseudophysics, as these relate to physical survival. Nevertheless, the two works define the sides in the central conflict in similar ways. Both protagonists seek assistance in defeating the invader. Mrs. May forces Mr. Greenleaf, her hired man, to kill the bull; Hank recruits his brother, Willy, to destroy the monster. In both works, the invader is associated with a reality alien to that of the protagonist. The bull violates Mrs. May's notion of "what *Reality* is," namely, the events over which she claims control (CS 320). Willy, "a scientist or something," tells his brother that the monster is really only a segment of a creature from the fourth dimension that has crossed over into our three-dimensional reality.[9]

Both works end with the death of the person who has been confronted directly with the alternative reality. The bull gores Mrs. May, disproving her belief that "I'll die when I get good and ready" (CS 321), and Willy dies when he travels into the fourth dimension by means of a machine he has developed. Both endings withhold from the reader the exact nature of the experience with the "other" reality. O'Connor does not divulge the "last discovery" that Mrs. May seems to be whispering to the bull (CS 334). Hank never learns what Willy saw in the fourth dimension – never learns the reason for the look of "sheer horror" on his brother's face.[10]

Both works, moreover, end with the destruction of the invader. Mr. Greenleaf shoots the bull; Willy succeeds in killing the creature, which Hank then buries. Each conclusion, however, reveals a Pyrrhic victory. The way of life rooted in the farm setting – and represented by it – is permanently compromised. Now that Mrs. May is dead, nothing remains to prevent the changes she has feared: "Soon as I'm dead," she says of her sons, "they'll marry trash and bring it in here and ruin everything . . . everything I've done" (CS 315). In the last panel of the comic-book narrative, in a statement that combines wistful regret and black humor, Hank announces his plans to leave his farm: "Living there's become unbearable! The odor of the decaying corpse of the fourth-dimensional creature . . . seems to be by-passing the 'line' I drew around it! Smells something terrible!"[11] The pastoral setting has lost its integrity. It has not been restored to its original condition, before its violation.

During the 1950s, Hollywood offered a more optimistic version of the scenario evident in "Greenleaf" and "It Was the Monster." Insofar as their endings mix triumph with loss, the two stories conform to the pattern underlying the best-known, most generically uniform examples of the invasion scenario: the alien-invasion films. A critic has noted the ambivalence conveyed by the closing images of these films: "Though humanity defeats the invader, life can never be the same after the experience; that which humanity has understood as real is amended to include things heretofore understood as unreal." The implicit message is that of humility: "The genre presents a vision of humanity no longer alone in the cosmos."[12] Nevertheless, the filmmakers differ from O'Connor in suggesting that the victims of invasion can fully regain control over their world. If a perceptual change occurs, humanity typically retains ownership of its territory in the invasion films. *Earth vs. the Flying Saucers* (1956) concludes with a vision, albeit tentative, of paradise regained. The scene that follows the destruction of the saucers in an urban setting, Washington, D.C., emphasizes the simplicity of physical existence in a natural setting, a pristine beach near Palm Springs. Dressed only in swimsuits, Dr. Russell Marvin (Hugh Marlowe) and his new wife, Carol (Joan Taylor), assume the roles of a prelapsarian Adam and Eve; they discuss the possibility of some future invasion but observe that they remain, for now, in possession of their world. "I'm glad it's still here," she remarks. "And still ours," he adds.[13] O'Connor undermines such confidence in "The Displaced Person" (1954), which also ends with the destruction of the foreign invader. The setting owned by the protagonist becomes less a paradise than a burden. When Mrs. McIntyre returns from the hospital, she sees that "the place would be too much for her to run now." Relinquishing her control, selling her cattle "at a loss," she retires "to live on what she had" (*CS* 235). She becomes an invalid, and the story leaves the reader with a sense of desolation.

One of the invasion films, *This Island Earth* (1955), locates the invasion in the very setting to which O'Connor returns in story after story: rural Georgia. An outpost has been established here, "thirty miles from nowhere," by alien scientists spearheading a mass migration. Other films of the genre present the rural countryside as the entry point for the invasion of U.S. society. The Martians in *The War of the Worlds* (1953) make their first landing outside a small town; later, a spaceship crashes into the farmhouse in which Dr. Clayton Forrester (Gene Barry) and Sylvia Van Buren (Ann Robinson) have sought refuge. In *The Blob* (1958), a backwoods farmer becomes the first victim of the invader. *Invasion of the Body*

Snatchers (1956) turns agriculture itself – the planting of seeds – into the means by which society will be subverted. Santa Mira, a town in the middle of a farming region, falls victim to "pods which have the power to reproduce themselves in the exact likeness of any form of life." One of the simulacra (Larry Gates) tells the remaining humans, Dr. Miles Bennell (Kevin McCarthy) and Becky Driscoll (Dana Wynter), that the invasion began when seeds from space "took root in a farmer's field." The invaders, having conquered Santa Mira by the end of the film, begin to extend their influence into large urban areas. When Miles runs onto the highway to escape his pursuers, he discovers a truck loaded with pods; the side of the truck announces its several destinations: Los Angeles, San Francisco, Portland, and Seattle. Similarly, in *The War of the Worlds,* the entry of the Martians into the rural California landscape will be followed by their attack on Los Angeles.[14]

Financial considerations may have dictated the use of rural locations in some of the invasion films; low budgets were the rule. But the choice that made sense in practical terms also made imaginative sense. The invasion of U.S. society would naturally begin in the setting identified with the "essential" America. This identification served as a guiding principle for the new academic discipline, American Studies, which came to prominence during the Cold War. Breaking with the New Critical "cult of pure literature,"[15] American Studies admitted popular culture into scholarly discourse. The visibility of the pastoral setting in the mass media of postwar America alerted scholars to its significance in literary works from the nineteenth century. The title of the book that marked the culmination of this trend in American Studies, *The Machine in the Garden* (1964), capsulizes the Cold War scenario of the invaded pastoral. The scholarly work, like the invasion films, associates "a reality alien to the pastoral dream" with technological power. *The Machine in the Garden* specifies industrial progress as "the counterforce in the American archetype of the pastoral design,"[16] while the films attribute a superior technology to the alien forces invading the pastoral. The critical presentation of episodes from nineteenth-century literature, such as "the steamboat bearing down on the raft" in *Huckleberry Finn* and "the train breaking in upon the idyll at Walden,"[17] has its counterpart in the cinematic presentation of spaceships entering the rural countryside.

The seminal texts of American Studies gave the pastoral setting a central position in national mythology. A critic observed in 1959, "The search for some single myth or hypothesis to explain American character and history has informed much of our recent criticism."[18] For Henry Nash Smith, Leo Marx, and R. W. B. Lewis, the pastoral ideal was this myth, basic to the American view of life. In *Virgin Land: The American West as Symbol and Myth,* Smith initiated the discussion regarding the image of an expanding agricultural society, "the Garden of the World," and the perception that it expressed "the assumptions and aspirations of a whole society." The agrarian myth, Smith wrote, "purported to set forth the character and destinies of the nation."[19] The year that *Virgin Land* was published, 1950, Marx completed the dissertation he would turn into *The Machine in the Garden*. In his 1964 book, Marx traced the emergence of the pastoral ideal "as a distinctively American theory of society." He described the ideal, which "has been used to define the meaning of America ever since the age of discovery," in the following terms:

> Beginning in Jefferson's time, the cardinal image of American aspirations was a rural landscape, a well-ordered green garden magnified to continental size. Although it probably shows a farmhouse or a neat white village, the scene usually is dominated by natural objects: in the foreground a pasture, a twisting brook with cattle grazing nearby, then a clump of elms on a rise in the middle distance and beyond that, way off on the western horizon, a line of dark hills. This is the countryside of the old Republic, a chaste, uncomplicated land of rural virtue.[20]

Lewis concentrated on the moral purity associated with the pastoral setting. In 1955 he argued that nineteenth-century Americans took their image of the "authentic American" from the biblical story of the Garden of Eden. He titled his book *The American Adam* after this "figure of heroic innocence and vast potentialities, poised at the start of a new history."[21]

Marx and Lewis followed Smith in noting the longevity of the pastoral ideal "as the accepted view of Western society." The myth persisted, Smith wrote, despite economic and technological changes in U.S. society:

> With the passage of time this symbol, like that of the Wild West, became in its turn a less and less accurate description of a society transformed by commerce and industry. . . . But the image of an agricultural paradise in the West, embodying group memories of an earlier, a simpler and, it was believed, a happier state of society, long survived as a force in American thought and politics. So powerful and vivid was the image that down to the very end of the nineteenth century it continued to seem a representation, in Whitman's words, of the core of the nation, "the real genuine America."[22]

In an essay published after *Virgin Land*, Smith noted the persistence of the image into his own time. "The West as an Image of the American Past," published in 1951, offers his analysis of a political cartoon that appeared the same year in the *Saturday Evening Post*. The cartoonist, Edmund Duffy, uses the standard Cold War imagery of rural setting and threatened invasion to depict Cold War hostilities. The landscape in the foreground includes a log cabin, pine trees, and the designation "U.S."

THESE RAMPARTS WE WATCH

Edmund Duffy, "These Ramparts We Watch," *Saturday Evening Post,* 20 Jan. 1951. Reprinted from *The Saturday Evening Post* © 1951.

The potential invader, dressed in the military uniform of a totalitarian regime, stares over a dark horizon line in the background. Returning this stare, across a body of water in the middle ground, is a figure looming over the cabin. Although his clothing identifies the American figure as an urban officeworker, "his roots," Smith observes, "are not defined by the skyline of a city or the smokestacks of a factory but by the conventional symbol of the agricultural frontier." The cartoonist, Smith concludes, proposes "that the meaning of our society is implicit in the cabin, or, in other words, that the essence of our institutions and our way of life is the frontier experience."[23]

For Lewis, the idea of pastoral innocence survived into the 1950s as a distrust of experience, whether motivated by "positive thinking" or by skeptical posturing. He related the Edenic myth to Cold War politics. "Ours is an age of containment," Lewis wrote, observing that "we huddle together and shore up defenses; both our literature and our public conduct suggest that exposure to experience is certain to be fatal."[24]

Smith's choice of cartoon and Lewis's use of the word "containment" make it clear that the perceived threat to the surviving pastoral ideal was now the Soviet Union. The threat took many forms in those popular works contemporaneous with the scholarship of Smith and Lewis. Whatever the form, however, the true identity of the invader was universally understood. The attack by creatures from outer space alluded to the quintessential invasion scenario of the 1950s, the Soviet plan to infiltrate and conquer the United States. Contemporary reviewers drew analogies between film plots and Communist plots. According to the critic who reviewed *Invasion of the Body Snatchers* at the time of its Italian release in 1957, "It is natural to see the pods as standing for the idea of communism which gradually takes possession of a normal person."[25] The filmmakers themselves could be fairly sly about the matter: the title of the movie that shared a double bill with *The Blob* in 1958, *I Married a Monster from Outer Space,* surely reminded audiences of the "red scare" film *I Married a Communist* (1949). In one of the earliest alien invasion films, *The Day the Earth Stood Still* (1951), the spaceman turns out to be peaceful; but a minor character, Mrs. Barley (Frances Bavier), hints that Klaatu (Michael Rennie) is in fact a Russian. "Well, if you want my opinion," she says, "he comes from right here on earth. And you know where I mean."[26]

Her meaning would not elude the characters who inhabit the pastoral setting in O'Connor's fiction. Fear of Soviet treachery is the psychological subtext in the stories O'Connor set on farms. "A Circle in the Fire" (1954) makes an explicit connection between the pastoral that has yet to be violated and the nation that has yet to succumb to Soviet aggression. Mrs. Cope, the owner of the farm in the story, says a daily "prayer of thanksgiving" for her "rich pastures." When she thinks about "all we have" in the pastoral setting (*CS* 177), Mrs. Cope associates that setting with American exceptionalism at a time of Cold War. She tells Mrs. Pritchard that "we ought to spend half our time on our knees" because, as Americans, they have been spared the suffering of national populations living under Soviet domination: "Why, think of all those poor Europeans . . . that they put in boxcars like cattle and rode them to Siberia" (*CS* 178). The advantages enjoyed by Mrs. Cope last only as long as the pastoral setting remains intact. Ultimately, the juvenile delinquents who invade her farm set fire to her woods.

The chief advantage of the pastoral setting, from the perspective of its fictional inhabitants, is the "rural virtue" identified by Marx. Characters like Mrs. Shortley in "The Displaced Person" (1954) believe that moral superiority depends on the continued integrity of the setting. An unquestioning faith in American innocence guides Mrs. Shortley, the farm wife who envisions herself as "a giant angel with wings as wide as a house," able to transcend the changes wrought by Mr. Guizac, the father of a family of European refugees, and "ten million billion" others like him (CS 200). Mrs. Shortley considers the United States morally superior to Europe, which she connects with newsreel footage of a Nazi concentration camp: "This was the kind of thing that was happening every day in Europe where they had not advanced as in this country." The Guizacs, the family whose name she gets wrong, seem to threaten American pastoral virtue: "Mrs. Shortley had the sudden intuition that the Gobblehooks, like rats with typhoid fleas, could have carried all those murderous ways over the water with them directly to this place" (CS 196). When Mr. Guizac smiles at her, "Europe stretched out in Mrs. Shortley's imagination, mysterious and evil, the devil's experiment station" (CS 205). The idea that "exposure to experience" is potentially fatal – the idea noted by Lewis when he connected Edenic isolation and Cold War containment – informs "The Displaced Person." Sure enough, a "great experience" (CS 214) proves to be the undoing of the woman who would have avoided experience. Mrs. Shortley suffers an attack that seems to bring her self-awareness even as it kills her.

Unlike Mrs. Cope, Mrs. Shortley never links the invasion with the Soviets. The threat she perceives is more general: the totalitarian threat to "a free country" (CS 204). Although she thinks in terms drawn from the Cold War rhetoric of disease,[27] she also represents a generation of Americans who had lived through two wars in which Germany was the enemy. Her husband fought the Germans in World War I, and images of Nazi atrocities haunt her imagination. As she suffers her fatal attack, Mrs. Shortley grabs at the limbs of her husband and daughter and hugs them to herself, thereby imitating the tangle of body parts she has seen in the newsreel of the concentration camp.

The Cold War narrative came into being when the Communists replaced the Nazis in the "political demonology" of Americans.[28] An essay published in early 1946 captures the moment at which the substitution occurred; to the essayist, nothing more than color distinguishes the "Red Fascism" of the Communists from the "Brown Fascism" of the Nazis.[29] Understood in the broader terms of totalitarianism versus freedom, the scenario of the invaded pastoral dates back to the early 1940s. One of Alfred Hitchcock's first Hollywood films, Saboteur (1942), features a Nazi espionage ring whose leader owns a ranch in the American West.[30] The year that Saboteur was released, Thomas Hart Benton painted the

Thomas Hart Benton, *Invasion*, 1942, oil on canvas, 48 × 78 in. State Historical Society of Missouri, Columbia.

prototypical image of the invaded pastoral. *Invasion,* one of eight paintings in his *Year of Peril* series, depicts the violation of the American rural landscape by foreign troops – a violation literalized in the rape of a woman near the center of the canvas. Benton equates the invasion of the countryside with the destruction of the family. As the woman struggles with her attackers, another soldier bayonets her farmer husband, or father; the younger members of the farm family lie dead or dying. Significantly, only the victims have faces that are fully visible. The soldiers, whose faces are hidden or cut off by their helmets, have no individual identity. Benton's composition suggests the centrality of the agricultural setting in terms of American identity. The primary target of the totalitarian invaders is the Midwestern farm, the site of the atrocities in the foreground, rather than the urban setting, whose Art Deco skyline appears in the distance, behind the slope of a hayfield.

The visual dominance of the farm connects Benton's wartime painting with the artistic movement that popularized a rural version of the "American Scene" in the decade before World War II. For all its propagandistic excess, *Invasion* reaffirms the values Benton had championed as a leading representative of regionalism. Among the regionalists, Grant Wood offered the most complete expression of these values; his Iowa

Grant Wood, *Stone City, Iowa*, 1930, oil on wood panel, 30¼ × 40 in. Joslyn Art Museum, Omaha, Nebraska.

landscapes suggest an ideal social order, similar to the one the Agrarians were then defending in the South. Order is the key to village life in *Stone City, Iowa* (1930), with its meticulous fields, pastures, and gardens. The near absence of human figures in Wood's painting suggests that the stability of the community derives as much from the natural setting as from human action. Wood's *Arbor Day* (1932) more explicitly links the maintenance of human culture with cultivation of the land: on the spotless lawn of a tidy white schoolhouse, located in an expanse of plowed fields, a teacher and her students plant a tree.[31] The regionalist painters of the Midwest, like the Agrarian writers of the South, founded their social vision on a right relation to nature.

Wood differed in one respect from the Southern Agrarians; while he typically depicted the imposition of human order on the natural world, they insisted on the contingency of nature.[32] Nevertheless, Wood's landscapes illustrate the Agrarian belief that the farmer who "identifies himself with a spot of ground" escapes "the dehumanization of his life" by industrial society.[33] Wood's artistic manifesto, published in 1935, high-

Grant Wood, *Spring Turning*, 1936, oil on masonite panel, 18¹/₈ × 40 in. Reynolda House, Museum of American Art, Winston-Salem, North Carolina.

lighted this idea. "Revolt Against the City" includes a poem about the envy that a farmer inspires in an urbanite; the speaker, who has "broken faith with field and pasture ground," listens eagerly when the farmer talks "of the things that happen where / The souls of men have kinship with the land."[34] *Spring Turning*, painted in 1936, depicts the envied harmony of nature and farmer – a harmony so great that rectangular clouds mirror the rectangles of plowed soil. The community idealized by Wood in a painting such as *Stone City, Iowa* is fully human, unlike industrial society, because of its location in a natural environment. Benton's *Invasion* makes the same point by withholding humanity from the invaders, whose tanks, guns, and planes ally them with industrialism.

Critics have long discussed the "sacramental" view of nature, rooted in Catholic theology, to which O'Connor gave literary expression.[35] "The River" (1953) supplies a clear example of the way in which O'Connor brings together the natural and the supernatural. Within her fictive world, "a pasture dotted here and there with black and white cows" leads to a site of religious significance – the baptismal stream of the title (*CS* 164). As an artistic choice, however, the pastoral setting in her fiction leads elsewhere. It points to changing views of nature, as expressed by American visual artists, in the 1930s, 1940s, and 1950s. The landscapes described by O'Connor gain new meaning when juxtaposed with landscapes painted by the regionalists, their contemporaries, and artists who came later.

It is useful here to note the political orientation of those painting the

Grant Wood, *Young Corn*, 1931, oil on masonite panel, 24 × 29⅞ in.
Cedar Rapids Community School District, Cedar Rapids, Iowa.

image of rural America in the 1930s. Their artistic aims were of a piece
with their nationalist sentiments, which, in turn, accorded with the isolationist foreign policy of the decade. "America has turned introspective,"
Wood announced in 1935 when he called for an indigenous art.[36] The
cultural isolationism he advocated in his manifesto has its visual counterpart in *Stone City, Iowa* and a similar painting, *Young Corn* (1931). Clearly, neither work excludes the viewer; in each, crop rows in the foreground lead the viewer into the valley that forms the middle ground. At
the same time, the viewer observes, neither work refers to a world
beyond its boundaries. However open and accessible they seem, the town
and the farm are self-contained. The abundance promised by the preg-
nant forms of the trees and hills guarantees the self-sufficiency of the
envisioned community. In "Revolt Against the City," Wood remarked of
the Midwestern farmer, "He is on a little unit of his own, where he
develops an extraordinary independence."[37] In his paintings, Wood
translated the idea of the "little unit" into pictorial terms.

Social realism, the other dominant movement in figurative painting
during the 1930s, provides the sharpest contrast with the isolationist

aesthetic of regionalism. The social realist work – for example, *Youngstown Strike* (c. 1937) by William Gropper – often depicts a confrontation between representatives of rival economic classes. The occasional landscape by a social realist projects this conflict into the outdoor setting. *Landscape with Tear Gas* (1937) by Joseph Hirsch shows police firing into a crowd of striking steelworkers. Even a specifically rural landscape, when it appears in a work of social realism, incorporates violence. Philip Evergood sets his *Lynching Party* (1935) in an otherwise bucolic pasture, and a wounded soldier dominates the foreground of *Where Next?* (1938) by Isaac Soyer, who shows a battle taking place in the Spanish countryside. If the work depicts only the victim or victims of economic oppression – rather than an actual confrontation – the work still directs attention to the oppressor beyond the edge of the canvas. Even as it encourages the viewer to sympathize with a disabled worker, Ben Shahn's *Man by the Railroad Track* (1935–6) condemns those unseen parties responsible for his condition.[38]

Spring Turning, by contrast, does not encourage the viewer to consider the relation between the Midwestern farm scene and the commodity markets of the East, which set the prices on the crops produced and thereby determined the quality of life of the farmers depicted. Rather, the quality of life within the painting transcends market values – what John Crowe Ransom denigrated as the "intangibles" into which "industrialism would translate the farmer's farm."[39] In *Spring Turning,* the farm exists on its own terms; the farmer's existence has an autonomous value; his identity is defined geographically rather than economically. Scenes of class conflict are rare in the regionalist canon. Benton, for instance, painted *Strikebreakers* (1931) before he declared himself a regionalist painter and left New York for Missouri.[40] In the few works that broach the topic, class divisions are elided, translated into geographical distinctions. The two women in Wood's *Appraisal* (1931) represent country and city, not poverty and privilege.[41] The self-sufficient, self-contained farm of regionalist art embodies a moral ideal that rules out internal conflict.

By the time O'Connor began her literary career, in the mid-1940s, the political implications of the regionalist project had alienated many art critics. To be precise, the isolationist stance of the painters seemed badly outdated. Like old Tarwater, the character who defends his "plowed ground" against urbanites in O'Connor's second novel (*VBA* 125), the artistic defenders of the pastoral ideal seemed insensible to political change. Just as old Tarwater ignores the presidents since Herbert Hoover (*VBA* 4), the regionalists appeared to ignore international developments since the early 1930s. Although Benton's *Invasion* clearly represented a response to the threat of fascism abroad, such paintings did little to alter the reputation that Benton, Wood, and their colleagues had gained as isolationists. Painters like Wood "are in eclipse," the editor of *Art Digest* explained in 1942, because "the United States is perhaps more international-minded than ever before."[42]

The outbreak of World War II had prompted U.S. political leaders to devalue the isolationism that the regionalists had identified with moral idealism. In June 1940, as German troops were advancing on Paris, President Franklin D. Roosevelt delivered an address in which he rejected "the now somewhat obvious delusion that we of the United States can safely permit the United States to become a lone island, a lone island in a world dominated by the philosophy of force." Isolationism, according to Roosevelt, no longer meant moral superiority and national security, but impotence and vulnerability:

> Such an island may be the dream of those who still talk and vote as isolationists. Such an island represents to me and to the overwhelming majority of Americans today a helpless nightmare, the helpless nightmare of a people without freedom; yes, the nightmare of a people lodged in prison, handcuffed, hungry, and fed through the bars from day to day by the contemptuous, unpitying masters of other continents.
>
> It is natural also that we should ask ourselves how now we can prevent the building of that prison and the placing of ourselves in the midst of it.[43]

The same logic governed U.S. diplomacy in the years after World War II, when the policy of containment held sway. In the midst of the Cold War, John Foster Dulles reiterated Roosevelt's attack on isolationism. In a 1952 essay for *Life* magazine, the future secretary of state criticized those "who would turn their backs on all the world's problems and wrap the United States in some magically 'impregnable' isolation." Like Roosevelt, Dulles treated isolationism as a source of vulnerability: "Such policies would really give 100% cooperation to the Soviet Communist effort to encircle and isolate us, as a preliminary to a final assault." Isolationism itself had its source in "a somewhat morbid state of mind." Nevertheless, Dulles retained the central assumption of the isolationist impulse, the moral idealism of Americans:

> Our dynamism has always been moral and intellectual rather than military or material. . . . We should be *dynamic,* we should use *ideas* as weapons; and these ideas should conform to *moral* principles. That we do this is right, for it is the inevitable expression of a faith – and I am confident that we still do have a faith.

The ultimate goal, in our confrontation with Communism, was to infuse "our practical decisions of policy"[44] with the rectitude that isolationist thinking had attributed to the American nation.

In the realm of culture, the Cold War narrative proved less conducive to moral idealism than to a "morbid state of mind." The political shift

Andrew Wyeth, *Christina's World*, 1948, tempera on gessoed panel, 32 ¼ × 47 ¾ in. Collection, The Museum of Modern Art, New York. Purchase.

from isolationism to interventionism had coincided with a shift away from moral statement in American painting. Abstract expressionists like Jackson Pollock rejected the narrative art through which the social realists had condemned U.S. capitalism. Despite their own radical political views, the abstract expressionists avoided politics and accentuated the individuality of the artist.[45] If individual expression replaced social criticism as the accepted function of art, it also superseded the regionalist commitment to a social ideal. In 1944 Pollock made explicit his break with the regionalist aesthetic of Benton, under whom he had studied a decade before. "The idea of an isolated American painting, so popular in this country during the 'thirties, seems absurd to me," Pollock told an interviewer.[46]

Even those artists who worked in a realistic idiom refrained from moral statement. Andrew Wyeth, for instance, painted numerous scenes of rural countrysides – but these landscapes convey no social vision. They reveal little more about the human figures located within them. The expansive compositions suggest the vulnerability of the figures without defining the terms by which the viewer is to understand this vulnerability. *Christina's World* (1948), like *Winter 1946* (1946) and *April*

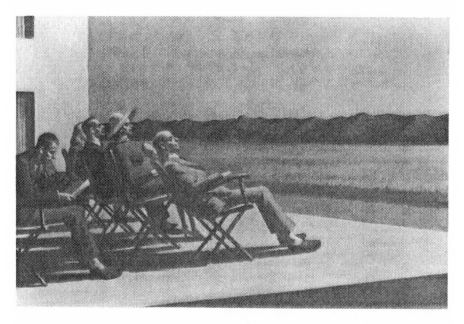

Edward Hopper, *People in the Sun,* 1960, oil on canvas, 40³/₈ × 60³/₈ in.
(102.6 × 153.5 cm). National Museum of American Art, Smithsonian
Institution, Washington, D.C. Gift of S. C. Johnson & Son, Inc.
(1969.47.61).

Wind (1952), places a lone figure in an open field. Christina's position on
the ground, the twist of her torso, and her gaze toward the distant
farmhouse suggest a frustrated longing for the safety of an interior setting. A similar frustration characterizes the viewing experience: Wyeth's
painting does not explain the vague sense of dread it inspires in the
viewer, who remains outside the painting as surely as Christina remains
exposed.[47]

The refusal to make the implicit narrative explicit connects *Christina's
World* with the paintings of Edward Hopper, who continued to produce
realistic landscapes during the postwar years. Works like *Seawatchers*
(1952), *Four Lane Road* (1956), *Sunlight on Brownstones* (1956), *Second Story
Sunlight* (1960), and *People in the Sun* (1960) provide only the fragments of
various narratives.[48] The human figures in Hopper's landscapes differ
significantly, however, from Christina. Whether seated in deck chairs or
perched on railings, they seem enthroned in isolation; they seem anything but helpless. From secure vantage points, directly in front of archi-
tectural structures, Hopper's figures survey a natural world that fails to
intimidate them.[49] Wyeth's figure, in contrast, seems overwhelmed by

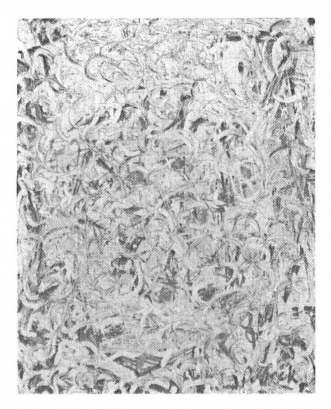

Jackson Pollock, *Shimmering Substance,* from the *Sounds in the Grass* series, 1946, oil on canvas, 30⅛ × 24¼ in. (76.3 × 61.6 cm). Collection, The Museum of Modern Art, New York. Mr. and Mrs. Albert Lewin and Mrs. Sam A. Lewisohn Funds.

the natural setting. Christina does not control Christina's world. While the title implies possession, the painting itself depicts dispossession.

The fear of losing control over nature helps explain the virtual disappearance of landscape as a major genre in the first decade after World War II. Wyeth and Hopper were the exceptions to the rule. Until Richard Diebenkorn turned to figurative painting in the second half of the 1950s, abstract expressionists did little more than allude to landscape in the occasional title. The landscape has disintegrated, in fact, in those works whose titles promise a pastoral vision. Pollock, for example, gave the evocative name *Sounds in the Grass* to a series of paintings unified by nothing more than his "allover" compositional style: frenzied brushstrokes cover each canvas, forming a tangle of colors rather than a recognizable scene. Two years after he completed his 1946 series, Pollock created a work to which he would also give a title evoking nature. This painting, *Summertime: Number 9A, 1948*, has the elements of a pastoral landscape but lacks the coherence. The shards of bright yellow could be sunshine; the dabs of green could be grass; the patches of dark blue could be spring water. The colors are caught in a tangle of curving black lines, which could have functioned as outlines, defining the forms within the landscape. Another work whose title refers to a natural season, *Autumn Rhythm: Number 30, 1950*, has a clear visual rhythm, but its autumnal colors do not coalesce into a perceptible harvest scene.[50]

Although Pollock discouraged viewers from bringing "a subject matter or preconceived idea" to his abstract paintings, his titles signal his continuing concern "with the rhythms of nature."[51] A new understanding of such "rhythms" accounts for the visual disintegration of landscape. In the 1930s a social order founded on a proper relation to nature had seemed viable to the regionalists. In 1945, with the bombing of Hiroshima and Nagasaki, nature suddenly lost its stability. The atom itself had been split. The nature that concerned Pollock was not peaceful, affording bucolic images of American moral virtue, but powerful beyond imagination. In the words of his art dealer, Pollock sensed "the power of it all – how scary it is."[52]

I acknowledge the possibility of reading too much into the visual texts under discussion. Paul Boyer points to the difficulties that attend the analysis of American "nuclear culture" in the years immediately following World War II. When he addresses the psychological impact of the atomic bomb, Boyer admits that "the evidence is scanty, murky, and indirect, involving impressionistic generalizations by social observers about other people's feelings, or vague speculation about possible future states of collective consciousness."[53] But at least one of Pollock's contemporaries saw the atomic age reflected in his painting *Out of the Web: Number 7, 1949*. A columnist for the *New York Sun*, writing in 1949, compared the effect of the painting to "that of a flat, war-shattered city, possibly Hiroshima, as seen from a great height in moonlight."[54] The following year, Pollock himself observed that the age he sought to express was the age of "the atom bomb."

This age, he said in 1950, demanded "new ways and new means" of expression. A genre in which Pollock chose to develop his "new techniques"[55] was the one in which Benton had instructed him: landscape. Not long after creating a number of regionalist scenes, including the Bentonesque *Cotton Pickers* (c. 1935), Pollock effaced a lithographic image of a literally pastoral subject. The result, *Landscape with Steer* (1936–7), hints at the direction his art would take over the next decade; the colors, red, blue, and gold, distract attention from the subject, the skeletal ox in the lower left-hand corner. As he moved farther away from the

Jackson Pollock, *Cotton Pickers*, c. 1935, oil on canvas, 24 × 30 in. Albright–Knox Art Gallery, Buffalo, New York. The Martha Jackson Collection, 1974.

regionalist aesthetic of his mentor, Pollock painted a work whose very theme was the destruction of landscape. Although this *Burning Landscape* (1943) is nonobjective, the colors are appropriate to the subject matter announced by the title. Bright yellow and reddish orange suggest the flames, while green and blue suggest the landscape itself; black lines, having lost their function as outlines, float throughout the composition like streamers of ash. In developing his own style, Pollock subverted the pastoral vision of his former teacher. Benton had issued a warning to Americans, a call to action, when he painted *Invasion* in 1942. He affirmed the pastoral ideal even as he showed its violation. Pollock, by contrast, suggested that the pastoral was no longer viable.

The pastoral setting became the site of annihilation in Pollock's work and the locus of ineffable dread in Wyeth's. The threat of nuclear destruction helped to shape these postwar variations on the pastoral. Another version, that of O'Connor, likewise conveys an imaginative response to the nuclear peril. The author who dreamed of "radiated bulls" in 1961

Jackson Pollock, *Landscape with Steer,* 1936–7, lithograph with airbrush, 13⅝ × 18⁹/₁₆ in. Collection, The Museum of Modern Art, New York. Gift of Lee Krasner Pollock.

(*HB* 449) had much in common with her contemporaries. The sense of imminent doom pervading her fiction derived not only from her awareness that lupus could kill her at any time, but also from her knowledge that a vast number of Americans and a vast area of U.S. territory could be destroyed at a moment of international crisis.

Death and the loss of territory come together in two stories by O'Connor. In "Greenleaf," the protagonist tries to maintain control over the setting with which she identifies herself. Mrs. May, who sees "the reflection of her own character" when she looks at her pastures (*CS* 321), tries to maintain control even after death. Afraid of what her sons might do with her land, she changes her will: "She had gone to her lawyer and had had the property entailed so that if they married, they could not leave it to their wives" (*CS* 315). But she cannot prevent the invasion of her property by the Greenleaf bull – the bull that kills her by piercing her heart. As she dies, in the "unbreakable grip" of the invader, the pastoral setting dissolves: "The tree line was a dark wound in a world that was nothing but sky" (*CS* 333). Mrs. Shortley in "The Displaced Person" also loses control over the land with which she identifies herself. Intro-

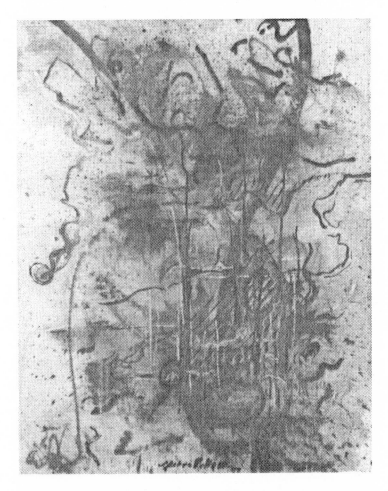

Jackson Pollock, *Burning Landscape,* 1943, oil on gesso on canvas, 36 ×
28⁷/₁₆ in. (91.4 × 72.2 cm). Yale University Art Gallery, New Haven,
Connecticut. Gift of Miss Peggy Guggenheim.

duced to the reader as a figure of power, "the giant wife of the countryside," Mrs. Shortley displays "the grand self-confidence of a mountain."
Standing on "the hill where she meant to stand," she seems to have a
secure vantage point. Like the human figures in Hopper's postwar landscapes, she stares into a natural setting that fails to impress her. The gaze
she casts from her position atop the natural "prominence" resembles the
gaze of the scowling woman in *People in the Sun.* O'Connor describes her
eyes as "two icy blue points of light that pierced forward, surveying

everything" (*CS* 194). When she dies, however, Mrs. Shortley shows a greater resemblance to the woman in *Christina's World*. She exits the story as a figure dispossessed. She suffers her fatal attack in the car as her family drives away from the McIntyre farm.

The sky appears to be the source of danger in both stories. The paragraph that opens "The Displaced Person" links "danger" and "trouble" in the countryside with an afternoon sun that assumes the role of "intruder" (*CS* 194). "Greenleaf" assigns the same role to the sun that will "burst through the tree line," the boundary line of the May property, in one of Mrs. May's dreams. Shaped "like a bullet," it races toward her (*CS* 329). For all their self-confidence, Mrs. Shortley and Mrs. May are as vulnerable as the figure that Wyeth places beneath an open sky.

"A Circle in the Fire" does not end with a death, as the other stories do, but it connects the loss of territory with a celestial threat. Mrs. Cope's daughter imagines that the "blank sky" itself is "pushing against the fortress wall" of trees, "trying to break through" (*CS* 176). Like other Americans in the atomic age, Mrs. Cope watches the skies anxiously. She shivers when she sees a "flame-colored" sun, "hung in a net of ragged cloud," that appears ready to "burn through any second and fall into the woods" (*CS* 184). The danger from the sky materializes at the end of the story; the woods go up in flames. Witnessing the conflagration she has feared for so long, Mrs. Cope loses faith in American exceptionalism. She wears an expression of misery that relates her to the European victims of Soviet aggression (*CS* 193).

Not everyone shared a pessimistic vision of the pastoral, as expressed in O'Connor's fiction. For many postwar Americans, the natural setting was the only one that promised security. Civil defense campaigns in the late 1940s and early 1950s carried this message: cities were atomic targets. At the same time, real estate advertisements presented the rural setting as a haven from nuclear attack. "Good bomb immunity" was among the selling points of some rural property listed in the *Wall Street Journal* in 1950.[56] The countryside would be spared the general destruction. Here, in the setting identified with its essence, the United States would survive. Richard Gerstell, author of *How to Survive an Atomic Bomb* (1950), had this advice for parents living in strategically important cities: "You ought to think about sending your children away to the country if we get into a big war."[57] In 1950 even a small war seemed to justify a move to the country. A Poughkeepsie real estate broker attributed an increase in farm purchases that year to "the fighting in Korea." The broker also reported, "One out of ten clients says he wants a place in the country because of the atom bomb."[58]

The image of a pastoral America, it seemed, could still influence public behavior. For this reason, cultural historians sought to deflate the myth they described. The image used to represent the United States, these intellectuals argued, betrayed fundamental misperceptions in American thought. Although the authors of "myth-symbol" studies affirmed the centrality of the pastoral ideal in American culture, they all emphasized its representational inadequacy. The centrality of the myth, for Henry Nash Smith, necessitated the criticism of the myth. The practical influence he ascribed to such "collective representations" raised the political stakes.[59] In *The Machine in the Garden*, Marx grouped Smith with two historians outside the "myth-symbol" school, Richard Hofstadter and Marvin Meyers, because "they all seem to agree that for some time now this tendency to idealize rural ways has been an impediment to clarity of thought and, from their point of view, to social progress." Marx continued, "They demonstrate that in public discourse, at least, this ideal has appeared with increasing frequency in the service of a reactionary or false ideology, thereby helping to mask the real problems of an industrial civilization."[60]

Smith denied the inclusiveness or comprehensiveness of the dominant cultural imagery and called attention to the cultural sin of omission. Americans, he argued in his 1951 essay, had mistaken the image of the agricultural frontier for "a complete account of American experience." This image, accorded "an almost sacrosanct status as the source of the highest value of our society," was "seriously misleading" because of "what it leaves out."[61] In *Virgin Land*, Smith wrote:

> The philosophy and the myth . . . ceased very early to be useful in interpreting American society as a whole because they offered no intellectual apparatus for taking account of the industrial revolution. A system which revolved about a half-mystical conception of nature and held up as an ideal a rudimentary type of agriculture was powerless to confront issues arising from the advance of technology.[62]

Smith was concerned primarily with the effect of the cultural image on historiography, but he also noted its "implications for present social policy." In fact, he saw a cause-and-effect relation between historical understanding and foreign policy: "If the historians themselves do not actively resist such an oversimplification of the American past, we need not be surprised if popular ideology turns the cultural image of the frontier West to the ends illustrated by Mr. Duffy's cartoon." He warned against the idea conveyed by the *Saturday Evening Post* cartoon, "the notion that we are now about to defend a log cabin against Asiatic aggression." Given the continuing power of the cultural image of the agricultural frontier, he wrote, "the American of the present day can be invited to identify with it at a level of the highest seriousness, as a means

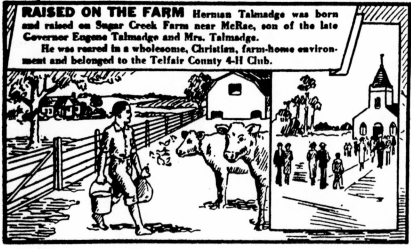

A pair of campaign ads from a 1948 issue of O'Connor's hometown newspaper, the Milledgeville *Union-Recorder,* demonstrated the continuing political value of the pastoral ideal. Each advertisement began with a panel that proclaimed the rural origins of the gubernatorial candidate. For anyone who might have missed the point, the opening panel of the ad for M. E. Thompson made explicit the connection between such origins and the American way of life. Reprinted from the Milledgeville *Union-Recorder,* 2 Sept. 1948.

of defining a position and perhaps even formulating national policy in a time of the most appalling crisis."[63] Smith's concerns resembled those expressed in Reinhold Niebuhr's *The Irony of American History* (1952) and C. Vann Woodward's "The Irony of Southern History" (1953), both of which linked the imaginative self-conception of Americans to an interventionist foreign policy. "Convinced of her virtue," Woodward wrote, "America may be tempted to exert all the terrible power she possesses to compel history to conform to her own illusions."[64]

If the pastoral myth encouraged a dangerous foreign policy, it also had domestic consequences, in terms of social consciousness. According to Marx, the postwar "flight from the city" exemplified the continuing influence of pastoralism, or at least its sentimental version, on American thought and behavior: "An inchoate longing for a more 'natural' environment enters into the contemptuous attitude that many Americans adopt toward urban life (with the result that we neglect our cities and desert them for the suburbs)."[65] The pastoral myth, supposedly realized by those who could afford to leave the cities for the suburbs, encouraged members of the middle class to ignore an America that seemed less "American" than their own.

From the perspective of middle-class suburbanites, U.S. prosperity was a blessing enjoyed by all. In 1962 the socialist author Michael Harrington had to remind his readers of the "other America," the "invisible land" of poverty. While a "familiar America" was "advertised on television," 40 to 50 million Americans "existing at levels beneath those necessary for human decency" were "slipping out of the very experience and consciousness of the nation." Harrington blamed "a new kind of blindness about poverty" on postwar changes in residential life: "The very development of the American city has removed poverty from the living, emotional experience of millions upon millions of middle-class Americans. Living out in the suburbs, it is easy to assume that ours is, indeed, an affluent society."

Harrington included the rural poor – small independent farmers as well as migrant workers – in his survey of "invisible" Americans. Although agriculture was "one of the major successes of the affluent society," Harrington wrote, the beneficiaries of this success were urban consumers and large corporate farms. Harrington pointed out the discrepancy between the mythic representation of the farm setting, identified with American character, and the economic reality: "In a nation where Fourth of July speeches about the virtue of the 'family farm' are still being made, there are nearly a million such farms that are centers of poverty and backwardness."[66]

By the middle of the 1960s, the image of the independent family farm no longer seemed sacrosanct. Paul Goodman, offering various plans for

"rural reconstruction" in a 1966 lecture, portrayed small farmers as marginal figures, "regarded as backward fools," who considered themselves
"deeply useless." The purpose behind rural reconstruction, as conceived
by Goodman, was not the rejuvenation of the pastoral ideal, not the
imaginative rebirth of the countryside "as the source of all moral virtue
and political independence," but the resolution of urban problems. Only
by serving an auxiliary function, by providing a means of "thinning out"
excessive urbanization, could the country "regain some importance in
the big society, which is urban."[67]

The pastoral now seemed viable only as a realm of escapist fantasy.
The intellectuals who worried about its continuing popular appeal as an
image representative of the United States failed to notice that the creators
of popular culture were also denying its representative function. On
network television, the family farm became a haven for eccentricity; the
farm family, a collection of social misfits. The discrepancy that concerned American intellectuals – the disagreement between pastoral myth
and contemporary social reality – served as a springboard for humor in
popular culture. A series of film comedies featuring Ma and Pa Kettle,
from 1947 to 1957, paved the way for a number of rural situation comedies on television.[68] The success of the situation comedies produced by
Paul Henning for CBS illustrates the ironies associated with the pastoral
setting in the 1960s. Judging by Nielsen ratings, the farm family still held
a central position in the American imagination. *The Beverly Hillbillies*
was the top-rated television series in its first two seasons, from 1962 to
1964, and ranked among the top twenty programs every season except its
last. In its first four seasons, *Green Acres* ranked among the top twenty.[69]
These programs owed their enormous popularity to their depiction of
rural characters as comic "characters," separated by language and by
logic from urban Americans. Verbal misunderstandings between the displaced Clampetts and the Los Angeles natives fuel many of the plots of
The Beverly Hillbillies. The skewed reasoning of the locals in *Green Acres*
frustrates the "normal" American, a lawyer from New York City, but
not his foreign-born wife. The lawyer, Oliver Douglas (Eddie Albert),
acknowledges this fact when he and his wife, Lisa (Eva Gabor), discuss
their hired hand, Eb Dawson (Tom Lester). "Everything he says makes
sense to you," Oliver tells Lisa. "Nothing he says makes sense to me."[70]

There was nothing new about playing "hicks" against city dwellers for
comic purposes. Indeed, the first American stage comedy, *The Contrast*
(1787) by Royall Tyler, places an unsophisticated farm boy named Jon-
athan among socially polished New Yorkers.[71] But the point had usually
been that the rural characters, like the American Adam delineated by
Lewis, were better representatives of our national identity than the urbanites could ever be. In *The Beverly Hillbillies,* by contrast, U.S. society

cannot assimilate the farm family. No member of the Clampett family ever detaches him- or herself from the "kinfolks" in order to join another social group. The Clampett family, moreover, is impermeable. No "normal" American can join the group. Their "rural idiocy," to borrow Goodman's phrase,[72] seals them off.

With the debut of *Green Acres* in 1965, the independent family farm became the locus of surrealist comedy.[73] The series concerns the attempt by a city couple to live out the agrarian ideal, which the husband frequently champions. "The farmer's always been the strength of the nation," Oliver declares in an early episode. On *Green Acres*, the postwar exodus from city to "pastoral" suburb is translated into its original terms; "farm living," rather than a suburban approximation of the same, lures Oliver away from the "city life" of Manhattan.[74] But the way of life the Douglases find in Hooterville falls short of the agrarian ideal as expressed in painting and literature. The run-down farm is a visual disappointment, a fact underscored at the end of the opening credits. Oliver and Lisa adopt the poses of the figures in *American Gothic* (1930), thereby suggesting the deviation from the tidy rural landscapes of Grant Wood. Eccentrics populate the countryside around Hooterville. One of the characters, Mr. Haney (Pat Buttram), does reprise a traditional role in the literature of American rural life, that of the shrewd Yankee trader. In general, however, nonsense replaces convention. Reality itself seems fluid in Hooterville, which secedes from the state – and, presumably, from the United States – in one of the last episodes. Snow falls in July; the Douglas farmhouse nearly suffocates under a new coat of paint; a farm family, the Ziffels, treats a pig named Arnold as its child.

The year that *Green Acres* debuted, a work by an "underground" playwright further disqualified rural characters as representative American figures. The title character in *Futz* (1965) by Rochelle Owens has a relationship with his pig that is far more intimate than the relationship between the Ziffels and Arnold. The "husbandman," Cyrus Futz, and his sow, Amanda, are lovers. On his "little plot of land," Cy Futz acts out a "sexual dream," which the narrator assures the audience "does not bear in the least to anything real in terms of yours or Cy's world."[75] The shock tactics of avant-garde theater, like the absurdities of television comedy, placed rural characters at the fringes of American life.

Grotesque characterizations perform the same function in the short stories and novels of O'Connor. The characters who populate her rural settings are not representative figures, but "maimed souls" (*MM* 43), the fictional counterparts of the Americans described by Harrington, Americans "maimed in body and spirit."[76] The residents of the "desolate" farm in "The Life You Save May Be Your Own" (1953) are a toothless old woman, "ravenous for a son-in-law," and her deaf, inarticulate daughter

Grant Wood, *American Gothic,* 1930, oil on beaverboard, 29⁷/₈ × 24⁷/₈ in. (76 × 63.3 cm). Friends of American Art Collection, 1930.934. Photograph copyright © 1992, The Art Institute of Chicago. All rights reserved.

(*CS* 145, 150). Urban society will not or cannot assimilate rural characters like Hazel Motes and Enoch Emery in *Wise Blood* (1952) and young Tarwater in *The Violent Bear It Away* (1960). "I been here two months," Enoch tells Hazel as they walk through downtown Taulkinham, "and I don't know nobody. People ain't friendly here" (*WB* 56). Tarwater, who notices that the eyes of city dwellers "didn't grab at you like the eyes of country people" (*VBA* 26), resists his uncle's attempt to make him adapt to urban life. When O'Connor published the first of her two novels, some reviewers compared its freaks and misfits to the inhabitants of Dogpatch, the rural community in which Al Capp set his popular comic strip "Li'l Abner." In a musical version of the strip, filmed in 1959, the federal government names Dogpatch "the most unnecessary place in the whole USA."⁷⁷ It is this sense of superfluousness that O'Connor emphasizes.

   In portraying her rural characters as freaks and misfits, O'Connor allied herself with those who called attention to the representational inadequacy of the pastoral myth. She suggested that Americans could no

Still from the opening credits of *Green Acres*, featuring Eva Gabor and
Eddie Albert, 1965. Artwork copyright © Orion Pictures Corporation.

longer base their national identity on a belief in pastoral innocence. Her
viewpoint resembled that of C. Vann Woodward, whom she admired as
a writer (*HB* 522). Woodward speculated in 1958 that the Southern experience of racial guilt and military defeat could "provide some immunity
to the illusions and myths of American nationalism," including the belief
in American innocence.[78] Four years later, O'Connor credited Southerners with "an inburnt knowledge of human limitations" and "a sense of
mystery which could not have developed in our first state of innocence –
as it has not sufficiently developed in the rest of our country" (*MM* 59).[79]

In her fictional countryside, it is always a bad idea to take for granted
the "rural virtue" of a rural character. In "Good Country People" (1955),
the owner of the farm professes her faith in such virtue. "I think there
aren't enough good country people in the world!" Mrs. Hopewell says.
"I think that's what's wrong with it!" Manley Pointer talks about "country people like me" in order to gain her confidence. "You don't see any
more real honest people," he says, "unless you go way out in the country" (*CS* 278–9). But "Manley Pointer" turns out to be an alias; the Bible
salesman is a thief. He steals the artificial leg that belongs to Mrs. Cope's
daughter, who has also been fooled by his act.

The rural characters in television programs of the 1960s retained some of the moral righteousness associated with their native setting. *The Beverly Hillbillies,* for example, is founded on "the conflict between Middle American virtue and Los Angeles decadence."[80] However cartoonish the Clampetts may be, they can claim an integrity that their banker and exploiter, Milburn Drysdale (Raymond Bailey), lacks. They are never morally implicated in his unethical maneuvers. Like network television, avant-garde theater reaffirmed the connection between the rural setting and purity of heart. Although the barn providing the backdrop for *Futz* combines "signs of the terrible city existence" with "the worst the country has to offer," the narrator valorizes the "dream" that motivates Cy Futz, the owner of the barn. Commenting on Cy's love for his sow, the narrator says, "It's pure sickness, but in its pureness it's a truth."[81]

O'Connor, by contrast, emphasizes the hypocrisy of her rural characters. The hypocrite in "A Circle in the Fire" is the defender of the pastoral setting. Mrs. Cope, the woman who thanks God for a pastoral haven in a world threatened by Soviet aggression, refuses to share this haven with the three boys from Atlanta. "It's not that I wouldn't be glad to have them," she claims; "it's their attitude." Her counterfeit generosity fails to convince her daughter, who observes, "You never like nobody's attitude" (*CS* 187). When she thinks she has scared the intruders away from her farm, Mrs. Cope feigns sympathy for the boys, calling them "poor things" and linking their situation with that of the Europeans deported to Siberia (*CS* 190). Her moral pretensions are obvious to everyone but Mrs. Cope herself. "I think I have been very nice to you boys," she tells them – right before she threatens to call the sheriff (*CS* 189).

Her desire to maintain control over her property leads one of the boys to joke that "she owns the sky over this place" (*CS* 186). "A Circle in the Fire" attributes her hypocrisy to her obsession with territorial security – the prevailing obsession of Cold War America, which placed supreme faith in its Air Defense Command. In her fiction, O'Connor issues a harsh judgment of Cold War America, suggesting that the preoccupation with national security had produced a great moral complacency. Her contemporaries had more reason than ever to conceive of themselves as a virtuous people. Appropriating the national myth of pastoral innocence, the Cold War narrative encouraged Americans to claim all goodness for themselves and to project all evil onto the Soviets. O'Connor undermined this simple moral dualism. She insisted that the self-conception of Americans, as grounded in the pastoral myth, was a form of self-deception.

2

The Domesticated Intellectual

Since the outset of her career, critics have removed Flannery O'Connor from the American literary mainstream, positioning her as a Southern, Catholic writer – as a writer whose regional and religious concerns diverted her from issues more politically salient to her intellectual contemporaries. O'Connor herself abetted this reading of her fiction, advocating a literary technique based on connections between local detail and universal significance, between "a point in the concrete" and "a point not visible to the naked eye" (*MM* 42). Theoretically, national politics would fall into the "gaps" left by such a technique (*MM* 40).

In practice, however, O'Connor does address questions of nationwide concern. Foremost among these is the political and cultural role the intellectual was supposed to play in a nation whose citizens felt threatened by Soviet aggression, in the form of military attack or internal subversion. O'Connor could hardly have ignored this new role. Her friends included the literary critic Granville Hicks, whose shift from Communism to anti-Communism exemplified the political reorientation of numerous American intellectuals, and the poet Robert Lowell, whose aversion to Communism prompted him to lead a 1949 "revolution" at Yaddo, the artists' colony in upstate New York (*HB* 11). O'Connor, a Yaddo resident at the time, joined Lowell in his protest against the politically suspect behavior of the executive director.

The anxiety that gave rise to the new role of the intellectual, the very anxiety Americans felt regarding an external threat, informs several stories in which national concerns appear to be remote. "Good Country People," "Greenleaf," and "The Enduring Chill" (1958) feature characters who enact the role of the Cold War intellectual. O'Connor locates these characters, Joy-Hulga Hopewell, Wesley May, and Asbury Fox, in the vulnerable setting of the invasion scenario: the family farm. This setting, in effect, provides a fictional analogue for the cultural situation in which postwar intellectuals found themselves. The choice of locale is

41

appropriate, given the ideological significance then attached to home and family. As the pastoral setting was identified with the essential America, so the domestic setting was identified with the American way of life.

In her study of domesticity during the Cold War, Elaine Tyler May calls attention to the propaganda value of the suburban home abounding with consumer goods. For many Americans – including Vice-President Richard Nixon, who turned propagandist in a 1959 "kitchen debate" with Soviet Premier Nikita Khrushchev – the home of the affluent nuclear family demonstrated the superiority of the American way. Moreover, by ensuring the moral strength of the nation, family stability would prevent the Communists from subverting that way of life.[1] The political ideology served by the image of a pastoral America, a nation morally pure as long as outside forces remained outside, was also served by the image of the self-contained family home. The ideology that governed the private as well as the public sphere, according to May, was the ideology expressed in the official policy of containment:

> With security as the common thread, the cold war ideology and the domestic revival reinforced each other. The powerful political consensus that supported cold war policies abroad and anticommunism at home fueled conformity to the suburban family ideal. In turn, the domestic ideology . . . further weakened the potential for challenges to the cold war consensus.[2]

For those who have examined this consensus, a 1952 symposium in *Partisan Review* has become a critical touchstone.[3] "Our Country and Our Culture" announced that intellectuals had shifted from a viewpoint antagonistic to U.S. society, in the decades before the Second World War, to a position affirming the American way of life, during the Cold War. As the editors remarked in their introductory statement:

> Most writers no longer accept alienation as the artist's fate in America; on the contrary, they want very much to be a part of American life. More and more writers have ceased to think of themselves as rebels and exiles. They now believe that their values, if they are to be realized at all, must be realized in America and in relation to the actuality of American life.

If mass culture made intellectuals feel they were "still outside looking in," the intellectuals characterized by the editors of the symposium knew where they needed to be: inside.

The spatial opposition basic to the invasion scenario – inside versus outside – dominated the discussion of the intellectuals' role. In redefining that role, the symposium contributors pointed to the geopolitical conflict between the United States and the Soviet Union. Recognizing that "the kind of democracy which exists in America . . . must be defended against Russian totalitarianism," intellectuals had no choice but to change their attitude and affirm the American way of life. The literary critic Newton Arvin agreed with this editorial view, arguing that "the habit of rejection, of repudiation, of mere exacerbated alienation, has ceased to seem relevant or defensible – inevitably, since the culture we profoundly cherish is now disastrously threatened from without." The greater the external threat, Arvin reasoned, "the intenser becomes the awareness of our necessary identification with [our culture]." In his contribution, Lionel Trilling observed, "Even the most disaffected intellectual must respond . . . to the growing isolation of his country amid the hostility which is directed against it." James Burnham also linked cultural concerns with political and military considerations. Intellectuals had changed their attitude toward the United States over the course of a generation, not because the national culture had improved, but because international relations had deteriorated: "The new context, and an understanding hardened by the fierce blows of these years, justify a renewed political affirmation."[4]

The *Partisan Review* symposium was not an isolated event. The assumptions of the editors typified the assumptions prevalent in the intellectual community during the Cold War. Indeed, visual as well as literary artists were expected to serve as cold warriors on the cultural front. In his study of the political ends served by abstract expressionism, a seemingly apolitical mode of painting, Serge Guilbaut maintains that "postwar American culture was placed on the same footing as American economic and military strength: in other words, it was made responsible for the survival of democratic liberties in the 'free' world." Culture, Guilbaut writes, "had become politicized and important in a world sharply divided between the forces of good and the forces of evil."[5] To win allies for the United States and to counteract Soviet propaganda, American artists were supposed to present their country in a positive light.

Although service as a cold warrior gained widespread acceptance, some members of the intellectual community refused to serve. The essay Norman Mailer contributed to the *Partisan Review* symposium announced his minority opinion; he rejected the fundamental assumptions of the introductory statement.[6] Disturbed by the implications of the dominant spatial metaphor, or "the curious space relations of politics which equates [*sic*] right to within and left to without," Mailer dismissed the argument that the American intellectual had to affirm national institutions because they were threatened from outside. Intellectual "exhaustion," rather than eagerness to defend democracy, motivated those writers who "now see it as their function to interpret American society from within."[7]

One critic has drawn a parallel between Mailer's objections to the introductory statement and the objections O'Connor raised concerning an editorial, "Wanted: An American Novel," which appeared in *Life* in 1955.[8] The *Life* editorial called for American novels that would mirror their time "faithfully," as *The Great Gatsby* had recorded the "frauds and deceits" of Prohibition or as *The Grapes of Wrath* had recorded the "unnecessary humiliations" of the Depression. According to the editorial, however, a "representative literature" for the 1950s would celebrate postwar America; given "the incredible accomplishments of our day," the need for social criticism was past.[9] In her essay "The Fiction Writer and His Country" (1957), O'Connor consigned the task of celebration to the advertising agencies: "No one has ever accused them of not being affirmative." O'Connor thus answered the question posed by the editorial: "Who speaks for America today?" (*MM* 34).

In doing so, she announced her own refusal to serve as a cold warrior on the cultural front. This refusal, she knew, went against the conventional political wisdom. According to a newspaper columnist whom O'Connor cited in a 1962 letter, even the private citizen traveling abroad had a duty to advance "our foreign policy" as "a salesman of the USA" (*HB* 482). At a time when Americans were so concerned about their image overseas, the writer who confirmed European prejudice against the United States could be accused of collaborating with the Communist propaganda effort. Although the *Life* editorial stopped short of calling American novelists politically subversive, it did reiterate most of the charges lodged against American painters by U.S. Representative George Dondero, a Michigan Republican, in a 1949 interview:

> Modern art is Communistic because it is distorted and ugly, because it does not glorify our beautiful country, our cheerful and smiling people, and our great material progress. Art which does not portray our beautiful country in plain, simple terms that everyone can understand breeds dissatisfaction. It is therefore opposed to our government, and those who create it and promote it are our enemies.[10]

In "The Fiction Writer and His Country," O'Connor disputed two of the criteria that the author of the *Life* editorial shared with Dondero: American artists needed to show "the joy of life" in the United States, and they needed to glorify "our unparalleled prosperity" since World War II. The adoption of such criteria, O'Connor warned, "will produce a soggy, formless, and sentimental literature," providing "a sense of joy for those who confuse that virtue with satisfaction" (*MM* 25–6, 30–1). The distinction between "joy" and "satisfaction" did not concern Dondero, for whom the danger of Communism outweighed the danger of sentimentality. Clearly, political anxieties gave the demands for literary "assurance" considerable political weight. Nevertheless, O'Connor resisted these demands (*MM* 34). Like Mailer, she defended the right of the artist to place him- or herself in opposition to American culture.[11]

In her fiction, O'Connor dramatizes the attempt to resist the demands for celebratory assent. Even though her intellectuals have been domesticated, they continue to think of themselves as "rebels." They try to realize the paradigm of intellectual exile and alienation, the paradigm declared obsolete by the editors of the *Partisan Review* symposium. Asbury Fox of "The Enduring Chill" left home to live in a "freezing flat" in New York (*CS* 358), despite the observation by William Phillips, a *Partisan Review* editor, that "such symbols of alienation as the cold-water flat are gone."[12] Phillips had helped found *Partisan Review* in 1934 as part of a Communist literary movement in the United States; over the next few years, he had helped deradicalize its editorial policy; now, he announced the end of intellectual alienation.[13] O'Connor's intellectuals may not espouse politically radical views, but they all reject the assessment offered by Phillips. They all resent their domestication.

Wesley May of "Greenleaf" feels nothing but contempt for the setting that unites the pastoral and the domestic: "He hated the country and he hated the life he lived; he hated living with his mother and his idiot brother and he hated hearing about the damn dairy and the damn help and the damn broken machinery" (*CS* 319). Asbury Fox shares Wesley's disdain for life on a family farm. On those rare occasions when Asbury works in his family dairy, he deliberately breaks the rules – by smoking a cigarette or by drinking unhomogenized milk. The environment toward which he directs his hostility proves hostile in return. One of the cows kicks him. From the milk he drinks, moreover, he contracts the undulant fever that will necessitate his final homecoming.

The intellectual characters remain in their rural setting against their will. They remain, specifically, because health problems have disabled them. Were it not for his illness, Asbury would still be in the "larger world" of New York City, where he moved in order "to escape the slave's atmosphere of home" (*CS* 358, 364). The heroine of "Good Country People," whose Ph.D. in philosophy certifies her kinship to Asbury and Wesley, wants to leave the farm her mother owns; but "a weak heart" keeps her confined there: "Joy had made it plain that if it had not been for this condition, she would be far from these red hills and good country people. She would be in a university lecturing to people who knew what she was talking about" (*CS* 276). In "Greenleaf," too, the character identified as an intellectual suffers from a heart condition. His mother, in fact, links this identity with sickness: "Wesley . . . had had rheumatic fever when he was seven and Mrs. May thought that this was what had caused him to be an intellectual" (*CS* 314).

The mothers in "Good Country People," "Greenleaf," and "The Enduring Chill" are the fictional counterparts of those who denied the American intellectual the option of expatriation, who tried to keep the intellectual within the boundaries of ideological consensus. Despite his unhappiness in the domestic setting, Mrs. May wants to keep her son confined there. When he talks about leaving home and living abroad, she warns Wesley about the dangers of Paris and Rome. "You'd go to those places and you'd get sick," she says (CS 320). Mrs. May likes the idea of controlling her son with her "iron hand" (CS 321). In "The Enduring Chill," Asbury blames the control his mother has exerted over his imagination – unintentionally, in her case – for his failure as a writer. "It was not that she had ever forced her way on him," O'Connor writes. "Her way had simply been the air he breathed and when at last he had found other air, he couldn't survive in it." Hoping to "liberate" his imagination by expatriating himself, Asbury discovers it has been "domesticated" (CS 364–5).

Obviously, the process of domestication to which O'Connor subjected her intellectual characters points to the central fact of her own life. Disseminated lupus, a hereditary disease for which O'Connor was first hospitalized in 1950, brought an end to her life away from home. After spending a few years in Iowa, New York, and Connecticut in the late 1940s, O'Connor was forced to live with her mother on the family farm, Andalusia, until her death in 1964. Critics have linked her depiction of family tensions – usually culminating in violence – to the frustration she must have felt as an adult who remained dependent on her mother.[14] What these critics have overlooked, however, is the fact that the confinement of her intellectuals to a setting both domestic and pastoral reflects the new conception of the role to be played by the intellectual during the Cold War. The sense of frustration conveyed by the situation common to "Good Country People," "Greenleaf," and "The Enduring Chill" had not only a personal origin but a cultural one. The facts of illness and confinement, of forced return to the family home and to the status of a child, dovetailed with the experience of an American intellectual conscripted into an ideological consensus.

"Good Country People" best illustrates the transformation of this experience into fiction. To be precise, "Good Country People" translates the debate between O'Connor and the author of the *Life* editorial into the struggle between the characters of Joy-Hulga and her mother. Joy-Hulga lives in an atmosphere of constant affirmation, an atmosphere her mother has created. Mrs. Hopewell delivers one optimistic cliché after another, each of which the hired woman, Mrs. Freeman, confirms: "The girl was used to this kind of dialogue for breakfast and more of it for dinner; sometimes they had it for supper too." The clichés repeated by Mrs.

Hopewell are those of democratic pluralism, the "most important" of which is the observation that "other people have their opinions too" (*CS* 273). Like the *Life* author, however, Mrs. Hopewell rejects any attitude but a positive one. "If you can't come pleasantly, I don't want you at all," she tells Joy-Hulga when they inspect their fields (*CS* 274). Joy-Hulga, whom O'Connor called "a projection of myself" (*HB* 106), refuses to conform to the narrow role assigned her by Mrs. Hopewell. "If you want me," Joy-Hulga tells her mother, "here I am – LIKE I AM" (*CS* 274). When her mother remarks elsewhere that "a smile never hurt anyone," her response suggests that Joy-Hulga equates affirmation with willful ignorance: "Do you ever look inside and see what you are *not?*" (*CS* 276). Like the contemporary novelists condemned by *Life,* Joy-Hulga rejects "yea-saying" in favor of "negation."[15] Her hyphenated name, which records the conflict between a mother who tried "to turn her dust into Joy" and a daughter who has tried "to turn it herself into Hulga" (*CS* 275), also reflects the split between the affirmative role assigned to the intellectual during the 1950s and the critical role that O'Connor would choose for herself. While *Life* demanded expressions of "joy," the writer sensitive to the materialism of life in the United States felt compelled to adopt a negative perspective. As O'Connor said in one of her talks, "The writer who emphasizes spiritual values is very likely to take the darkest view of all of what he sees in this country today" (*MM* 26).

As her statement indicates, O'Connor departed from the Cold War ideological consensus at the level of the most basic assumptions. She attached a negative value to the material abundance that signified American cultural superiority for the adherents of domestic ideology. In her 1957 essay, O'Connor postulated "some ugly correlation between our unparalleled prosperity and the stridency of these demands for a literature that shows us the joy of life." She asked whether "these screams for joy would be quite so piercing if joy were really more abundant in our prosperous society" (*MM* 30).

In her fiction, O'Connor answers the question she raised about the quality of American life. She answers it, specifically, in the context of the home; domestic existence in her farm stories is insufferable, with family members constantly antagonizing one another. There are exceptions: the mother in "A Temple of the Holy Ghost" (1954) treats her daughter as her confidante. But the typical relation between parent and child, or among siblings, is one of spite and resentment. Of all the stories, "Greenleaf" presents the divided, dysfunctional family in the harshest light. The bickering that runs through the other stories here escalates into a brawl between brothers. Wesley, one of the brothers, has already made it clear that the May family is wholly devoid of love and loyalty. He has informed his mother, "I wouldn't milk a cow to save your soul from hell" (*CS* 321). The families inhabiting O'Connor's pastoral settings lack the moral virtues that made the domestic ideal so emotionally powerful, so psychologically reassuring, to postwar Americans. Here again, O'Connor undermines an assumption basic to the ideology of domestic containment – in this case, the integrity of the American family. For adherents of this ideology, Elaine Tyler May notes, the self-contained home promised "security in an insecure world." Only an external threat could corrupt or fragment the family; the home therefore required "heavy protection against the intrusions of forces outside itself."[16] Before such intrusions, the family existed in a state of innocence, of purity and harmony. O'Connor, in contrast, shows families that are already corrupt, already fragmented, by the time their members become aware of external threats. Outside forces, in other words, are not to blame for the evils of family life in her fiction. Corruption precedes invasion.

O'Connor subverts the ideological construct that had normative value for defenders of the self-contained home. A polemicist writing in 1954 could take for granted a uniform understanding of the phrase "ordinary home life" and a widespread acceptance of the norm it adumbrated. The psychiatrist Fredric Wertham, the best-known opponent of crime and horror comics in the decade after World War II, appealed to this norm in *Seduction of the Innocent,* his most extended attack on the comic-book industry. Speaking for many parents who saw the comic book as a domestic intruder, a threat to the integrity of the family, Wertham incorporated elements of the invasion scenario into *Seduction.* His use of garden imagery, for example, conjoins the image of the invaded home with that of the invaded pastoral: "blight and weeds" threaten American children, who are likened to flowers. "We could learn from the specialists in agriculture," Wertham told parents. "They would know how to deal with the comic-book pest." Wertham made explicit reference to the scenario when he expanded his attack on the comics to include other mass media. He warned his readers that the American family "is invaded with an all-round amphibious offensive" by the media:

> Take a peaceful American family on a quiet evening. Papa . . . is reading Mickey Spillane. Junior . . . settles down to look at one of those good crime television shows where a man is beaten up so mercilessly that he is blinded for life. His older sister, just this side of puberty, is engrossed in the comic book *Reform School Girl!*, which blends sex, violence and torture in its content.

Although the mother of this nuclear family is reading books on child psychology, she receives the same message: "Papa, mama, and the two children are all subjected to the impact of the same current fashion, the extolling of hostility and violence." The family has been corrupted by the media, or, in the words of another writer, negatively "influenced" by "these outside forces."[17]

A story by O'Connor, "A Good Man Is Hard to Find" (1953), opens with a family scene similar to the one described by Wertham. The scenes differ, however, in what they suggest about the quality of family life, and this contrast illustrates O'Connor's rejection of the ideological assumption underlying Wertham's attack on the media – the idea that the family, before invasion, existed in a state of pastoral innocence. The first few paragraphs of "A Good Man" show an American home penetrated by one of the mass media. Various sections of the Atlanta *Journal,* including the crime news and "the funny papers" (*CS* 117), engross the family members as they spend a Sunday morning at home. The scene has a strong current of hostility. The two older children, John Wesley and June Star, are rude to their grandmother, whose relationship to her son, Bailey, is obviously strained. She nags him, and he ignores her. In a later scene, Bailey says "something to his mother that shocked even the children" (*CS* 127); he blames her for the acts of violence that will destroy the family, the shootings prompted by her announcement that she recognizes The Misfit. The newspaper in the opening scene of "A Good Man" serves as a device for introducing The Misfit to the grandmother and to the reader. As a mere prop in this scene, the newspaper does not call attention to itself. It does not represent one of the "outside forces" that concerned Wertham. The family members in the story by O'Connor do not seem to have been "influenced" to any great degree by the mass media. More specifically, the narration never suggests that their meanness derives from their reading. The "hostility and violence" that the media smuggled into the home, according to Wertham, are inherent in family life, according to O'Connor.

Her literary subversion of the domestic ideal reflects her critical perspective on the American way of life. O'Connor seems ambivalent, however, when she portrays intellectual characters who adopt, or claim to adopt, the perspective she defends in her nonfiction. As critics, her intellectuals do little more than grumble and whine. Joy-Hulga makes "ugly" remarks (*CS* 274); when he talks about Timberboro, his hometown, Asbury has an "ugly" voice (*CS* 359); Wesley has a voice "he could not help making deliberately nasty" (*CS* 319). Joy-Hulga's attacks on her mother's worldview are sporadic, incomprehensible to Mrs. Hopewell, and, consequently, ineffectual. Her state of "constant outrage" never weakens the complacent optimism of her mother, who recites her clichés "in a tone of gentle insistence" (*CS* 273). The outrage has no effect on Mrs. Freeman, either: "A direct attack, a positive leer, blatant ugliness to her face – these never touched her" (*CS* 274). From the viewpoint authorized by *Life* and *Partisan Review,* the intellectual who did not affirm American life, first and foremost, did not merit serious attention. Surprisingly, O'Connor here seems to concur with *Life* and *Partisan Review.* The manner in which she portrays her intellectuals discourages the reader from taking them seriously.

In tying their domestication to their disability, O'Connor communicates her own frustration over the limited role she felt she had been assigned. At the same time, however, she reduces sympathy for her intellectual characters by making them vain, self-pitying, ridiculous. Asbury, for instance, has never published any of his work, which consists of "lifeless novels," "stationary plays," "prosy poems," and "sketchy short stories" (*CS* 365); still, he considers himself to be without intellectual peer. Asbury founds his intellectual identity on his isolation – even from a sister, Mary George, who "posed as an intellectual" (*CS* 363). He believes in the myth O'Connor mentions in "The Regional Writer" (1962), the romantic notion that "the writer exists in a state of sensitivity which cuts him off, or raises him above, or casts him below the community around him" (*MM* 52–3).

For O'Connor, this myth was no better than the idea that had supplanted it, the idea of the intellectual as cold warrior. Having rejected the affirmative, socially integrated role in her 1957 essay, O'Connor went on to reject the older notion, "the idea of the artist as Sufferer and Rebel," in her 1962 lecture. The apparent discrepancy between her position in "The Fiction Writer and His Country" and her position in "The Regional Writer" suggests that American authors, like American politicians during the Cold War, faced a choice between impossible alternatives.[18]

Authors who sought a critical stance found themselves in a double bind. If the role of cold warrior seemed too narrow, the role of social rebel seemed no longer viable. The image of the intellectual as romantic rebel had fallen victim to the anxieties of the atomic age. Before World War II, a faith in the intelligentsia as agents of revolutionary social change had figured in the writings of many American leftists, including those at *Partisan Review.*[19] After World War II, many intellectuals worried that they operated only at the margins of U.S. society – a society more concerned about survival than about change. The atomic bomb had revealed the true impotence of the writer as rebel: such was the argument with which Marshall McLuhan opened a 1947 essay. In "The Southern Quality," which O'Connor recommended to a friend in 1954 (*HB* 70), McLuhan said, "The atom-bomb has laid forever the illusion that writers and artists were somehow constitutive and directive of the holy *zeitgeist*." McLuhan contrasted the situation before the war with the situation afterward. It was easy, he wrote, "to indulge in the lyrical megalomania of being a 'revolutionary' writer when mere political affiliation . . . assured reputation and audience." Now, however, the writer had to acknowledge a "destructive energy" far greater than that "postulated by the revolutionaries," an energy "vastly in excess of any available human wisdom or political ingenuity to accommodate it."

Understandably, McLuhan wrote, the fact of "their futility and insignificance" proved to be "more than the very vigorous and very human egotism of artists and writers [was] prepared to swallow." After all, the myth of romantic rebellion had promised empowerment as well as segregation. From their position outside bourgeois culture, artists and writers had planned "to perturb the unyielding bovines" by dropping "a plastic or poetic bomb."[20] From their new position within bourgeois culture, they had to give up their plans.

The intellectuals who appear in O'Connor's farm stories share not only the desire to drop bombs, but also the frustration of that desire. Asbury writes his mother a lengthy letter, patterned after the one Franz Kafka wrote to his father, so that "she might experience a painful realization" (*CS* 364). At the end of "The Enduring Chill," however, Asbury decides against dropping his bomb; he keeps the letter locked in his desk. He abandons the romantic role in which he has cast himself. The trouble is, the story ends before he identifies a role he *can* play.

A viable role for the American intellectual is conspicuous by its absence from O'Connor's fiction. In a 1960 lecture, "Some Aspects of the Grotesque in Southern Fiction," O'Connor proposes a middle way between the complete integration and the complete isolation of American writers; ideally, literature would constitute a "guide" for society by criticizing that society (*MM* 46). In her 1957 essay, O'Connor claims that the fiction writer is of "value . . . to his country" as long as he maintains a critical stance (*MM* 35). In the stories, unfortunately, such a writer nowhere appears. A story published in a journal called *The Critic*, "The Partridge Festival" (1961), shows the difficulty of positioning oneself as a social critic in Cold War America. If the figure of the romantic rebel was now obsolete, it was still the only oppositional figure available to the imagination of American intellectuals; McLuhan had offered no substitute. "The Partridge Festival" features an intellectual actively engaged in cultural criticism. Calhoun is visiting the hometown of his relatives, Aunt Bessie and Aunt Mattie, to write an exposé of the community. He blames the town for a recent tragedy, a multiple killing that occurred during a town celebration. In his desire to enact a role critical of society, Calhoun adopts Singleton as his ideal, casting the murderous loner as "the Outsider" (*CS* 429). To some extent, Singleton is an appropriate choice; insofar as he spurns the cultural act of celebration, he departs from the approved model of the postwar intellectual. Having refused to buy an Azalea Festival badge, Singleton is jailed in "an outdoor privy borrowed for the occasion by the Jaycees." He then "mars the festive spirit" by shooting five local dignitaries and a member of the crowd (CS 422). Singleton, Calhoun believes, disdains any form of consensus. Calhoun calls him a "non-conformist" and an "individualist" who "would not allow himself to be pressed into the mold of his inferiors" (CS 431). Aunt Bessie's observation, "He never conformed" (CS 423), seems to reinforce the image of Singleton as a radical idealist, as the kind of intellectual that Calhoun wants to be.

The punchline is that Singleton is no idealist, no intellectual. He is, instead, a "mental case" who claims to own Partridge (CS 423, 443). Calhoun turns the lunatic into a social critic because he wants "to mitigate his own guilt," to atone for his involvement in a commercial culture whose values Singleton apparently rejects. Calhoun, who envies "Singleton's purity," feels guilty about his position as an intellectual in the capitalist system:

> For the three summer months of the year, he lived with his parents and sold air-conditioners, boats and refrigerators so that for the other nine months he could afford to meet life naturally and bring his real self – the rebel-artist-mystic – to birth. (CS 424)

Calhoun feels especially guilty because "he could have fared without the orgy of selling he cast himself into in the summer." The truth is, "he *enjoyed* selling. . . . He was so good at it that the company had given him an achievement scroll" (CS 425).

His subsequent abuse of the scroll – specifically, his placement of "quotation marks around the word *achievement*" (CS 425) – indicates his dissent from capitalist ideology, one of whose tenets, according to an economic textbook published in 1960, was personal incentive.[21] However, Calhoun criticizes Partridge less for economic or political reasons than for aesthetic "sins" that demand a scapegoat (CS 431). After all, his aversion to the citizens of Partridge predates their mistreatment of Singleton. Calhoun hates them because they appreciate the wrong things. They like beauty contests, and they prefer the "pathetic store displays" of downtown Partridge to the "best" azaleas of the neighborhoods away from the "bare commercial scene." The town motto, "Beauty is Our Money Crop," signifies the "taint of the place" for Calhoun (CS 426). Mary Elizabeth, like Calhoun, bases judgment on aesthetics rather than politics; this female "scholar" (CS 433), with whom he forms an uneasy alliance, condemns the citizens of Partridge for their crimes against beauty. "They prostitute azaleas!" she exclaims (CS 434).

The standard of judgment applied by Calhoun and Mary Elizabeth prevailed among postwar intellectuals. During the Cold War, writes

Jackson Lears, "the touchstones of cultural criticism became questions of style and taste."[22] Although Calhoun's vocal support for the right "to be different" and "to be yourself" (*CS* 429) might conceivably have served as the rallying cry for substantive acts of dissent, it should be remembered that "the endless chatter about conformity" in the 1950s coexisted with "the tendency to redefine questions of power as matters of taste."[23]

When she and Calhoun visit Singleton, Mary Elizabeth brings a paperback *Revolt of the Masses*, a translation of *La rebelión de las masas* (1930) by José Ortega y Gasset. O'Connor has her character bring this particular book because the type of individual that Ortega commends, *el hombre selecto*, parallels the Emersonian nonconformist that Mary Elizabeth and Calhoun imagine Singleton to be. The book is also significant because it gave American intellectuals a philosophical rationale for their new devotion to aesthetic concerns. In their introduction to a passage from *La rebelión*, the American editors of a Spanish literary anthology published in 1960 summarized its thesis in the following terms:

> By *rebelión* Ortega does not refer to political revolution; he means, rather, that when democracy, which he holds to be valid only within the limits of law, is applied indiscriminately to art, literature, social comportment, taste, religion, and education, there is a perversion of values. This is what happens when the *hombre-masa*, complacent and undistinguished, seeks through sheer numbers to impose his mediocre standards upon the *minoría selecta* or élite. The result is a tyranny of the masses, a tyranny as oppressive as the political tyrannies of the *ancien régime*, of oligarchy or plutocracy.[24]

The idea that the leveling of cultural standards could be "as oppressive as" the abuse of political power had a practical value for intellectuals who felt compelled to affirm U.S. political institutions but who wanted nonetheless to maintain a critical stance: mass culture became the object of their criticism. In the *Partisan Review* symposium, Andrew Ross observes, many of those who agreed with the editorial statement concerning the new attitude of American intellectuals "expressed their anxiety about the likely erosion of their traditional critical and independent vantage point upon social and cultural affairs."[25] Some intellectuals, like Dwight Macdonald, might assign a political significance to mass culture as "an instrument of social domination,"[26] but the tendency was to discuss cultural products instead of political issues.

This tendency was most evident in the New Criticism, which came to dominate the teaching of literature at U.S. colleges and universities during the 1950s.[27] In a 1949 lecture, a leftist professor known for his political activism singled out the movement as a source of "self-enclosed knowledge." Using the image common to "Greenleaf," "Good Country

People," and "The Enduring Chill," the image of the intellectual contained within a pastoral setting, F. O. Matthiessen warned against political quietism:

> The dilemma for the serious critic in our dangerously split society is that, feeling isolated, he will become serious in the wrong sense, aloof and finally taking an inverted superiority in his isolation. At that point criticism becomes a kind of closed garden.
>
> My views are based on the conviction that the land beyond the garden's walls is more fertile, and that the responsibilities of the critic lie in making renewed contact with that soil.[28]

A decade later, William Esty called attention to the political quietism of Americans engaged in the production of literature. Esty charged that "younger" American writers were "politically rather numb." They had succumbed, he wrote in 1958, to "the extreme temptation of us all in the fifties: the forsaking of politics and, indeed, life, for an intellectual bomb shelter." He included O'Connor among writers who had opted for self-containment. In her case, political statement had been replaced by literary trickery; Esty faulted O'Connor for converting "the very real and cruel grotesquerie of our world . . . into clever gimmicks for *Partisan Review*." In "Good Country People," for example, Esty found only "overingenious horrifics."[29]

I have been arguing otherwise: O'Connor does make a political statement with this story, though in the form of political allegory. "Good Country People" and the passage from Matthiessen's essay share not only the situation of intellectual containment, but also the resulting sense of frustration. O'Connor, whose concern over "the Manichean spirit of the times" (*MM* 33) recalled the anxiety Matthiessen had expressed regarding a society "dangerously split" over questions of political loyalty, agreed with his assertion that a criticism limited to the purely formal aspects of cultural productions would be irresponsible.

Of course, Matthiessen and O'Connor differed vastly in terms of partisan politics. Matthiessen was a socialist shadowed by government agents in the late 1940s, a leftist attacked by other leftists, including Irving Howe, who called him "our outstanding literary fellow-traveller" and "an apologist for a brutal totalitarian state."[30] The few times that O'Connor recorded her opinion on a partisan political issue, she threw her support behind mainstream Democratic candidates: Stevenson in 1952, Kennedy in 1960 (*HB* 42, 404). O'Connor, moreover, remained faithful to the New Critical precepts that Matthiessen associated with political apathy and critical irresponsibility. *Understanding Fiction*, "a book that has been of invaluable help to me" (*HB* 83), taught O'Connor how to apply these precepts to the short story form. In the original 1943 edition, Cleanth Brooks and Robert Penn Warren articulated the autotelic standard of the New Criticism. A story is successful, they wrote, "when all of the elements are functionally related to each other, when each part contributes to the intended effect." The elements, in other words, "are so related that we feel an expressive interpenetration among them, a set of vital relationships." Adherence to this standard of "organic" internal unity would seem to lead the fiction writer into the error for which Matthiessen faulted the New Critics: inattention to sociopolitical realities beyond the text. Brooks and Warren, however, nowhere encouraged the fiction writer to produce self-contained works; they insisted, rather, that "all fiction implies a meaningfulness beyond the particular instances which it presents. The meanings involved in characters and events can be extended to apply to other characters and events."[31]

This last assertion comes from a passage in which Brooks and Warren discuss allegory, a mode of expression that experienced a resurgence throughout postwar culture. In the theater, *The Crucible* (1953) by Arthur Miller transported McCarthyism from Washington, D.C., to seventeenth-century Salem. The genre of the Western film enabled Carl Foreman, a writer-director and former Communist Party member, to make a statement about the political situation that would force him to work under pseudonyms. *High Noon* (1952), the last Hollywood film he scripted, has been interpreted as "an allegory about existential man standing alone in the McCarthy era."[32] In painting, Cécile Whiting notes, the allegorical mode adopted by social realists during World War II enabled them to address the political controversies of the postwar years. *Witch Hunt* (1950) by William Gropper and *Second Allegory* (1953) by Ben Shahn convey their attitudes toward the House Committee on Un-American Activities, before which both painters had been called to testify.[33] Allegory gave artists in the various media a versatile mode of protest and self-protection.

The desire for self-preservation was a major reason for intellectuals to adopt the new affirmative role announced by *Partisan Review*. However, only one contributor to the symposium made this connection. While Arvin, Trilling, and Burnham followed the lead of the editors and pointed to foreign totalitarianism as the reason for integration, C. Wright Mills called attention to the domestic political climate, a climate that discouraged dissent from the status quo: "Impatience with things as they are in America," Mills wrote, was often judged to be "mutinous."[34] For intellectuals, the consequences of such judgment were serious. American universities, which embraced the New Critics and their apolitical "scholasticism,"[35] had no place for those professors with ties to political groups of the radical Left. During the first fifteen years of the Cold War, hundreds lost their teaching positions over allegations of Communism or fellow traveling, or for their refusal to cooperate with government inves-

Ben Shahn, *Second Allegory*, 1953, tempera on masonite, 53 3/8 × 31 3/8 in. Krannert Art Museum and Kinkead Pavilion, University of Illinois, Champaign. Festival of Arts Purchase Fund, 1953.

tigations into political subversiveness.[36] Responding to the dismissal of several professors at Olivet College, Matthiessen warned that "once official opinion embarks on the course of stamping out dangerous views, every shade of dissent becomes dangerous."[37]

The domestication of American intellectuals was part of a wider phenomenon, the prohibition of dissent at a time of political paranoia. But the situation of the intellectual seemed especially precarious. Anti-Communism often merged with the anti-intellectualism that Richard Hofstadter would later identify as a sentiment to which Americans had long been susceptible.[38] Edward A. Shils, who considered the *Partisan Review* symposium a well-intentioned but futile effort to "overcome the long tradition of withdrawal and alienation," connected postwar fears about Communist infiltration with long-standing prejudice against intellectuals. "The agitation of the past decade about secrecy and subversion," Shils wrote in 1956, "has been only the flaring up on another front of the long war between, on the one side, intellectuals and, on the other, politicians and businessmen." Although he predicted "the death of this obnoxious tradition," Shils observed that "McCarthyism has slowed down and harmed the process of reconciliation between politicians and intellectuals."[39] To Leslie A. Fiedler, writing in the early 1950s, McCarthyism represented "hostility between the community and its intelligence" and drew its strength from a populist suspicion of intellectuals. Fiedler recalled the "troubled silence" that greeted Whittaker Chambers when he remarked, during his 1948 testimony against Alger Hiss, that he had once spent a whole week reading: "How could anyone read so long? It is the suspicious vagary of the kind of man who once believed in Stalin and now believes in the Devil."[40]

The suspicion of intellectual activity fuels the character struggles dramatized by O'Connor. In "Good Country People," Mrs. Hopewell has a "troubled" reaction to the reading Joy-Hulga has been doing. A textual passage underlined by her daughter "worked on Mrs. Hopewell like some evil incantation in gibberish" (CS 277). Although Joy-Hulga has been domesticated, confined to the family farm, she continues to be a source of anxiety. In this respect, her situation resembles that of the local schoolteacher described by Shils:

> The teacher is often an outsider, at least in the sense of having been away to a normal school or a teachers' college, and might be reading a periodical otherwise unknown in the town. The teacher is suspected of being too distant, thinking he or she is better than the "ordinary people" of the place.

When even "the humblest representative of the intellectuals" could arouse suspicion, their acceptance as insiders could prove elusive. According to Shils, neither artists nor scientists "seem to fit into the scheme of things in which the politician has confidence."[41] It is not enough for Joy-Hulga to *be* in the setting identified with the American way of life. "In America," Shils observed, "being American is not a primordial fact attendant on residence." Instead, "there is more of a tendency to define a person as American by the extent to which he acts and feels and thinks in a way defined as American." Shils added, "There is more of a tendency in the United States, as compared with Great Britain, to think of differences in terms of loyalty and disloyalty, in terms of liking and disliking America."[42]

At the start of her career, the question of intellectual loyalty arose for O'Connor herself. Early in 1949, in the suitably rural setting of Yaddo, she became involved in a controversy centering around an American intellectual linked with "un-American" activities. The *New York Times* reported in February that the U.S. Army had identified a former Yaddo resident, Agnes Smedley, as a contact for a Soviet spy ring.[43] The army admitted a few days later that it had no evidence against Smedley, a journalist and novelist who supported the Chinese Communists; but the four guests in residence asked the board of the Yaddo corporation to fire the executive director, Elizabeth Ames, for being "deeply and mysteriously involved in Mrs. Smedley's political activities." Speaking for O'Connor and the other two guests, Elizabeth Hardwick and Edward Maisel, Robert Lowell attacked the director in the Cold War language of disease. After he compared Yaddo to a "body," he called Ames "a diseased organ, chronically poisoning the whole system." The scenario of the invaded pastoral had clearly influenced his thinking. In an open letter written to defend Lowell's conduct, Robert Fitzgerald said that Lowell had attributed "something unpleasant in the atmosphere of the place" to "long permeation by moods or influences that were politically or morally committed to communism."[44]

The four guests left Yaddo in protest. In a letter written a decade later, O'Connor would recall the "magnificent" scenery of Yaddo (*HB* 362), but the correspondence published in *The Habit of Being* reveals little about her feelings regarding the controversy or, more specifically, her participation in one of the many "witch hunts" of the Cold War period. In her account of the incident, Sally Fitzgerald absolves O'Connor of any guilt: "Nothing in it reflects discredit on her motives or her intelligence." O'Connor, she writes, "behaved honestly throughout and in accord with her convictions" (*HB* 12). What Fitzgerald ignores are the moral complexities of behaving "honestly" at a time when informing on friends and co-workers had become a patriotic duty.[45] The outrage of the former Yaddo guests who supported Ames, the outrage they expressed in a petition against "the use of a smear-technique,"[46] cannot be dismissed. One of these former guests, Alfred Kazin, knew O'Connor professionally and admired her fiction. Despite his admiration, which never diminished, Kazin felt she had overreacted at Yaddo. In his 1971 review of *The Complete Stories,* he recalled meeting O'Connor "during the McCarthy period, under circumstances that persuaded me that she – or her friends – would have considered Jefferson Davis a Communist."[47]

For her part, Elizabeth Ames expressed dismay over the change she had seen in a group of people who had lived "in great apparent harmony and good will toward me," a group that included a secretary who turned out to be an FBI informer. At the Yaddo board meeting, Ames attributed the behavior of Lowell, O'Connor, Hardwick, and Maisel to "fear and hysteria," as well as immaturity: "They are young people, in their 30's; I can understand it, faced with a world such as we have."[48]

O'Connor's participation is understandable, if not entirely honorable, given the uncomfortable position of Cold War intellectuals who sought to maintain a critical stance: they had to distinguish theirs from any stance that would be labeled "un-American." When liberals agreed to act as informers, claims Victor S. Navasky, the purpose was to prove that "liberalism was free of any Communist taint." Those who cooperated with investigators and "named names" hoped "to preserve and fortify their 'liberal' outpost by means of this ultimate anti-Communist gesture."[49] For this reason, too, liberals dissociated themselves from Matthiessen. William E. Cain summarizes the argument of leftists who attacked the Harvard professor in the late 1940s: "By refusing to denounce the totalitarian evils of Stalinist Russia, Matthiessen had dirtied the very cause of democratic socialism he took himself to be supporting."[50]

Opposition to Communism, domestic as well as foreign, was central to the ideology of Cold War liberalism.[51] Liberals agreed with conservatives that the Communist Party in the United States had no right to be heard.[52] Granville Hicks, with whom O'Connor became friends in the late 1950s, claimed that every U.S. Communist was "actually or potentially a Soviet agent."[53] For Sidney Hook, this justified the antidemocratic excesses of anti-Communism. In his contribution to the *Partisan Review* symposium, Hook wrote, "Our own vigilantes and reactionaries are much more like witches and straw scarecrows than are the paid and unpaid agents of the Kremlin who constitute the membership of the Communist Parties in all countries."[54]

At the same time, Cold War liberals had to account for their own history of Communist Party membership in the 1930s. Hicks, for instance, had joined a party unit at Harvard.[55] While Ames blamed the youth of the four Yaddo guests for their anti-Communist fervor, the postwar liberal community blamed its prewar Communist sympathies on political immaturity. Fiedler observed in 1955 that regular contributors to *Partisan Review,* which began as a Communist publication, had taken "a long time to grow up," partly "because they have almost all been forced somewhere between 1935 and 1940 to make a radical shift in their political allegiances." Members of "the *Partisan* academy," having undergone the change to which Fiedler and others attested in the 1952 symposium, now provided "evidence of a movement toward a literature of maturity."[56]

The domestication of American intellectuals supposedly demonstrated this maturity. As Mailer noted with disgust, "The American writer is being dunned . . . to grow up, to accept the American reality, to integrate himself."[57] O'Connor expressed her own dissatisfaction by reversing the formula that Cold War liberals used to explain their changing political allegiances. The intellectuals who have been domesticated in her fiction are characterized – by their relatives and by the narration – in terms of childishness. In "Good Country People," the mother refuses to recognize the adult identity the daughter has chosen for herself. Joy changed her name to Hulga at the age of legal majority, twenty-one, when she was "away from home" (CS 274). Only away from the family farm could Joy-Hulga be an adult. At home, "Mrs. Hopewell thought of her as a child though she was thirty-two years old and highly educated" (CS 271). Placement within the domestic setting infantilizes the intellectual. When Aunt Bessie greets her nephew Calhoun at the beginning of "The Partridge Festival," she calls the aspiring novelist "our baby" (CS 421). She and Aunt Mattie repeatedly address Calhoun, who lives at home during the summer, as "Baby Lamb." Mary Elizabeth, the "scholar" who is "home for her spring holidays," has a face that is "still childish" (CS 433).

According to Hook, domestic Communism showed American intellectuals the limits they had to place on their social and political criticism. Although he paid lip service to the idea of intellectual dissent, Hook urged intellectuals to distance themselves from the extremism of the radical Left: "The task of the intellectual is . . . to criticize what needs to be criticized in America, without forgetting for a moment the total threat which Communism poses to the life of the free mind."[58] The limits that did not bother Hook did bother O'Connor. Despite her aversion to the politics of a radical leftist like Smedley, O'Connor shared Matthiessen's concern that "every shade of dissent" would prompt charges of subversiveness in the political climate of Cold War America. The role of dissenter held great appeal for O'Connor, who approached it from two directions – one religious, one regional. When she rejects the idea of literary exile in her occasional prose, O'Connor seems to echo the majority view in "Our Country and Our Culture." She redefines the key term, however, so that "country" signifies far more than the United States. In "The Fiction Writer and His Country," the term points to a set of conflicting loyalties: nation, region, and the "true country" of Christian faith (MM 27). As her essay continues, it becomes clear that allegiance to the South and fidelity to the Catholic Church concerned O'Connor more than any representative service she might have performed for the nation – the service required of the American writer as cold warrior. Her status as a Southern, Catholic writer, the very status that meant her removal from the literary mainstream, meant a great deal more. It gave her a position, a territory, from which she could criticize U.S. society.

3

Jesus Fanatics and Communist Foreigners

The way of life that O'Connor refused to celebrate had a slippery meaning in Cold War rhetoric. When the editors of *Fortune* magazine tried to define "the American way of life" in 1951, they described the phrase as "a vague but tantalizing abstraction . . . used by every orator on every side of every issue." Those who demanded celebration usually defined the American way by contrasting it with life under Communism, the rival system in the Cold War narrative. The 1955 editorial in *Life* magazine, published by the same corporation that published *Fortune*, identified the superiority of the United States with material abundance. Capitalism, as the recognized source of national prosperity, seemed synonymous with the American way.[1]

Some definitions, however, contrasted this way of life with systems other than Communism – belief systems that commanded the devotion, or at least the respect, of most Americans. In this regard, religion informed the various attempts to define the ubiquitous phrase. The editors of *Fortune* equated "Christian" and "American" ideals, but some writers rejected the "spurious wedding" signified by the phrase – the wedding of Christianity and capitalism.[2] These writers saw the American way as a belief system competing with established religions. Will Herberg, for example, called it "the operative faith of the American people." As such, it constituted the national religion, "the framework in terms of which the crucial values of American existence are couched." At the same time, Herberg noted, several groups were unwilling to profess this "common faith." The "hold outs" included Catholics who refused to let their traditional creeds "be dissolved into an over-all 'American religion,'" and Protestants who espoused the "religions of the disinherited," or the "many 'holiness,' pentecostal, and millenarian sects of the socially and culturally submerged segments of our society."[3]

The two varieties of religious dissent came together in the creative process of O'Connor, the Catholic writer whose fictional characters

61

show the influence of Protestant fundamentalism. As a Catholic novelist, she sympathized with "those aspects of Southern life where the religious feeling is most intense and where its outward forms are farthest from the Catholic" (*MM* 207). In her fiction, the "human aspiration" shared by Catholicism and fundamentalism (*MM* 206) unites them against the American way of life. O'Connor believed in an existential "framework" other than that of the American way: Christian dogma as "an instrument for penetrating reality" (*MM* 178). Simply put, her reason for dissenting from the Cold War consensus was religious.

A scene from her first novel, *Wise Blood,* is emblematic of the cultural scene in which religious dissent took place – when it did take place – during the Cold War. In the third chapter, Asa and Sabbath Lily Hawks interrupt the sales pitch of a street vendor and confront the people gathered around the man. While Sabbath hands out religious tracts, Asa rattles a tin cup and offers his listeners a choice between repentance and charity. "Help a blind preacher," he says. "If you won't repent, give up a nickel" (*WB* 40). His listeners have come downtown "to see what was for sale" (*WB* 37), and this intrusion of religious rhetoric into a commercial setting makes them uncomfortable; the small crowd begins to disperse. The vendor, who is selling potato peelers, yells at Asa: "What you think you doing? Who you think you are, running people off from here?" (*WB* 40). After looking at one of the tracts, the vendor calls Asa and Sabbath "damn Jesus fanatics." Then, for good measure, he charges them with political subversiveness: "These goddam Communist foreigners!" he screams (*WB* 41).

A 1949 draft of the chapter, published as "The Peeler" in *Partisan Review,* places even greater emphasis on the link between religious suasion and political subversion. The vendor here refers to Asa and Sabbath as "goddam Communist Jesus Foreigners" (*CS* 65). If the political reference comes as a surprise in a narrative that departs so radically from "the customary kind of realism" (*MM* 40), the reasoning behind the reference seems more arbitrary still. At the time, however, the link was not uncommon. Indeed, it reappeared in the 1952 *Newsweek* review of *Wise Blood.* Along with "a satire on the secularization of modern life," the *Newsweek* reviewer found "a subtle parody of Communist soapboxing in Haze's street sermons." Hazel Motes never mentions politics, but the negativism of his message prompted the reviewer, undeterred by "the deliberate unreality of her tale," to read O'Connor's narrative as political commentary; the point about "Communist soapboxing" follows the observation that the "primitive evangelism" of Hazel's grandfather has become "purely destructive."[4]

For many of O'Connor's contemporaries, religious rhetoric that carried a message of "rejection" was politically suspect. Religious figures who failed to celebrate capitalist society – setting themselves in opposition to the cultural status quo and making a rival claim for the allegiance of U.S. citizens – could expect to meet with the same response as American intellectuals who failed to enact the new role of cold warrior, the affirmative role endorsed by the *Partisan Review* symposium. In religious as well as intellectual discussions, the totalizing dualism of Cold War rhetoric equated dissent with disloyalty. That is, with only two political alternatives, any form of dissent from the ideology of capitalism seemed to promote the opposite ideology, Communism. An essay by a Presbyterian minister, published in 1957, suggests that O'Connor's street vendor spoke for many Americans. John H. Marion observed that the "front-line participation" of American Christians in "certain sharp battles over social customs and group relationships" opened them to the charge of subversiveness when their convictions placed them "on the less popular side of these battles." Such "hard-pressed disciples," Marion wrote, "know that to buck certain powerful social forces . . . is to get oneself labeled, more than likely, as a 'fool,' a 'crackpot,' an 'agitator,' and maybe as a 'pro-Communist.'"5

Marion's vagueness regarding "certain" battles and "certain" forces underlines the seriousness of the problem facing those who dissented on religious grounds. The specific issues on which they challenged the political consensus seemed less important, to those who upheld this consensus, than the challenge itself. In *Wise Blood,* the content of the street sermons hardly matters to the secular audience that is distracted from its window-shopping. Asa Hawks seeks contributions more than converts, and Hazel Motes preaches against religious faith; but the mere fact that they speak the language of fundamentalist religion, calling people away from the consumerism that signified the superiority of the American way of life, alienates them from their listeners.

The shoppers in the commercial setting of downtown Taulkinham are not completely averse to religious rhetoric. They simply prefer the preaching of Onnie Jay Holy, who offers no challenge, actual or perceived, to their values. Hoover Shoats, who abandons his assumed identity when he advises Hazel on marketing strategy, keeps his message "sweet" to attract listeners and, ultimately, to collect money (*WB* 157). His sermons focus attention on the individual; his "up-to-date" church, he claims, calls forth the "natural sweetness" of the individual. What he counsels, then, is self-improvement based on positive qualities that have been suppressed by negative emotions. As a child grows up, Hoover says, "its sweetness don't show so much, cares and troubles come to perplext it, and all its sweetness is driven inside it. Then it gets miserable and lonesome and sick." When the individual learns "to unlock that little rose of sweetness," social success will result. Pointing to a baby in the crowd, Hoover cajoles his listeners: "Why, I know you people aren't going to let that little thing grow up and have all his sweetness pushed inside him when it could be on the outside to win friends and make him loved" (*WB* 150–1, 153).

O'Connor's readers would have been familiar with this brand of religious rhetoric. Hoover's preaching condenses a distinct body of religious thought in Cold War America. Hoover Shoats surpasses Hazel Motes in audience appeal because he speaks in the widely popular idiom of the "cult of reassurance," the movement to which O'Connor alluded when she criticized those Christians who "think faith is a big electric blanket" (*HB* 354). Norman Vincent Peale, the best-known representative of this postwar trend in religion, offered Americans a message almost identical to the one delivered by Hoover.[6] In *The Power of Positive Thinking* (1952), a best-seller published the same year as *Wise Blood*, Peale preached a gospel of self-realization. "It is a pity that people should let themselves be defeated by the problems, cares, and difficulties of human existence," Peale wrote, "and it is also quite unnecessary." The solution, he maintained, was to stop thinking negatively about "your personal powers." Urging his reader to "believe in yourself and release your inner powers," he promised that "faith in your abilities" would bring success and happiness.[7]

In effect, the cult of reassurance translated the message of the 1952 *Partisan Review* symposium and the 1955 *Life* editorial from cultural into personal terms: the individual was basically good, as U.S. society was fundamentally sound, so there was no need for criticism. "This cult," Paul Hutchinson told readers of *Life* earlier in 1955, "says that the bedeviled victim of today's pressures should discipline his thoughts to reject all pessimistic ('negative') ideas and encourage optimistic ones."[8] Such discipline narrowed the focus of religion to the merely personal, shifting attention away from society. For this reason, a contributor to the journal edited by Hutchinson, the *Christian Century,* objected to the emphasis on "personal adjustment." A. Roy Eckardt wondered "how much the social order is *worth* adjusting to" and derided the cult for its failure to ask the same question:

> An evil aspect of peace-of-mind religion is its acceptance, by default, of the social status quo. An unannounced assumption is that the present condition of the social order is irrelevant to one's true needs and outside the scope of one's obligations.[9]

John C. Bennett and Will Herberg suggested that the nationwide religious revival of the 1950s had produced an American "culture religion," which Bennett blamed for the "loss of any basis of criticism on our culture as a whole."[10] Herberg, the author of *Protestant – Catholic – Jew*

(1955), lamented the transformation of Judeo-Christian faith into "the cult of culture and society, in which the 'right' social order and the received cultural values are divinized by being identified with the divine purpose." Christian faith, he wrote, "can be used to sustain the civic religion of 'laissez-faire capitalism.'" In general, "the new religiosity pervading America" validated "the social patterns and cultural values associated with the American Way of Life."

The religious revival not only encouraged "social irresponsibility," according to Herberg, but also supported U.S. nationalism: "This religiosity very easily comes to serve as a spiritual reinforcement of national self-righteousness and a spiritual authentication of national self-will." Herberg worried about the "national messianism" generated by "this identification of religion with national purpose," a messianism "which sees it as the vocation of America to bring the American Way of Life, compounded almost equally of democracy and free enterprise, to every corner of the globe."[11] Bennett, too, complained that the revival had brought about "the close alliance of religion with the forces of nationalism." The American culture religion, Bennett maintained, served these forces by "capitalizing on the fact that communism is atheistic" and by suggesting that "because we are against communism, God must be on our side."[12]

Hutchinson noted the use of religion for nationalistic ends, but his assessment differed from that of Herberg and Bennett. He credited the cult of reassurance with boosting American morale during the Cold War. "This cult is making a contribution to the survival of American optimism," Hutchinson wrote, "and in today's world it is important to have some optimism somewhere outside the Communist orbit."[13] His assessment was the more typical in a nation concerned about the external threat of Communism. The civic value of religion was widely accepted; in fact, all three branches of the federal government helped to promote the religious revival of the 1950s. Congress, for instance, passed legislation changing the pledge of allegiance to include "under God" and placing "In God We Trust" on all currency.[14] A month before his presidential inauguration, Dwight D. Eisenhower declared that "our form of Government has no sense unless it is founded in a deeply felt religious faith."[15]

The religious aspect of U.S. political rhetoric struck O'Connor when she listened to a radio broadcast of the 1956 Democratic National Convention. In a letter to Frances Cheney, whose husband served as a public relations officer for Tennessee Governor Frank Clement, O'Connor parodied the invocation with which Clement ended his keynote address: "All my subconscious has come up with this past week is Prahhhshuss Lord, take my hand and lead me awnnnnn!" (C 41).

In Wise Blood, O'Connor incorporates lines of dialogue alluding to the

Cold War alliance between nationalism and theism. Hoover Shoats tells his listeners they can trust his new sect, the Holy Church of Christ Without Christ, because "it's nothing foreign connected with it" (WB 152). Mrs. Flood suspects that the original Church Without Christ is "something foreign," and she will not show Hazel Motes a room in her boardinghouse until he assures her otherwise (WB 106). Such dialogue is in keeping with the insular attitude of the rural protagonist, who would have been content to remain in Eastrod "with his two eyes open, and his hands always handling the familiar thing," and "his feet on the known track" (WB 22). But the dialogue also conveys the suspicion with which Cold War Americans viewed ideologies originating "outside" their culture. As they prized ideological consensus in the political sphere, so they prized the "thoroughly American" religion described by Herberg – the religion with "no taint of foreignness."[16]

During the period in which O'Connor produced her fiction, the suspicion of "foreign" ideologies governed religious as well as intellectual discussions. Like the secular intellectual – who "stayed at home and even found himself feeling at home," according to a 1956 cover story in Time magazine – the American Christian was supposed to accept his or her position within American culture.[17] A conservative Methodist minister, writing in 1964, told his readers that their "universal" religious faith did not make them outsiders. Charles M. Crowe insisted that "American Christians are not homeless creatures without a country," but citizens with a "duty to be patriotic," a "positive" role to play in "offsetting Communist influence." Crowe had the same advice for the clergy in 1964 that Life magazine had for novelists in 1955. "Instead of being so critical and apologetic," Crowe argued, "American Christian leaders need to be profoundly grateful for this land of ours – and not be ashamed to say so!"[18] Like American intellectuals, American Christians were expected to serve as cold warriors.

Religious leaders who failed to perform their assigned patriotic duty, their task of defending capitalist institutions against the Communist threat, often encountered political harassment. If it had become "un-American to be unreligious," as Eckardt observed,[19] it could also be deemed un-American to criticize the U.S. economic system on religious grounds. The situation had changed dramatically since the Depression, when many in the clergy had lodged such criticism, using the criterion specified in a 1934 poll: "Which economic system appears to you to be less antagonistic to and more consistent with the ideals and methods of Jesus and the noblest of the Hebrew Prophets?" Out of nearly 21,000 ministers and rabbis who responded to this question in the World Tomorrow poll, less than 5 percent selected capitalism; more than half of the respondents wanted to see the capitalist system "drastically reformed."[20]

The desire for fundamental reform found expression in statements issued by major religious bodies. In 1932 the General Conference of the Methodist Episcopal Church declared the "present industrial order" to be "unchristian, unethical and anti-social because it is largely based on the profit-motive."[21] In 1934 the General Council of the Congregational Christian Churches passed a resolution condemning "our present competitive profit-seeking economy." During the Cold War, however, both groups retracted their demands for systemic change. In one year, 1952, the General Conference of the United Methodist Church revised its social creed, softening its criticism of the "profit-motive," and the Congregational council disclaimed its 1934 resolution.[22]

Like those secular intellectuals who had joined the Communist Party or otherwise supported the cause of the radical Left during the Depression, those in the clergy who had criticized the capitalist system in the 1930s faced charges of political subversiveness in the 1950s. Even "the official Establishment theologian"[23] had a political past for which to account. Reinhold Niebuhr, who served as an official consultant for the U.S. Department of State under President Truman, had belonged to several leftist organizations during the Depression – including the Socialist Party, which he represented as a state senatorial candidate in 1930 and as a congressional candidate in 1932.[24] In "Communism and the Clergy" (1953), Niebuhr apologized for the "political errors" of the American clergy during the 1930s and confessed his own "complicity in these errors." The religious critics of capitalism, Niebuhr wrote, had been "too uncritical of the Marxist alternative."[25] Despite his published mea culpa, his vocal anti-Communism, and his service in the presidential administration that had devised the policy of containment, Niebuhr continued to face allegations of disloyalty in his public life. The loyalty check that the FBI conducted after the State Department asked Niebuhr to become a consultant in 1950 was not the first such investigation into his political activities and affiliations; and it lasted longer than his tenure in office, largely because "Niebuhr had belonged to, spoken for, or signed the petitions of countless left-leaning groups that the attorney general's staff had seen fit to declare subversive."

Political conservatives distrusted Niebuhr, not only for his past "Marxian" views,[26] but also for his present refusal to affirm the American system uncritically. On the surface, his political evolution had followed the course described by the *Partisan Review* symposium, to which he contributed an essay; as a public figure, Niebuhr had gone from alienation to integration. But Niebuhr maintained an oppositional stance, criticizing the American system on religious grounds. He joined Norman Mailer and C. Wright Mills in departing from the editorial assumptions of the 1952 symposium. Although he adopted its dominant spatial metaphor – inside versus outside – he used the metaphor to emphasize American complacency. Like Mailer, whose essay preceded his, Niebuhr called into question the editorial assumption that the external threat of Communism compelled American intellectuals to affirm a political, economic, and cultural status quo. Niebuhr wrote that "we are almost in greater peril from the foes within than from the foe without. . . . We are engaged in such a perpetual liturgy of self-congratulations about the vaunted virtues and achievements of the 'American way of life' that we . . . make ourselves odious to the world."[27] Even as he offered his mea culpa for political naïveté in the 1953 essay, "Communism and the Clergy," he declined to celebrate U.S. capitalism. Though "ready to confess" that the religious advocates of Marxism had misplaced their trust, Niebuhr insisted that "the Marxist errors do not make more true the ridiculous dogma of laissez faire, which our conservatives have used to prevent the political and moral criticism of the workings of power monopolies in the economic sphere." Niebuhr saw his break with the radical Left as a change in strategy, not in principle. Refusing to praise "our already too complacent nation and culture," he urged Christians to make "our 'prophetic witness' against its complacencies more telling by eliminating political errors from its essentially religious judgments."

The occasion for "Communism and the Clergy" was the appearance by another Protestant leader, G. Bromley Oxnam, before the House Committee on Un-American Activities. Niebuhr praised Oxnam, a Methodist bishop, for challenging the committee to "clean up its files and eliminate the lies and slander contained in them."[28] At the 1953 hearing – which Oxnam himself had requested – the bishop accused committee members of slandering him for nearly seven years, through the release of information "prepared in a way capable of creating the impression that I have been and am sympathetic to communism and therefore subversive."[29] A reporter for the *Nation* noted the disadvantage under which Oxnam had come before the committee:

> As a liberal bishop he was almost ex officio – and this point is basic – a sponsor for many groups organized to support worthy causes. He has fought for civil rights and freedom of conscience for many years, speaking and writing without fear. Such activities make a man a sitting duck for the witch-hunters.[30]

Such activities, Niebuhr conceded, had brought liberals into contact with Communists. To the forces of "modern vigilantism," this meant guilt by association.[31]

Earlier in 1953, a member of the House committee denounced Oxnam as a minister who had long "served God on Sunday and the Communist front for the balance of the week." For U.S. Representative Donald L. Jackson, a California Republican, Oxnam's expressions of concern regarding possible violations of civil liberties merely proved his guilt: "It is no great wonder," Jackson sneered, "that the bishop sees an investigating committee in every vestry."[32] In fact, there were several calls that year for the investigation of the American clergy. Harold H. Velde, the House committee chair, suggested the need for congressional investigation.[33] J. B. Matthews, a former chief investigator for the committee, argued in the July *American Mercury* that the clergy deserved no special treatment:

> Preachers, too, are people. As such, they are citizens to be held responsible for their civic and political acts. If professors and government employees are held to strict accountability for collaboration with the Communist-front apparatus, why not clergymen? Do clergymen have their own little Yalu River – their professional status – beyond which they have sanctuary? Why should they be allowed to participate, without investigation and exposure, in the "campaign to disarm and defeat the United States"?

Matthews opened his *American Mercury* article, "Reds and Our Churches," with the contention that members of the Protestant clergy formed the "largest single group supporting the Communist apparatus in the United States today." Matthews declared that the Communist Party had recruited more "agents, stooges, dupes, front men, and fellow-travelers" from among the clergy than from among the intelligentsia: "Clergymen outnumber professors two to one in supporting the Communist-front apparatus of the Kremlin conspiracy." Over the past seventeen years, Matthews wrote, some seven thousand ministers had "allowed their zeal for social justice to run away with their better judgment and patriotism," and for this he blamed "the vogue of the 'social gospel' which infected the Protestant theological seminaries more than a generation ago."[34]

The article by Matthews appeared about a month before the House committee conducted its "inquisition" of Oxnam, a proceeding by which the committee inadvertently damaged its own reputation. One editorial cartoonist depicted its "files" on Oxnam as garbage cans. Copies of the July *American Mercury* were on newsstands when Senator Joseph R. McCarthy named Matthews executive director of his Internal Security Subcommittee; the article prompted "thunderbolts of protest," according to *Time*, and turned many of McCarthy's supporters against the senator, who accepted the resignation of his new "hatchet man" under pressure from President Eisenhower. The *Commonweal* suggested that "Senator McCarthy may have made his first serious political blunder in the case of J. B. Matthews and his headline-making article on the Protestant clergy." From the perspective of Eisenhower and others angered by "Reds and Our Churches," Matthews had made "a wholesale attack on the Protestant clergy," not just on those individual ministers with ties

THE FILES COLLAPSED

Congressional investigators underestimated the faith that Cold War America placed in Protestant ministers like G. Bromley Oxnam. Daniel Fitzpatrick, "The Files Collapsed," *St. Louis Post-Dispatch*, 23 July 1953. State Historical Society of Missouri, Columbia.

to "subversive" organizations. Such a charge, it seemed, slandered those Protestant ministers who had been performing the patriotic service assigned to them. After all, the Cold War seemed to many Americans, as it seemed to Charles M. Crowe, "a conflict between two mighty faiths, Christianity and communism." In this conflict, *Time* reported, "U.S. Protestants trust their clergy."[35]

If the clergy had its detractors, it also had its defenders. In 1961 the chief inspector of the FBI vouched for "the loyalty of the overwhelming majority of the American clergy." William C. Sullivan ranked the members of the clergy "among the most consistent and vigorous opponents of

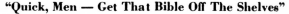

"Quick, Men — Get That Bible Off The Shelves"

This Herblock cartoon, on the controversy sparked by the publication of "Reds and Our Churches" in 1953, suggests that religious concerns did not necessarily transcend politics during the Cold War. Herbert Block, "Quick, Men – Get That Bible Off the Shelves," *Washington Post,* 7 July 1953. Reprinted from *Herblock's Here and Now* (Simon & Schuster, 1955).

communism."[36] Charles Crowe went further in 1964, saying that Christians constituted "the strongest single antidote" to Communism. Two obstacles to the Communist conspiracy, he wrote, were "America's economic and military strength and, ultimately, the moral character of the nation as reflected in and supported by the Christian church."[37] On this point, the liberal Methodist, Oxnam, agreed with the conservative Methodist, Crowe. Oxnam voiced his belief in the practical ideological power of the churches when he appeared before the House committee in 1953: "The churches have done and are doing far more to destroy the

Communist threat to faith and to freedom than all investigating commit-
tees put together."[38]

Many Protestants, liberal and conservative, did not consider the Catholic
Church to be one of the Christian bodies that would strengthen the
United States against Communism. Although he affirmed the value of
institutional religion in terms of national defense, Crowe distinguished
Protestant bodies from the Catholic Church: "Protestantism, rather than
Catholicism, is more of a bulwark against communism."[39] In making
this distinction, Crowe challenged the image of the Church promulgated
by its most prominent representatives and embraced by much of its
membership – the Church as the foe of Communism. During the 1940s
and 1950s, the American Catholic hierarchy was vehemently anti-
Communist. The head of the American hierarchy, Francis Cardinal
Spellman, declared that "Communism Is *Un-American*" in a 1946 magazine article. Bishop Fulton J. Sheen, the most visible member of the
hierarchy from 1952 to 1957, hosted a network television series that
combined lessons in morality with attacks on Communism. Senator
McCarthy, the most visible member of the Catholic laity, enjoyed widespread support within the Church. The controversy involving his executive director, J. B. Matthews, seemed ready to become a "sectarian issue," setting McCarthy's Catholic supporters against those Protestants
offended by "Reds and Our Churches."[40]

The anti-Communist rhetoric of the American Catholic Church did
not impress Crowe: "The claim of many elements in the Roman church,
that it is the bulwark of free men against communism, is unwar-
ranted."[41] Writers both religious and secular advanced this argument:
Americans could not rely on the Church as a political ally in the present
crisis. Some writers argued, moreover, that the Church itself posed a
threat to the United States. Paul Blanshard suggested that the anti-
Communist stance of the Church was self-serving, in that the Vatican would "gain increased prestige from co-operation with us in the
emergency, and then use that prestige to weaken our democratic culture." To Blanshard, the American way of life was "predominantly non-
Catholic."[42] One subject in particular – the constitutional separation of
church and state – prompted writers to express "a conviction that there is
a fundamental antagonism between Catholicism and the American way
of life, between democratic liberty and our ideas of freedom."[43] According to John Cogley, those who criticized the Church feared "that im-
probable day when Catholics as a majority in the United States have the
legal power to destroy the democratic way of life as it is now understood
among us and to erect the classical 'Catholic State' in this country."[44]

Of course, there was nothing new about Protestants seeing "the shadow of Rome descending upon American culture" or fearing Vatican influence in national politics. Vincent F. Holden, a Paulist father, compared the "assault" on the Church in the 1940s to the "flood of anti-Catholic literature . . . let loose upon the American electorate" during the 1928 presidential campaign of Alfred E. Smith.[45] Indeed, the question of loyalty that would arise in 1960 had arisen in 1928: would a Catholic president answer to the pope or to the U.S. Constitution? Long before the Cold War, Protestant Americans had invested the Catholic Church with sinister powers. In *The Ambassadors* (1903), Henry James parodied this Protestant tendency in the character of Waymarsh, who fears "the recruiting interests of the Catholic Church . . . the enemy, the monster of bulging eyes and far-reaching quivering groping tentacles."[46] The female evangelist who appears briefly in *The Violent Bear It Away*, relating her experience as "a missionary in Rome where minds are still chained in priestly darkness" (*VBA* 128), can claim numerous predecessors like Waymarsh. And the image of the Church as "the Scarlet Woman," from whom an admirer hoped to save O'Connor (*HB* 380), predated the United States itself.

If anti-Catholic sentiment had a long history, however, it acquired a new vocabulary during the Cold War. Those who attacked the Church did so in terms specific to the political discussions of the period. John Cogley, writing in 1953, noted a shift from theological to political terminology: "In days gone by, Catholic doctrine was condemned as being un-Biblical or superstitious: the judgment was theological. Today, it is more often branded as 'un-democratic' or 'un-American.'"[47] The shift seemed to confer intellectual respectability on the anti-Catholic position. A case in point was the treatment of Catholicism in the pages of a prominent liberal journal, the *Nation*, during the late 1940s. The *Nation* regularly warned its readers that the Roman Catholic hierarchy had political ambitions in the United States. At the same time, the journal distinguished its alarmist rhetoric from that of conservative extremists: responding to the accusation that a 1947 series on the social policies of the Church demonstrated journalistic "bigotry," an editorial writer for the *Nation* maintained that "our opposition to the Klan and other hate-Catholic groups is surely as unequivocal today as it has ever been." In line with its liberal editorial policy, the *Nation* claimed to criticize the Church on constitutional grounds. "If we are narrow-minded now because we interpret the First Amendment to mean the literal separation of church and state," reasoned the editorial writer, "then we have always been narrow-minded, for in common with the Supreme Court of the United States we have always held to that interpretation."[48]

Paul Blanshard, the author of the 1947 *Nation* series, told the readers of further installments in 1948 that the "fear of being associated with A.P.A.

fanatics," with anti-Catholic prejudice, should not deter liberals "from an honest analysis of the implications of Catholic rule."[49] Blanshard framed his criticism of the Church in political rather than theological terms, and he emphasized this after Robert Fitzgerald voiced objections in 1948. Fitzgerald, the Catholic poet whose friendship with O'Connor would begin the following year, answered Blanshard's charge that the Church was "un-American" by calling it "more than American," by insisting that the "catholic and universal" Church transcended nationality and saw "one world . . . of men under God."[50] In his reply to Fitzgerald, Blanshard said he had tried to avoid questions of "pure theology" in the *Nation* series by confining his discussion to "the social effects of Catholic policy in the fields of politics, medicine, the family, welfare, education, and science." He now addressed doctrinal issues only because Fitzgerald had forced him to do so: "He will not permit me to be non-theological in my reply because his defense is primarily denominational and sacerdotal."[51]

Cold War anxieties informed the *Nation* articles by Blanshard, but remained implicit. In 1951, however, Blanshard devoted an entire book to "the fundamental resemblance between the Vatican and the Kremlin." For Blanshard, the threat posed by "political Catholicism as a world power" paralleled the Communist threat to the American way of life. In *Communism, Democracy, and Catholic Power,* Blanshard held that "the climate of authoritarian rule over the human mind" characterized both the Catholic Church and the Soviet Union. Because they practiced "thought control," both systems were opposed to democracy "as a system of free choices and a gospel of free minds." The shared institutional practice indicated a shared institutional structure. If the Catholic system was "soft" and the Soviet system "hard," both were dictatorships, "totalitarian agencies whose aims and methods are incompatible with democratic ideals."

Xenophobia underlay the analogy between Catholicism and Communism. Although most Catholics in the United States were probably "good Americans," according to Blanshard, the Church itself, like the Soviet Union, was a "foreign government." In this respect, the Catholic Church and the Communist Party were interchangeable elements of the invasion scenario. In each case, the "invading power" refused "to submit its ideas and policies for free discussion and choice in the market place of ideas." Reducing the "legitimate exchange of ideas" to "cultural and political imperialism," the invader achieved its ends surreptitiously:

> Both the Kremlin and the Vatican have learned to conquer nations
> without majorities by using the methods of infiltration and combina-
> tion. Today the most dangerous kind of imperialism is that which may

develop inside a nation through the technique of penetration by a determined minority controlled by an outside power. This strategy of penetration is far more effective than the old strategy of frontal attack.

The image of penetration appeared throughout Blanshard's book. As
"missionaries of the Kremlin penetrate the jungles of capitalism," so
"missionaries of the Vatican penetrate all non-Catholic countries."
Blanshard even saw the high birthrate among Catholics as a form of
"biological penetration" by "Catholic power into non-Catholic territory."[52]

The editor of the *Christian Century* likewise employed the scenario of
invasion and subversion in writing about American Catholicism. In a
1946 series of articles, Charles Clayton Morrison insisted on the political
implications of religious affiliation:

> A strong religious faith that claims universality is bound to affect the
> culture of its habitat. It infiltrates into the political, the economic, the
> intellectual, the artistic areas of life and tends to mold the laws and
> customs of its culture into an ethos marked by its own spirit, its own
> ethic and its own ideology.

Catholicism, Morrison wrote, "has become a formidable system spreading out into all the states and exercising a powerful influence in public
and cultural life." He added, "Its policy has been to infiltrate the faithful
into public office and so gain, if not direct control, a privileged relation
to political power." Protestantism, too, hoped to "penetrate" a secular
American culture; but it was a religion seeking to regain its proper status,
"its former ascendancy in the national culture." Morrison valorized Protestantism as the religion whose presence in America dated "from the
beginning of our national history," and, by implication, he devalued
Catholicism as a relative newcomer.[53]

Blanshard complained that American writers had ignored the "fundamental resemblance" between the Catholic Church and the Soviet
Union. As a matter of fact, the analogy had become a rhetorical convention by the time he published *Communism, Democracy, and Catholic Power*.
When the managing editor of the *Daily Worker* abandoned Communism
for Catholicism in 1945, the *Christian Century* took his conversion as
evidence that the two systems cultivated the same mentality: "It is not
very surprising that a man who has been disillusioned about one totalitarian system which makes lofty claims as the defender of 'true freedom'
by regimentation should seek refuge in another."[54] In a 1947 issue of the
Nation, Harold J. Laski wrote that "the influence of a militant Roman
Catholic church" in U.S. politics "is as much the expression of the
purposes of a foreign power as any influence exerted by the Communist
Party."[55] In a 1949 lecture, a retired Harvard professor identified an

"impressive parallelism of theoretical principles and of institutional features in a totalitarian church and in a totalitarian state."[56]

Conversatives sometimes employed the analogy. Crowe, for instance,
considered Protestantism "more of a bulwark against communism" because the "authoritarian habit of mind of Catholics is no protection
against the authoritarian habit of mind of Communists."[57] Primarily,
however, the analogy suited the rhetorical purposes of Cold War liberals
– even those who protested the smear tactics of government informers
and investigators. Writing in 1954, Bishop Oxnam argued that the sort of
informer who had linked him with Communism was "as un-American
as . . . the Russian commissar."[58] In 1949, by contrast, Oxnam used the
analogy to underscore his charge that the Catholic Church intended to
destroy the separation of church and state: "The American Roman Catholic hierarchy, as well as the American Communist Party, is bound by
directives from a foreign capital."[59] If Oxnam was best known in the
early 1950s for his criticism of the House Committee on Un-American
Activities, in the late 1940s he was "perhaps more widely known for his
attacks upon the Catholic Church than for any other reason."[60]

This, then, was the position from which O'Connor wrote: she belonged
to a church that many Americans perceived as a foreign power, a would-
be invader, a threat analogous to the Soviet Union. Her comments on a
contemporary work by C. G. Jung, the Swiss psychoanalyst, show
her awareness of the analogy. Discussing *The Undiscovered Self* (1958) in a
1959 letter, O'Connor deprecated those passages "equating the Communist idea of community with the Church's and Communist methods
with Loyola's." O'Connor advised her correspondent, Father John Mc-
Cown, to read Jung's book "just to see what you have to combat in the
modern mind" (*HB* 362–3). The issue, as O'Connor saw it, was the
institutional rather than the theological nature of Catholicism. Religious
readings of O'Connor have focused on Catholicism as a timeless, autonomous body of doctrine, neglecting the Church as an institution, a com-
petitor in the arena of changing public opinion. But O'Connor and her
literary contemporaries did not overlook the influence of Catholicism as
an institution. Responding to a 1955 symposium on "the dearth of Catholic writers among the graduates of Catholic colleges," the novelist Philip Wylie repeated Blanshard's argument that the Church rejected the
democratic principles of "free choices" and "free minds." In a statement
quoted by O'Connor, Wylie maintained that the Church denied its members the freedom necessary for literary creativity: "A Catholic, if he is
devout, i.e., sold on the authority of his Church, is also brain-washed,
whether he realizes it or not" (*MM* 143–4).

Many Catholics felt obliged to "combat" the widespread image of a church opposed to U.S. democratic principles. Members of the American hierarchy, including Archbishop Richard J. Cushing, made statements affirming Catholic support for the constitutional separation of church and state.[61] In his 1946 essay, "Communism Is *Un-American*," Cardinal Spellman took pains to establish his credentials as a "true American." Anticipating the charge that he represented a foreign institution, Spellman professed his faith "in America, her freedoms, her ideals, her traditions" and pledged his allegiance to "our American way of life."[62] Father Holden, in his 1947 essay, declared that "our American way of life is not inimical to Catholic teaching."[63] Academics joined clerics in defending the Americanism of the Church. James M. O'Neill, a professor at Brooklyn College, wrote *Catholicism and American Freedom* (1952) as an answer to Blanshard's published attacks on the Church; and he challenged the idea, expressed by Morrison in 1946, that Catholicism was a newcomer to the United States. "The beginnings of Catholicism in America," O'Neill wrote, "are coincident with the American beginnings of Christianity and education." After calling attention to the role Catholics had played in framing and ratifying the U.S. Constitution and the Bill of Rights, O'Neill praised "the consistent record of American Catholic endorsement of our total constitutional situation," from the eighteenth century to the twentieth.[64]

Another approach recommended itself to Catholic writers. Instead of serving as apologists, they could play on the fears that made apologetics necessary. The role of the Catholic Church in the popular imagination could be a tempting one to exploit, despite its sinister nature. Insofar as it attributed irresistible power to the Church, the role appealed to American Catholics who felt culturally marginalized. In an address delivered at the 1947 Catholic Press Convention, James M. Gillis gave a standard defense of Catholic Americanism, claiming that no one "really understands . . . our American civilization, unless he is a Catholic." Later in the speech, however, he celebrated the power that non-Catholics feared, the power of the Church to influence minds:

> We have a superlative mechanism of propaganda . . . the like of which could not be obtained if . . . the entire personnel of Standard Oil, General Motors and of a half dozen other world-wide industries were combined and directed from a central source.

Extolling the ideological power of the Church over against the economic power of capitalist America, Gillis confirmed the liberal fears he mentioned in another passage: "Our rivals entertain and often exploit the curiously mythical notion that our Church and with the Church, our Press, has developed regimentation, standardization, even mechanization to the nth degree." Rather than protest the myth, he lamented the fact that the institutional power of the Church was largely potential, that "we don't use the fullness of the power of the world-wide, intricate, highly disciplined Catholic organization." Elaborating on the analogy between Communism and Catholicism, Gillis speculated, "If Soviet Russia had . . . 350 millions of convinced and loyal adherents such as ours, she would by this time hold dominion . . . over 'The Great Globe Itself.'"[65]

As a regular contributor to the local diocesan papers, O'Connor could claim membership in the Catholic press. In this capacity, she voiced concern over the public image of the Church. Reviewing a collection of essays in 1959, O'Connor cited with approval a statement regarding the "public role" of religion in the United States:

> A Church may be absolutely sure of its own mandate and spiritual authority, yet it cannot publicly act as though that mandate and authority were generally accepted by the civil society. Forms of religious behavior or assertions of religious power that in theological terms may be quite logical and just, or in other societies, in other times and places, might even have been expedient, become dangerously imprudent in the pluralist society that is America.

After citing this passage, O'Connor remarked, "More such statements as this coming from Catholics might tend to curb some of the just suspicion created in the minds of non-Catholics by certain Catholic excesses in social action" (*PG* 69). Furthermore, O'Connor attacked the public image when it discouraged a non-Catholic from joining the Church. In a 1955 letter to a friend considering conversion, she expressed dismay over "your feeling of the voluptuous seductive powers of the Church" and "your effort not to be seduced by the Church," and she called this effort "the devil's greatest work of hallucination" (*HB* 93).

When she wrote her book review and her letter to "A," O'Connor followed the lead of those clerics and academics who tried to assuage liberal fears regarding Catholic power. As a fiction writer, O'Connor took the opposite approach. Following the example set by Gillis, she chose to exploit the image of the Church as invader. "The Displaced Person," specifically, concerns an invasion carried out under the auspices of the Church. The cleric who appears in this story, overseeing the invasion, bears little resemblance to the prelates like Cardinal Spellman who affirmed the American way. O'Connor's fictional priest is an agent of change, not an apologist for the status quo.

Since the narrative focuses on the Protestant characters and their attempts to resist change, the priest in "The Displaced Person" seems to be an incidental figure. Generally speaking, the clerics portrayed by O'Connor seem to play a minor role in her fiction; as Robert Fitzgerald noted in 1962, her readers "are aware of the Roman or universal Church mainly by its absence."[66] The priest is crucial, however, to the literary strategy

O'Connor outlined in her essays. When she wrote that the Christian novelist must "draw large and startling figures" in order to communicate a religious vision (*MM* 34), she knew that the figure of the Catholic Church in the popular imagination was one of the most startling. From personal observation, she had learned that the scenario of the invading Church could provoke strong emotions. "You ought to hear all the Baptists down here hollering about the Separation of Church & State," she told the Fitzgeralds, Robert and Sally, in 1951. "You'd think the Pope was about to annex the Sovereign State of Georgia" (*CW* 892). However "exaggerated" it seemed "to the Catholic mind," the image of a politically aggressive Church struck a nerve with non-Catholics. In this regard, it enabled the Catholic writer "to get his vision across to a hostile audience," a secular audience "that is unprepared and unwilling to see the meaning of life as he sees it" (*MM* 185).

The judgment O'Connor passed on the American way of life, the way of life her audience revered, was central to the vision she conveyed by "violent literary means" (*MM* 185). The scenario of a foreign Church subverting the American way provided the element of "shock" she felt she needed in order to reach non-Catholics (*MM* 34), but it also gave dramatic form to her belief that "Catholicism is opposed to the bourgeois mind" (*CW* 862). In "The Displaced Person," she brings the Church and its representative into conflict with those who inhabit the pastoral setting, the setting identified with the essential America. The priest, who speaks "in a foreign way" (*CS* 198), arranges for the Guizacs to come to the Georgia dairy farm owned by Mrs. McIntyre. Father Flynn thereby disrupts the pastoral way of life, for which the farmhand, Mr. Shortley, claims to have "fought and bled and died" in World War I. The claim that Mr. Shortley risked "life and limb" defending a democratic proposition, "All men was created free and equal" (*CS* 232), underscores the political significance of the pastoral setting. For the characters themselves, it embodies the American way of life. They are wary, therefore, of Catholic efforts to locate displaced persons "on the land." As a commentator on the story has pointed out, the postwar resettlement of European refugees in the United States aroused fears of political subversiveness; the opponents of resettlement suspected that many of the new immigrants were coming "to infiltrate this country and to serve alien causes."[67] In the story, domination by a foreign church is the ultimate threat to the pastoral setting – as to the "free country" for which it stands (*CS* 204). "I ain't going to have the Pope of Rome tell me how to run no dairy," Mr. Shortley declares. To the Shortleys, the arrival of the Catholic family is only the first stage of a larger invasion planned by the Church. Their fears are aggravated by the fact that their employer, Mrs. McIntyre, is helping to further the ambitions of the Church. "She says it's ten million more like them, Displaced Persons," Mrs. Shortley tells Mr. Shortley; "she says that there priest can get her all she wants" (CS 201).

Mrs. McIntyre feels that she controls the pastoral setting, that she is "the one around here who holds all the strings together" (CS 217), but the Shortleys believe that the "slick" priest is taking over. Mrs. Shortley speculates on his plans for Mrs. McIntyre: "First he would get her into his Church and then he would get his hand in her pocketbook" (CS 208). Mr. Shortley, alerted to "the dangerous presence of the priest" by Mrs. Shortley, "had no doubt that the priest had got some peculiar control over Mrs. McIntyre and that before long she would start attending his Masses. She looked as if something was wearing her down from the inside" (CS 211, 230). For Mrs. McIntyre, more confident in her power to resist indoctrination, the behavior of the priest merely confirms her prejudices: "After he had got her the Pole, he had used the business introduction to try to convert her – just as she had supposed he would" (CS 225).

The priest behaves as Paul Blanshard expected priests to behave. The story by O'Connor, like the scenario outlined by Blanshard, links invasion and indoctrination. Whenever he visits the farm to see the Guizacs, Father Flynn spends time instructing Mrs. McIntyre, "forcing a little definition of one of the sacraments or of some dogma into each conversation." Mrs. McIntyre "had not asked to be instructed but he instructed anyway" (CS 229). Blanshard argued that the mind cultivated by the Church, "that authoritarian mind which leans for support on received dogma," would render Americans vulnerable to an external threat: "Habitual, uncritical obedience to superior authority disqualifies men as fighters against Communism because it incapacitates their minds." Calling for a closer look at "our alleged ally," Blanshard advised Americans to distrust a Church guilty of hypocrisy, a Church that took advantage of democratic freedom "while working to destroy it."[68] Mrs. Shortley, who "felt that her business was to watch the priest," ascribes ulterior motives to Father Flynn; his innocent appearance, she believes, cloaks his sinister aims: "leading foreigners over in hordes to places that were not theirs, to cause disputes, to uproot niggers, to plant the Whore of Babylon in the midst of the righteous!" (CS 209). The priest has come, she believes, "to destroy" (CS 210).

"The Displaced Person" ends with the image of Father Flynn explaining "the doctrines of the Church" to Mrs. McIntyre, who is now too weak to resist her indoctrination (CS 235). Another story with a rural setting, "The Enduring Chill," features a priest lecturing an invalid. Father Finn quizzes the protagonist, Asbury Fox, on the catechism and calls him "a lazy ignorant conceited youth" for not knowing it. While Asbury moves his arms and legs "helplessly," Father Finn threatens him with "eternal damnation" should he refuse to accept the teachings of the Church and submit to its discipline (CS 377). In each case, the scene illustrates priestly coercion, as described by Blanshard, rather than "the *voluntary* acceptance of the Church's guidance," as described by O'Neill. Father Finn's brand of "guidance" corroborates the charge that O'Neill dismissed, the idea that the Church dictated thought by claiming "to *punish in the next world* those who go against Catholic teaching."[69] Those representatives of the Church who enter the pastoral setting, in O'Connor's fiction, are single-minded in their desire to gain converts and to enforce obedience.

By the end of "The Displaced Person," the priest has become the dominating presence. The characters who think of themselves as defenders of the pastoral setting – the Shortleys – have departed. The setting has lost its integrity; the pastures are empty, for the cows have been sold. The story follows to completion the scenario of the invading Church. But even as she lets the scenario play itself out, O'Connor revises its meaning: in her version, invasion seems fortunate. The pastoral setting is anything but Edenic. The inhabitants are morally inferior to the newcomers who threaten their social order, the foreigners against whom "there ought to be a law," according to Mrs. Shortley (CS 205). For all their moral posturing, the Americans are guilty of "collusion" in the death of Mr. Guizac, the Polish laborer (CS 234). The xenophobia that found expression in the invasion scenario inspires such hostility toward the "Displaced Person" that neither Mrs. McIntyre nor Mr. Shortley calls his attention to the tractor heading in his direction. For O'Connor, a way of life whose preservation demands such drastic measures is not worth saving. In a 1955 letter, she referred to the McIntyre farm as an "evil" place (HB 118).

In the same letter, O'Connor linked the invasion scenario with religious salvation: "The displaced person did accomplish a kind of redemption in that he destroyed the place . . . and set Mrs. McIntyre on the road to a new kind of suffering" (HB 118). Early in the story, Mrs. McIntyre exclaims, "That man is my salvation!" From the xenophobic viewpoint of Mrs. Shortley, it is "salvation got from the devil" (CS 203), but a later remark by Mrs. McIntyre suggests that the invader who brings destruction is divine rather than diabolic. Interrupting the priest, who has been discussing the nature of Christ "as a Redeemer to mankind," Mrs. McIntyre objects that "Christ was just another D.P." (CS 229). With this statement, O'Connor reverses the moral poles of the invasion scenario. Where Blanshard treated the Catholic Church as a sinister invader, analogous to the Soviet Union, O'Connor established a parallel between the invasion sponsored by a foreign Church and the intrusion of divine grace. In other words, O'Connor imagines an invasion that benefits the

In this 1965 cartoon, Ed Renfro noted the overlap between religious concerns and the invasion scenario. *Nation,* 13 Sept. 1965. Courtesy of Edward R. Renfro.

invaded. Mrs. McIntyre suffers, but as O'Connor suggested in the 1955 letter, her suffering will presumably lead to her redemption. Her weakness in the presence of clerical authority – at the end of the story – makes spiritual redemption possible. O'Connor elides the distinction on which Blanshard insisted: Catholicism as a "great structure of political, diplomatic, medical, and cultural authority" versus "Catholicism as a theory of the relationship between man and God."[70] In her fiction, the institutional merges with the theological.

O'Connor was not alone in imagining a fortunate invasion. Many of her contemporaries developed the idea, which had considerable appeal as an alternative to the dominant Cold War scenario. The idea received its clearest expression in an unlikely context – speculative literature on extraterrestrial life. Since 1947, widely publicized reports of unidentified flying objects (UFOs) had generated nationwide interest in the topic. By 1952 the Catholic Church had joined in the speculation, formulating its own position "on the question of invaders from outer space." A Catholic educator quoted by *Time* admitted the possibility of benevolent invaders. If they existed, he said, extraterrestrial beings might even possess "supernatural gifts" such as "the immortality of body once enjoyed by Adam & Eve."[71] The possibility of benevolent extraterrestrials inspired numerous works in the literary genre of science fiction.[72] *Invaders of Earth*, a 1952 collection of alien invasion narratives, included stories about "Those Who Guide" as well as "Those Who Take Over."[73] The alien in one of these stories, "Angel's Egg" by Edgar Pangborn, belongs to a morally advanced race and educates the human protagonist in "goodness." The protagonist, "convinced that our human case is hopeful," asks at the end of the story, "Who can doubt that in another fifty million years we might well be only a little lower than the angels?"[74]

The connection between Catholicism and science fiction may seem odd, but it is hardly tenuous. Indeed, some of the classic works in this genre make Catholicism central to the narrative. In *A Canticle for Leibowitz* (1960) by Walter M. Miller, Jr., a Catholic religious order tries to preserve the remnants of human culture in a world devastated by the "Flame Deluge" of nuclear war. Catholic missionaries travel to another world, Mars, in "The Fire Balloons," a story from *The Illustrated Man* (1951) by Ray Bradbury.[75]

From a psychoanalytic perspective, the connection between religious belief and the idea of extraterrestrial invasion was important enough to merit extended study. In the late 1950s, Jung offered a psychological interpretation of the UFO phenomenon, published under the title *Flying Saucers: A Modern Myth of Things Seen in the Skies*. Jung concluded that the wave of UFO sightings over the past decade indicated an actual longing for invasion. In his preface to the first English edition of *Flying Saucers* (1959), he observed:

> News affirming the existence of Ufos is welcome, but . . . scepticism seems to be undesirable. To believe that Ufos are real suits the general opinion, whereas disbelief is to be discouraged. This creates the impression that there is a tendency all over the world to believe in saucers and to want them to be real.

According to Jung, the "*living myth*" of alien invaders fulfilled the same psychic need that the Christian concept of a divine mediator in human form had fulfilled.

Jung identified Cold War tensions as the source of this configuration – this imaginative convergence of the extraterrestrial and the supernatural. The obsession with UFOs reflected "the need for a saviour" at a time when "half the world" had been turned into "the State prison of Communism." Political anxiety thus fueled religious desire: "The present world situation is calculated as never before to arouse expectations of a redeeming, supernatural event," Jung wrote.[76]

At the imaginative juncture of the alien and the divine, political anxiety could be translated into a sense of otherworldly possibility. The mystique of Catholicism, in a non-Catholic society, could therefore be translated into imaginative power. As a source of political concern, the Church offered a position "outside" American culture, and this position seemed to merge with the otherworldly. Such a merger is evident in one of the stories from the science fiction collection *Invaders of Earth*. "'Will You Walk a Little Faster?'" has an alien leader reveal his invasion plans to a group of Americans; "the anti-Catholics," among others, "identified him colorfully with their peculiar concepts of the opposition."[77]

The educator who stated the Catholic position on extraterrestrials assumed that Cold War America would greet such visitors with hostility, regardless of any connection between the alien and the divine. He took it for granted that "our superjet or rocket pilots" would "try to shoot them." At the same time, he noted that such action would be "foolish" if the invaders did, in fact, possess supernatural gifts: "They would be unkillable."[78] He could have been describing the cultural situation of the Church itself. Cold War liberals attacked the Church despite its claim to supernatural authority. In launching their attack, however, they demonized the Church, crediting it with transcendent power – conspiratorial power that magically bypassed the democratic process.[79] Criticism only reinforced the image of Catholic power. The hyperbolic rhetoric of liberals like Blanshard and Oxnam made the Church seem unstoppable.

As an American Catholic, O'Connor knew what it meant to be considered an alien. "The things that bind us together as Catholics are known only to ourselves," she observed in a 1963 lecture. "A secular society understands us less and less" (*MM* 201). The same idea informs a short story written a decade earlier. "A Temple of the Holy Ghost" translates the lack of understanding, as experienced by non-Catholics, into an actual linguistic barrier. In a comic episode, the Catholic teenagers who call themselves "Temple One" and "Temple Two" literally speak a foreign language. Because they attend a convent school rather than a "regular school," Susan and Joanne know their Latin (*CS* 236). The girls shock Wendell and Cory, the Protestant farm boys who are taking them to a fair, by singing a Latin hymn in "their convent-trained voices" (*CS* 241). To the Wilkinses, who respond with "perplexed frowning stares," a foreign language means an alien culture. "That must be Jew singing," Wendell says, suggesting there is little difference between one group of cultural outsiders and another. In the rural society sketched by O'Connor, the Wilkinses are truly insiders. When they become Church of God preachers, as they apparently plan to do, Wendell and Cory will join a Protestant clergy that validates and enforces the social status quo. The "regular" public school calls on a Baptist preacher to give the devotional at commencement, and the police department submits to the will of those preachers who want the fair shut down. "All kinds of freaks" populate the fair (*CS* 244), but one in particular seems to offend the clerical representatives of the status quo: the hermaphrodite. O'Connor underscores the alien status of Catholicism by associating the freak with Catholic ceremony. The main character in "A Temple," the anonymous cousin of Susan and Joanne, makes this connection during her visit to the convent chapel: "When the priest raised the monstrance with the Host shining ivory-colored in the center of it, she was thinking of the tent at the fair that had the freak in it" (CS 248).

The vulnerable position of a Catholic in a society dominated by Protestant ministers helps explain why the main character in "A Temple" fantasizes about various forms of martyrdom. "She could stand to be shot but not to be burned in oil," O'Connor writes. "She didn't know if she could stand to be torn to pieces by lions or not." When the imaginary lions refuse to attack the girl, the imaginary Romans try other methods: "Finding she was so hard to kill, they finally cut off her head very quickly with a sword" (CS 243). Despite her fantasies, however, the girl is grateful to be Catholic. In her prayers, she repeats the words "Lord, Lord, thank You that I'm not in the Church of God, thank You Lord, thank You!" (CS 244). Here the character speaks for the author. O'Connor recognized and appreciated the imaginative resources available to her as a Catholic writer – a writer cast in the role of cultural outsider. Chief among these was the scenario of the fortunate invasion, which enabled O'Connor to project a religious alternative to the Cold War consensus.

Her desire to project such an alternative determined her choice of literary strategy. Since Catholicism was "opposed to the bourgeois mind," according to O'Connor, the appropriate mode of expression for a Catholic writer was the grotesque, "the true anti-bourgeois style" (MM 43). Working within this mode, O'Connor produced what Congressman Dondero had condemned as politically subversive. Resisting his demand for "cheerful and smiling people" in art, she created characters "who are afflicted in both mind and body" and "who have little – or at best a distorted – sense of spiritual purpose" (MM 32). For Dondero, "distorted and ugly" art served the same ends as Communist propaganda; for O'Connor, distortion was an "instrument" crucial to her purpose in writing: "The novelist with Christian concerns will find in modern life distortions which are repugnant to him, and his problem will be to make these appear as distortions to an audience which is used to seeing them as natural" (MM 33, 162).

As defined by O'Connor, the literary grotesque features outsiders – freaks, misfits, characters lacking "a coherence to their social framework" (MM 40). What sets them apart is the "invisible burden" of fanaticism (MM 44). Blanshard saw fanaticism as another parallel between Catholicism and Communism – another reason for condemning both systems. From his viewpoint, fanaticism meant resistance to progress:

"While the rest of the world was busy with the great expansion and development of modern liberalism and science, the Papacy . . . stood fast against the tides of modern culture." It was at the time of the Counter-Reformation, Blanshard wrote, that the Church arrived at its present totalitarian structure.[80] Mrs. Shortley of "The Displaced Person" holds the same opinion. Catholicism is not an "advanced religion," she believes, because "none of the foolishness had been reformed out of it" (CS 198).

For O'Connor, by contrast, fanaticism meant resistance to the status quo. Conceived as "a reproach, not merely an eccentricity" (MM 44), the fanaticism of characters like Hazel Motes points to a moral standard at odds with consensus ideology. Even a murderous "Christian malgré lui" has more "integrity" (CW 1265) than a spokesman for the cult of reassurance, the religious movement that served the national political consensus. Hazel kills Solace Layfield, the associate of Hoover Shoats in Wise Blood, but the narrator clearly prefers the sincere nihilist to the "hired Prophet." Hazel becomes a "pin point of light" at the end of the novel; Solace departs from the novel after pleading for help from Christ, whom he has betrayed for "three dollars an evening" (WB 201, 205, 232). Dissent becomes the moral standard in fiction by O'Connor, regardless of any crimes her dissenters commit. It was, moreover, the standard she espoused for the Catholic writer in her nonfiction: O'Connor was comfortable in the role of dissenter, regardless of the political stigma attached to that role during the Cold War.

4

The Segregated Pastoral

The farm setting in the works of O'Connor has a dual significance. O'Connor, I have argued, exploits the cultural meaning long attached to the site: her fiction identifies the pastoral setting with the essential America. At the same time, in the same works of fiction, the pastoral is identified with the South as a region distinct from the nation. One critic has recently discussed "The Displaced Person" in relation to social change in the postwar South.[1] This emphasis on regional rather than national history helps to illuminate the specifically Southern nature of the setting in narratives that present the Southern way of life as a deviation from the American way.

Among these narratives, "The Displaced Person" best illustrates the contradictory meanings of the pastoral setting. Nationality is uppermost in the minds of the characters who feel threatened by the European newcomers to the McIntyre farm. The fact that the Guizacs are foreigners translates the local conflict into an international contest: the Americans versus the Poles. The contested territory, the farm itself, functions as a synecdoche for the United States; it represents the "native land" for which Mr. Shortley fought as a U.S. soldier. When Mrs. McIntyre thinks of "her own people," she thinks of Americans like Mr. Shortley, "who had fought in the world war for his country" (CS 228). But the concept of "her own people" also applies to Southerners as a group set apart from other Americans. It is not the national defense, but the defense of a social order peculiar to the South, that concerns Mrs. McIntyre, Mr. Shortley, and Mrs. Shortley. By proposing a marriage between his cousin and one of the black laborers, Mr. Guizac threatens the institution of racial segregation. His attempt to do what "can't be done here" costs Mr. Guizac his only ally on the farm. Mrs. McIntyre, who previously considered him "a kind of miracle," now calls Mr. Guizac a "monster" (CS 219, 222). Forbidding any further mention of intermarriage, she makes an explicit connection between maintaining the racial order and maintaining her farm. "I will not have my niggers upset," she says. "I cannot run this place without my niggers" (*CS* 223). The segregated pastoral of "The Displaced Person" points to the region that founded its social structure on racial division.

As a Southern writer, O'Connor had access to a pastoral tradition whose central theme was race. Lewis P. Simpson has noted the way in which the Southern version of pastoralism departed from the version identified with the U.S. republic; antebellum Southern writers tried "to accommodate the pastoral mode to the antipastoral novelty of the South as expressed by the institution of African chattel slavery." In her farm stories, O'Connor updated the "garden of the chattel"[2] by replacing slavery with segregation – another institution that signified the Southern deviation from the American norm. Three years after the U.S. Supreme Court redefined the national norm on race in *Brown v. Board of Education* (1954), a reporter for the *Saturday Evening Post* made the same connection that O'Connor made, between the Southern pastoral and an anomalous racial policy: "The Rural South – this is the heart of the segregation problem." The pastoral setting, when found in the South, seemed aberrant rather than representative: "This is an island, a backwater, in twentieth-century America."[3]

The racial hierarchy evident in the Southern pastoral was central to the discussion of Southern regional identity in the decades after World War II. Many Southerners, including the advocates of racial integration, repeated the argument that Ulrich B. Phillips had advanced in the 1920s. The South owed its regional distinctiveness, they said, to its policy of white supremacy. In *The Burden of Southern History* (1960), a book O'Connor admired (*HB* 522), C. Vann Woodward quoted Phillips on "the cardinal test of a Southerner and the central theme of southern history." The essence of Southernism, Phillips contended, was "a common resolve indomitably maintained" that the South "shall be and remain a white man's country." Woodward feared that the "Phillipsian doctrine" would discourage Southern liberals from defending their regional identity:

> If Southernism is allowed to become identified with a last ditch defense of segregation, it will increasingly lose its appeal among the younger generation. Many will be tempted to reject their entire regional identification, even the name "Southern," in order to dissociate themselves from the one discredited aspect.[4]

A book by a Southern integrationist, published in 1958, seemed to confirm this fear. Harry S. Ashmore offered *An Epitaph for Dixie,* instead of a defense, because he tied Southernism to racial segregation. When black Southerners completed their transition "from second- to first-class citizenship," Ashmore predicted, the South would no longer be special: "The transition can be accomplished only at the expense of the qualities that made the South distinctive, and cast it in the remarkable role it has played in the history of the Republic."

Afterward, Ashmore speculated, "we shall be able to see the vanishing age more clearly, to examine its virtues without being distracted by its faults."[5] The language here is virtually identical to the language in a passage from "The Fiction Writer and His Country." In her 1957 essay, O'Connor lamented "that every day we are getting more and more like the rest of the country, that we are being forced out not only of our many sins, but of our few virtues" (*MM* 29).

The similarity between the two passages underscores the political dimension of the issue that engaged O'Connor in much of her occasional prose – the issue of "fading" Southern "manners" (*MM* 29). Racial segregation was foremost among the regional characteristics whose demise she announced in her 1962 lecture, "The Regional Writer." Given the widespread acceptance of the "Phillipsian doctrine," O'Connor saw no need to mention segregation by name: "In the past, the things that have seemed to many to make us ourselves have been very obvious things" (*MM* 57). The lecture from 1962 shows that O'Connor wanted to deemphasize politics in her defense of Southern identity. Believing that "the development of power obeys strange laws of its own," she chose not to use "the antics of our politicians" as an exhibit of this identity (*MM* 58). Nevertheless, her fiction is informed by the political drama of Southerners maneuvering to preserve segregation. Defending a regional identity that was "obscured and in doubt" (*MM* 57), O'Connor adapted a rhetoric that opposed the region to the nation on the issue of race.

The memory of the Civil War gave Southerners a means of interpreting this opposition. To be precise, they had their own invasion scenario: the South was the territory threatened from outside, and the United States itself posed the threat. Before World War II, the scenario had served a group critical of "the common or American industrial ideal." The Agrarians, united by their desire "to support a Southern way of life against what may be called the American or prevailing way," attacked industrialism as a form of cultural invasion.[6] Frank Lawrence Owsley spoke for the other contributors to the Agrarian manifesto, *I'll Take My Stand* (1930), when he described industrialism in these terms:

> After the South had been conquered by war and humiliated and impoverished by peace, there appeared still to remain something which made the South different – something intangible, incomprehensible, in the realm of the spirit. That too must be invaded and destroyed; so there commenced a second war of conquest, the conquest of the Southern

> mind, calculated to remake every Southern opinion, to impose the
> Northern way of life and thought upon the South.[7]

John Crowe Ransom called industrialism "a foreign invasion of Southern
soil, which is capable of doing more devastation than was wrought when
Sherman marched to the sea." Ransom argued that "the attitude of resistance on the part of the natives" needed to be revived:

> From this point of view it will be a great gain if the usually-peaceful
> invasion forgets itself now and then, is less peaceful, and commits indis-
> cretions. The native and the invader will be sure to come to an occasion-
> al clash, and that will offer the chance to revive ancient and almost
> forgotten animosities.

As their name suggests, the Agrarians imagined the South in pastoral
terms, and they used the image of a violated countryside to signify the
reduction or loss of regional identity. Ransom predicted, gloomily, that
factories would soon be included "among the charming features of
Southern landscape."[8] Clearly, the scenario of the invaded pastoral
served regional as well as national purposes. After World War II, the
invaded pastoral as a figure of threatened Southern identity reappeared in
a volume of essays edited by Allen Tate, one of the contributors to the
Agrarian manifesto. In *A Southern Vanguard* (1947), a book that O'Connor discussed with her correspondents (*HB* 70, 174), Robert B. Heilman
answered the "outsider" who criticized Southerners for their "blanket
defensiveness." Heilman countered by asserting that Southerners were
reasonably "concerned with the fundamental spiritual well-being" of
their region, and he connected the loss of that well-being with the Satanic
violation of Eden:

> After long indifference to a barrage of critical club-blows from abroad,
> the South . . . is now listening to the serpentine voice of its critics, who
> say, "Be like us, and rejoice"; it has bitten into the apple of conformity;
> it has become self-conscious and put on the fig-leaves of standardiza-
> tion; it has fled its naked individuality.[9]

By the 1950s, the scenario of Northern invasion and Southern defensiveness had become associated with the international conflict that concerned Northerners and Southerners alike. The larger geopolitical opposition – East versus West – provided new terms in which to understand
the attempted preservation of regional identity. The scenario, in short,
now reflected Cold War anxiety over foreign totalitarianism. In addition,
the focal point of Southern resistance had shifted by the 1950s. Education
replaced industrialism as the specific issue that rallied the defenders of
Southern identity. One of the Agrarians, John Gould Fletcher, had argued that Northern ideas about public education reinforced the detrimen-

tal effects of Northern industrialism; in his contribution to *I'll Take My Stand*, he attacked "the revolution in educational theory and practice, that, set in motion after 1865, has worked as effectively to destroy the culture and leisure of our section as the present plague of factories and rash of cheap automobiles."[10] In 1930, however, such protest was fairly isolated. Twenty-four years later, the Supreme Court decision in the *Brown* case provoked massive Southern protest against Northern educational ideas. The controversy came to a head in 1957 when President Eisenhower sent federal troops into Little Rock, Arkansas, to enforce the integration of Central High School. The rhetoric prompted by that action illustrates the influence of Cold War thinking on the defenders of Southern identity.

In a *Life* magazine article that preceded *An Epitaph for Dixie,* Harry Ashmore placed the struggle between the president of the United States and the governor of Arkansas against the background of the Cold War. Ashmore opened his article by noting the coincidence of two major events, the launching of *Sputnik* by the Soviets and the desegregation crisis at home: "When the first earth satellite appeared in the sky, emitting the unnerving sounds of the future, a man named Orval E. Faubus was busily occupied in Little Rock, Ark., trying to re-create the sounds of the past."[11] Governor Faubus compared his own situation to that of Robert E. Lee at the outset of the Civil War. "Lee decided to remain loyal to the people of his state," Faubus told a *New York Times* reporter. "I will remain with the people of Arkansas."[12] Not surprisingly, analogies with the Civil War abounded; to many Southerners, the deployment of federal troops in a Southern city represented nothing less than a military invasion. One Little Rock resident lamented, "The South has been occupied again."[13] But Southerners also compared the troop deployment to recent Soviet military actions. Segregationist rhetoric cast the U.S. government in the role of totalitarian invader. In a speech broadcast during the crisis, Faubus drew an analogy between Little Rock and Budapest – between the intervention of federal troops in Arkansas and the suppression of Hungarian anti-Communists by Soviet troops in 1956. The tactics of the federal authorities, Faubus told his audience, were those of totalitarian governments: "These combined actions on the part of the judicial, executive and military departments of the Federal Government, are 'police state' methods in a form never before seen in America."[14] One of the most prominent segregationists, Senator Herman E. Talmadge of Georgia, drew the same analogy between the situation in Arkansas and the situation in Hungary the previous year:

> We still mourn the destruction of the sovereignty of Hungary by Russian tanks and troops in the streets of Budapest. We are now threatened

with the spectacle of the President of the United States using tanks and
troops in the streets of Little Rock to destroy the sovereignty of the
State of Arkansas.[15]

The other senator from O'Connor's home state, Richard B. Russell,
warned that "millions of patriotic people in this country . . . will strong-
ly resent the strong-armed, totalitarian, police-state methods being employed at Little Rock."[16]

Faubus, Talmadge, and Russell all suggested that the U.S. government
had abandoned its own fundamental principles. As Faubus observed,
"School attendance at bayonet point is not compatible with the American
way of life."[17] By extension, Southern resistance to federal aggression
equaled true patriotism. The segregationists acknowledged no conflict
between defending Southern racial policy and defending U.S. democracy; Russell, for instance, worked to ensure the national security as chair
of the Senate Armed Services Committee. Their position embodied the
central contradiction in the rhetoric of Southern identity: the region that
deviated from the national norm bore a striking resemblance to the essential America. To its defenders, the South seemed distinctive yet representative, exceptional yet exemplary.

Even the Southern opponents of segregation identified the region with
the essential America. A collection of essays published in 1960 bore the
title *The Southerner as American*. The essayists collapsed the distinction
"between Southernism and Americanism" by affirming a consensus at
the level of basic values. The editor, for instance, referred to the region as
"the fundamentally liberal, Christian, American South." Challenging the
idea that "somehow the South escaped the intellectual forces which
shaped American thought and action," the essayists claimed that "in
most ways faith in democracy developed in the South as it did in other
parts of America." The Old South may have defended slavery, but it
never rejected "the Revolutionary tradition of liberty." In other words,
"the Southerner was too American to be convinced by his own arguments" justifying slavery. Southern history had a "tragic dimension"
because antebellum Southerners went against beliefs they held in common with other Americans; the Southerners of the 1960s needed to recognize this dimension if they were to "recover the viable in their tradition."[18]

One writer called the South "the *essence* of the nation" so as to under-
mine Northern complacency. In *The Southern Mystique* (1964), Howard
Zinn took issue with the idea that the South "is distinct from the rest of
the nation – a sport, a freak, an inexplicable variant from the national
norm." Instead, Zinn argued, "the South crystallizes the defects of the
nation," chief among which was racism: "Although the symptoms show
mostly in the South, the entire mind and body of the American nation are

Latest Reports

The rhetoric of Southern identity, which identified "Southernism" with "Americanism," found visual expression in this *Nashville Banner* cartoon. Noting the coincidence of two major events in October 1957, the cartoonist presented *Sputnik* and enforced racial integration as parallel threats to U.S. democracy. Indeed, President Eisenhower's decision to deploy federal troops in Little Rock seems to anger Uncle Sam far more than the Soviet technological victory. Jack Knox, "Latest Reports," *Nashville Banner*, 8 Oct. 1957. Courtesy of the *Nashville Banner*.

afflicted." Zinn wrote, "Those very qualities long attributed to the South as special possessions are, in truth, *American* qualities, and the nation reacts emotionally to the South precisely because it subconsciously recognizes itself there."[19]

For the most part, however, those who identified the South with the essential America did not intend to criticize American life. Indeed, the defenders of Southern identity tended to be fervent cold warriors.[20] James O. Eastland, a Mississippi senator who encouraged segregationists to defy the federal government, served as the ranking Democrat on the Internal Security Subcommittee of the U.S. Senate. In 1954 he conducted a subcommittee hearing to uncover Communist activity in the South; coincidentally, the targets of investigation turned out to be advocates of racial integration. One historian has observed, "It is hard to resist the view that, as Senator Eastland diligently pursued southern communists, he had very much in his mind the need to destroy the credibility of those white southerners who opposed the prevailing system."[21]

In this way, racism and anti-Communism converged. Segregationists linked integration with foreign political subversion. Robert Patterson, the organizer of the first Citizens' Council, stated a rhetorical commonplace when he called desegregation a "communistic disease" in the mid-1950s.[22] "It is now standard practice for the professional pamphleteers to equate integration and Communism," Ashmore wrote in 1958; "most of the racists . . . proceed directly to the conclusion that the South is beset by some sort of gigantic conspiracy, and since the current synonym for conspiratorial evil is Communism, they employ it for all it is worth."[23]

One of the pamphleteers was Tom P. Brady, the "intellectual father" of the Citizens' Council movement.[24] Brady put out a booklet, *Black Monday* (1955), attacking the "socialistic" decision of the Supreme Court in the *Brown* case. According to Brady, U.S. Communists adopted their "plan to abolish segregation" after the failure of an earlier plot "to destroy the South." The Communists targeted the South in the 1930s because they recognized its link with the essential America:

> A black empire was to be established in the Southern States of this nation, ruled by negroes. . . . Back of all this was but one motive, not the welfare of the negro, but the splitting away and controlling of a fine section of this nation, the segment which gave to democracy Thomas Jefferson, Washington, Madison, Monroe and Andrew Jackson. It was and is being done in behalf of Communist Russia. If the South, the stronghold of democracy, could be destroyed, then the nation could be destroyed.

Having failed to upset the racial balance of power, the Communists now intended to weaken the United States by producing "a mongrelized race," which Communists knew to be "an ignorant, weak, easily conquered race." Clearly, Brady was engaged in the rhetoric that tied Southern regional identity to true Americanism. Although he focused on the racial composition of the South, Brady claimed to write as a concerned American:

The inter-racial angle is but a tool, a means to an end, in the overall effort to socialize and communize our Government. The grading down of the intelligence quotient of one-third of the people of this country through amalgamation of the white and negro race would be a great asset in the communizing of our Government.

Brady wrote *Black Monday*, he said, "to alert and encourage every American . . . who loves our Constitution, our Government and our God-given American way of life."[25]

Like their opponents, integrationists discussed domestic race relations in the global context of the Cold War. When they did so, however, they reassigned the roles: segregation advanced Communist aims, while integration helped to strengthen the United States. Rejecting the claim that Patterson and his followers were "just plain patriotic Americans,"[26] national political figures charged Southern segregationists with damaging the reputation of the United States abroad. President Eisenhower himself leveled this charge against the Arkansans who resisted the integration of the Little Rock public schools:

In the South, as elsewhere, citizens are keenly aware of the tremendous disservice . . . that has been done to the nation in the eyes of the world.

At a time when we face grave situations abroad because of the hatred that Communism bears toward a system of government based on human rights, it would be difficult to exaggerate the harm that is being done to the prestige and influence – and, indeed, to the safety – of our nation and the world.

Our enemies are gloating over this incident and using it everywhere to misrepresent our whole nation.[27]

Politicians outside the South supported integration as a way to gain U.S. allies in the Third World. This argument had a "hollow ring" to a Mississippi segregationist like Patterson. "Hubert Humphrey says we should integrate because of Russia and the cold war and the opinion of the Asiatics," Patterson remarked. "So I'm to destroy my children here in Sunflower County in order to impress the Asiatics."[28] But many Southerners agreed with Eisenhower and Humphrey on the propaganda value of race relations at a time of Cold War. Two years after the *Brown* decision, Robert Penn Warren asked whether "we can afford, in the present world picture, to alienate Asia by segregation here at home."[29]

A certain irony inhered in the rhetoric of Southerners who defended their region but held views on race more moderate than those of the segregationists. Despite their disdain for the "provincial Southerners" whose "cultural shortcomings" invited criticism throughout the world,[30] their rhetoric valorized the existing social order of the South. The key term in their rhetoric was individualism, which had a clearly defined ideological value during the Cold War. When Arthur M. Schlesinger, Jr., articulated the ideology of Cold War liberalism in *The Vital Center* (1949), he tied "an unconditional rejection of totalitarianism" to "a reassertion of the ultimate integrity of the individual."[31] The South, claimed its more moderate defenders, performed a crucial service to the nation: it exemplified the American ideal of individualism at a moment of political crisis. Louis D. Rubin, Jr., praised the South as a region that cherished the individual over the mass. The Southerner, he wrote in 1957, emphasized "one's existence as a recognizable individual in a social fabric designed above all to provide for the individual identity."[32] Richard M. Weaver praised the South in terms identical to those of Schlesinger: "Its people still have no desire to be pulled in and made to conform to a regimented mass state." Weaver attributed an "intransigent patriotism" to the Southerner, whose region would play a decisive role in the global conflict of the Cold War:

> If the future of the world shapes up as a gigantic battle between communism and freedom, there is not the slightest doubt as to where the South will stand. It will stand in the forefront of those who oppose the degrading of man to a purely material being, and it will continue to fight those who presume to direct the individual "for his own good" from some central seat of authority. . . . By all the standards that apply, the South has earned the moral right to lead the nation in the present and coming battle against communism, and perhaps also in the more general renascence of the human way of life.

Ultimately, Weaver predicted, the "unyielding Southerner" would "emerge as a providential instrument for the saving of this nation."

Detailing the qualifications of the Southerner as a cold warrior, Weaver stressed the importance of the existing social order: "The South has never lost sight of the fact that society means structuring and differentiation." On this point, the rhetoric of his essay showed considerable overlap with the segregationist rhetoric of *Black Monday*. Like Brady, Weaver maintained that the Communists sought to destroy the social order of the South:

> Because the mass looks with hatred upon any sign of the structuring of society, the South has been viewed with special venom by Socialist and Communist radicals, past and present. One of their prime goals is to break down the South's historic social structure and replace it with a mass condition reflecting only materialist objectives.

Weaver included the "dictates" of the Supreme Court among the "fresh assaults" on the regional social order. Discussing the potential consequences of the *Brown* decree, Weaver supported the Southern decision "to resist the new forward motion of the centralizing and regimenting impulse."[33] He claimed that the issue of governmental authority took prece-

dence over the issue of race relations. Nevertheless, the defense of regional identity boiled down to the defense of segregation. The most visible
example of Southern resistance in the year that Weaver published his
remarks, 1957, was the attempt to circumvent federally mandated integration in Little Rock. The irony in the rhetoric of Southern identity was
inescapable. The "social fabric" that promoted individuality, according
to Rubin, also kept the races separate. In this rhetoric, individualism and
the "Phillipsian doctrine" could not be disentangled. The ideas of individual, racial, and regional "difference" reinforced one another.

As a group, Southern literary artists seemed unwilling to enact the role of
cold warrior. They appeared to resist the demand for a celebratory treatment of American life; in the *Partisan Review* symposium, Irving Howe
observed that fiction by young Southerners showed no evidence of any
"acceptance" of their country.[34] One drama critic, writing in 1961,
faulted Tennessee Williams for tarnishing the international image of the
United States: the plays by Williams that were touring Latin America
depicted a "rotted world" that "does not seem worthy of defending."
The Brazilian critic complained, "It is sad to think that Williams represents a country which is Western and 'Christian,' whose style of life they
want to convince us should be defended against the Communist threat."
The *Time* reporter who quoted the critic agreed with his assessment:
while "serious, liberal-minded intellectuals" worried "about the unat-
tractive impression the U.S. often makes abroad," the Southern playwright who had created *Suddenly, Last Summer* and *Sweet Bird of Youth*
was acting as one of "the worst ambassadors of all."[35]
     Although Williams made her "plumb sick" (*HB* 121), O'Connor like-
wise declined to represent the United States positively. Despite her misgivings about the term "Southern school" (*MM* 28), O'Connor identified
herself as an author whose regional concerns ruled out the celebration of
American life. She explicitly rejected the advice offered by the celebrants:
"Don't be a Southern writer; be an American writer." To O'Connor, the
observation of "our fierce but fading manners" in the South outweighed
the literary alternative: "Express this great country – which is 'enjoying
an unparalleled prosperity,' which is 'the strongest nation in the world,'
and which has 'almost produced a classless society'" (*MM* 29–30).
     The fiction of O'Connor displays the ironies inherent in the rhetoric
available to her as a defender of Southern identity during the Cold War.
These ironies provide much of the humor in "The Displaced Person,"
but they also account for much of the moral resonance. "The Displaced
Person" conveys a clearly negative attitude toward the rhetoric that identified the segregated South with the essential America. The convergence
of racism and anti-Communism in a tract like *Black Monday* explains the

confusion evident in the story by O'Connor – specifically, the jumble of racist and nationalist sentiments in the minds of the white characters who inhabit the pastoral setting. The dual function of the pastoral in the story – as a synecdoche for the region, as a synecdoche for the nation – derives from the rhetorical identification of Southernism and true Americanism. Displaced persons, or "Communist-minded immigrants," played a major role in Brady's scenario of racial "amalgamation" and political subversion. "The continued bringing into our country of this old world flotsam is going to destroy our American way of life and Government," Brady wrote in *Black Monday*. "Rigid immigration restrictions should be enacted and enforced."[36] In "The Displaced Person," O'Connor indicts those who held Brady's views. She portrays Brady's fictional counterparts as conspirators in the death of Mr. Guizac, the immigrant who proposed intermarriage.

Such an indictment is rare in her fiction. Other works by O'Connor show no attempt to discredit the rhetoric of Southern identity. Her second novel, in fact, validates the idea that a distinctively Southern way of life realizes the American ideal of individualism. The rural Southern setting in *The Violent Bear It Away* is a stronghold of individuality. Old Tarwater has raised his great-nephew at Powderhead, the clearing in "the farthest part of the backwoods," for this reason: "I saved you to be free, your own self!" (*VBA* 5, 16). The boy himself connects his independence with the rural setting. Young Tarwater feels he can "smell his freedom, pine-scented, coming out of the woods" (*VBA* 20).

At Powderhead, Tarwater receives a "good education" from his great-uncle. Although his schooling includes "Figures, Reading, Writing, and History," it deviates from the instruction he would have received in the city. The curriculum at Powderhead is hardly standard. The history lessons begin with "Adam expelled from the Garden," continue "through the presidents to Herbert Hoover," and conclude with "speculation" about "the Second Coming and the Day of Judgment" (*VBA* 4). The extent of the deviation from the educational norm worries the invisible "friend" who speaks to Tarwater:

> And how do you know the education he give you is true to the facts? Maybe he taught you a system of figures nobody else uses? How do you know that two added to two makes four? Four added to four makes eight? Maybe other people don't think so. (*VBA* 46)

But the eccentricity of Tarwater's education is its chief virtue. His private schooling guarantees his uniqueness. To young Tarwater, who values an existence set "apart from the ordinary one" (*VBA* 41), Powderhead represents a haven from a public educational system that homogenizes students:

While other children his age were herded together in a room to cut out paper pumpkins under the direction of a woman, he was left free for the pursuit of wisdom. . . . The boy knew that escaping school was the surest sign of his election. (*VBA* 17)

In public school, Tarwater would be "one among many, indistinguishable from the herd" (*VBA* 18).

The character who wants to put Tarwater there is Rayber, whose regular identification as "the schoolteacher" emphasizes his role as the representative of public education. To Rayber, the primary goal of education is the socialization of children. "I want you to be educated," he tells Tarwater, "so that you can take your place as an intelligent man in the world" (*VBA* 110). He intends to help his nephew make "progress toward being a normal person" (*VBA* 193). According to Rayber, old Tarwater did just the opposite: "He kept you from having a normal life, from getting a decent education" (*VBA* 103).

Rayber condemns "the brand of independence the old man had wrought" in Tarwater. Rayber considers it "irrational, backwoods, and ignorant." But his own idea of a "constructive independence" (*VBA* 100) proves hollow. The "chance" that Rayber offers his nephew, the opportunity "to do what you want to do" (*VBA* 92), hinges on Tarwater's compliance with Rayber's expectations. Near the end of the novel, Rayber decides to issue an ultimatum. Tarwater must "cooperate, fully and completely," by adopting a new attitude, submitting to a series of personality tests, and entering public school in the fall (*VBA* 200). Despite his promise of freedom, Rayber embodies the threat to individuality posed by public education. He is the expert on standardized testing at his high school: "All his professional decisions were prefabricated and did not involve his participation" (*VBA* 114). As old Tarwater has warned young Tarwater, the tests given by Rayber reduce the individual to mere "information" (*VBA* 16). They turn individual difference into "emotional infection" (*VBA* 111).

Rayber places his faith in the average, the general, the abstract. "There are certain laws that determine every man's conduct," Rayber tells Tarwater. "You are no exception" (*VBA* 196). He disposes of individual traits, calling his uncle "a type that's almost extinct" (*VBA* 29). Thinking of his nephew, Rayber rejects the actual personality: "He eliminated the oppressive presence from his thoughts and retained only those aspects of it that could be abstracted, clean, into the future person he envisioned" (*VBA* 179).

Toward the end of her 1960 novel, O'Connor brings out a few of the products of the public educational system. The dancers at the Cherokee Lodge are the same age as Tarwater, "but they might have belonged to a different species entirely." Homogenization has gone so far as to reduce gender differences: "The girls could be distinguished from the boys only by their tight skirts and bare legs; their faces and heads were alike." They respond with an "angry silence" when they see Bishop, Rayber's mentally retarded son: "Their look was shocked and affronted as if they had been betrayed by a fault in creation, something that should have been corrected before they were allowed to see it" (*VBA* 189–90). Refusing to make any allowance for "special" children, the teenagers mimic the educational system that has formed them. When young Tarwater pretends to be retarded, a truant officer decides against enforcing the school attendance policy; as old Tarwater has predicted, the school representative suggests that "it might be best to leave him in peace. . . . I speck he better stay at home" (*VBA* 18).

Rayber may want to swing a chair into the faces of the teenagers at the lodge, but his reaction to Bishop is pretty much the same. He tells Tarwater to ignore Bishop, who is "just a mistake of nature" (*VBA* 117). He has little patience for nonconformity, whether willful, like Tarwater's, or innate, like Bishop's. Rayber is a Southerner, like his rural relatives, but he has no regard for their "backwoods" individualism. Even his place of residence reflects his commitment to conformity. He lives in a section of town where the houses are "almost identical" (*VBA* 31). To Southern writers in the 1950s, suburbia had become a symbol for the loss of regional identity. Interpreting the phenomenon of "almost identical ranch homes in almost identical housing projects," Louis Rubin foresaw the future of the South as "a thriving but undistinguished replica of the North and West."[37] Rayber's disregard for individuality aligns him with the forces from outside the South that seemed to diminish its identity.

The educational system that Rayber represents is also aligned with these forces. By enforcing conformity, the novel suggests, public education works against Southern identity. O'Connor makes this opposition explicit in a short story she finished not long before starting work on *The Violent Bear It Away*. "A Late Encounter with the Enemy" (1953) posits a conflict between regional identity and educational ideas originating from outside the region. The story concerns the effort by Sally Poker Sash to have her grandfather, "General" George Poker Sash, attend her graduation from a state teachers' college. For the past twenty years, Sally Poker has been resisting its progressive curriculum. Though she has taken all the required classes, "she always taught in the exact way she had been taught not to teach" (*CS* 135). On one level, the character speaks for the author, who felt that the education courses she had taken in college had been "Pure Wasted Time" (*HB* 564). But Sally Poker also speaks for those who felt that Northern educational ideas, including the forthcoming decision in the *Brown* case, threatened Southern society. She wants her grandfather at the commencement ceremony because he symbolizes the "old traditions" of the South:

> She wanted the General at her graduation because she wanted to show what she stood for, or, as she said, 'what all was behind her,' and was not behind them. This *them* was not anybody in particular. It was just all the upstarts who had turned the world on its head and unsettled the ways of decent living. (*CS* 135)

The General himself has forgotten the Civil War, in which he served as a major, but he has proven useful as a symbol of Southern identity: "Every year on Confederate Memorial Day, he was bundled up and lent to the Capitol City Museum where he was displayed from one to four in a musty room full of old photographs, old uniforms, old artillery, and historic documents" (*CS* 139).

After the 1954 *Brown* decision, public education figured prominently in the rhetoric of Southerners defending their regional identity. But the terms in which the defenders reproached the "upstarts," the supporters of educational progress, antedated the Supreme Court ruling. The essay that John Gould Fletcher contributed to *I'll Take My Stand*, "Education, Past and Present," furnishes a paradigm for the discussion. Arguing that the Northern system of public education was "not adapted to Southern life," Fletcher eulogized the private academies of the Old South. The students in these academies, Fletcher wrote, had received individual attention. They had enjoyed "direct contact" with their teachers, "not with undisputed masses of information and up-to-date apparatus." According to Fletcher, private education nurtured regional as well as individual identity. While the public schools "ignored local and functional differences" and produced "a being without roots," the private schools produced "the balanced character . . . the man with spiritual roots in his own community." Moreover, Fletcher merged the concepts of individual distinction and regional distinctiveness with the concept of racial "difference." Fletcher complained that the public school system discouraged intellectual excellence; even a black student could "pass easily through the high school and college mill," he wrote, noting parenthetically that "such a task does not require any profound knowledge of self or determination of mind." Still, blacks were to remain separate. Integration was "simply a waste of money and effort," Fletcher held. The desire to recognize individual distinction, or "to select out of the mass the saving remnant who might under proper encouragement become masters in their several fields," was consistent with segregation on the basis of the intellectual "capacity" attributed to each race.

Fletcher admitted that his ideal of private education belonged to the past: "We cannot, apparently, destroy the public-school system. That is now rooted, whether for good or evil, in our midst, just as the industrial system is."[38] By contrast, the segregationists of the 1950s and 1960s saw private education as a viable political strategy. They believed it would help them defend their way of life against an immediate political threat – federally mandated integration. By the spring of 1958 – a few months after the Little Rock showdown – Georgia and several other Southern states had announced plans to close their public schools should the federal government try to enforce integration. Under these plans for "massive resistance," newly created private schools would assume the educational burden.[39] As a method by which Southern state governments could circumvent the federal government, the creation of private educational systems would enable the South to preserve its racial order and thus its regional identity.

The threat of school closings in Tennessee prompted one of O'Connor's friends, Brainard Cheney, to resign as public relations officer for Governor Frank Clement. Because of "his pitch on Segregation," Cheney told O'Connor in 1958, "I cannot stomach the Clement candidate for Governor." The candidate, Buford Ellington, "made a backhanded invitation to the Ku Klux Klan, et al to the effect that he would close down any school at their behest before they would let it be desegregated." Cheney observed, "That may be necessary in Mississippi, or Georgia, but it isn't in Tennessee" (C 69).

The "massive resistance" movement created no statewide systems of private education. Acting independently, however, many Southerners turned to private education as a means of preserving a segregated society. The white Citizens' Councils established a number of "segregation academies," which became increasingly popular after Congress passed the Civil Rights Act in 1964; over the next five years, the Southern Regional Council reported, enrollment underwent at least a tenfold increase.[40]

Private schools appealed to those Southerners like Fletcher who conjoined individualism, racial "difference," and regional identity. Benjamin Muse, assessing the impact of the *Brown* decision after ten years, noted this rhetorical conjunction in some of the arguments for closing the public schools:

> A few enthusiasts, like the *Richmond News Leader,* argued that a proliferation of private schools, with their release from uniformity of curriculum and philosophy, was a desirable end even apart from the aim of preserving racial segregation, and they suggested that the South eventually might have this crisis to thank for an educational advance.[41]

In the *Brown* decision, by contrast, Chief Justice Earl Warren valorized public education as a force for conformity, as a "principal instrument" for "awakening the child to cultural values" and "helping him to adjust normally to his environment." From Warren's perspective, the education that promoted conformity was "the very foundation of good citizenship."[42] As a legal analyst noted in 1957, the Supreme Court found "a national interest in education" that transcended local concerns; without public education, Arthur S. Miller explained, "the national security would be imperiled."[43] This assumption led Congress to pass the National Defense Education Act (1958) over the objections of Southern legislators who worried that federal aid to education would be used to advance racial integration.[44] "Intercontinental competition in education," or "the new 'cold war' of the classrooms,"[45] took priority over the struggle to preserve Southern regional identity. For this reason, one educator criticized the 1959 closing of the public schools in Prince Edward County, Virginia: "Here people took a step to hamper educational effort at a time when the American people were being urged to make greater educational effort to preserve civilization itself."[46]

This, then, is the rhetorical context of *The Violent Bear It Away*. The conflict between private education, as a means of promoting "backwoods" individualism, and public education, as a means of forming a "good citizen" (*VBA* 108), is basically a conflict between regional and national goals. The result of the narrative conflict is clear. The Southerner who defends individuality triumphs over the Southerner who preaches conformity. Tarwater becomes an "oppressive presence" to Rayber; "the boy's cold intractability" wears down the schoolteacher, who comes to realize that "the only feeling he had for this boy was hate." Rayber gives up on his plan to make Tarwater conform: "He no longer felt any challenge to rehabilitate him. All he wanted now was to get rid of him" (*VBA* 179, 196, 199). He never has a chance to deliver his ultimatum to his nephew, who escapes into the woods across the lake from the Cherokee Lodge. Rayber finally recognizes the extent to which the private education at Powderhead has taken hold of the boy. Tarwater, Rayber knows instinctively, "was headed for everything the old man had prepared him for" (*VBA* 203). Rayber's departure from the novel underscores Rayber's defeat: the schoolteacher collapses.

A short story by O'Connor, "The Lame Shall Enter First" (1962), shows the defeat of another spokesman for conformity. Like Rayber, who wants to "save" Tarwater "from being a freak" (*VBA* 170), Sheppard wants to "save" a juvenile delinquent by eradicating his religious "ignorance" and bringing him into "the space age" (*CS* 451, 474). Sheppard is the good citizen that Rayber wants Tarwater to be. He is the recreational director for the city, and he volunteers his time for public service: "On Saturdays he worked at the reformatory as a counselor, receiving nothing for it but the satisfaction of knowing he was helping boys no one else cared about" (*CS* 447). Even as he serves his local community, he champions a national goal: U.S. superiority in the space

race with the Soviets. When he counsels Rufus Johnson, the boy he hopes
to reform, Sheppard describes "the space capsules that were whirling
around the earth faster than the speed of sound and would soon encircle
the stars" (*CS* 451). His optimism surpasses even that of President John
F. Kennedy, who announced plans in 1961 to put an American on the
moon by the end of the decade. "In ten years," Sheppard says, "men will
probably be making round trips there on schedule" (*CS* 461). Sheppard
encourages Rufus to become an astronaut. But Rufus, like Tarwater,
successfully resists the attempt to reform him. Rufus, a juvenile delinquent who speaks the language of Southern religious fundamentalism,
refuses to surrender either aspect of his personality. He continues to
break the law, and when the police catch him, he claims he "wanted to
get caught" in order to escape from Sheppard: "I'd rather be in the
reformatory than in his house, I'd rather be in the pen!" At the same
time, he continues to espouse the religious teachings of his grandfather,
the leader of a Christian survivalist group in the hills. Rufus rejects the
salvation offered by Sheppard. "When I get ready to be saved," he says,
"Jesus'll save me, not that lying stinking atheist" (*CS* 479, 480). Sheppard
has already realized "that there could be nothing now but a battle of
nerves and that Johnson would win it." Sheppard recognizes his own
defeat: "He wished he had never laid eyes on the boy. The failure of his
compassion numbed him." He simply wants Rufus to leave: "He longed
for the time when there would be no one but himself and Norton in the
house" (*CS* 474–5). The ending of the story, however, leaves Sheppard
completely alone; his son, having come under the influence of Rufus
Johnson, kills himself.

In other works of fiction by O'Connor, Southerners attempting to preserve their individual identity are less successful than Rufus or Tarwater.
The logic informing these stories is the logic inherent in the rhetoric of
Southern identity: the South could promote individuality only as long as
it retained its distinctive regional character, which depended, in turn, on
the legal recognition of racial "difference." In her reading of "Everything
That Rises Must Converge" (1961), the novelist Alice Walker notes the
connection O'Connor made between the loss of regional identity and
the destruction of racial hierarchy: "O'Connor thought that the South,
as it became more 'progressive,' would become just like the North.
Culturally bland, physically ravished, and, where the people are concerned, well, you wouldn't be able to tell one racial group from another."[47] But the end of segregation, as dramatized by O'Connor, also
means the loss of individual identity. "Everything That Rises" features a
debate on the question of individual identity in a setting representative of
the perceived threat to Southern regional identity – an integrated bus.

The participants in this debate are a mother who contends that "who you are" remains constant, despite economic hardship, and a son who discredits any identity based on past social status. "Knowing who you are," he says, "is good for one generation only" (CS 407). The mother believes that "reduced circumstances" make no difference to Southerners who can claim an aristocratic heritage: "reduced or not," she says of her family, "they never forgot who they were" (CS 408). She lives with her son, Julian, in a neighborhood that has gone from "fashionable" to "dingy" (CS 406, 407). She disregards the change in the neighborhood because she bases her sense of self on the achievements of her family, a family identified with the peculiar institution of the Old South. "You remain what you are," she tells Julian. "Your great-grandfather had a plantation and two hundred slaves." She argues that blacks were "better off" under slavery, and she wants to keep them "on their own side of the fence" (CS 408). As a threat to her sense of self, racial integration outweighs poverty. However far she descended the economic scale during the "hard times" in the past (CS 411), she could take for granted her position at the top of the racial hierarchy. But now, she complains, "the bottom rail is on the top" (CS 407). She has lost her identity, according to Julian, because she can no longer expect blacks to concede her superiority. "You aren't who you think you are," Julian informs her. To maintain her sense of self, she persists in treating blacks as inferiors. When she and Julian leave the bus, she demonstrates her aristocratic "graciousness" (CS 419) by giving a black child a penny. By means of this condescending gesture, "as natural to her as breathing" (CS 417), the granddaughter of slaveholders asserts an authority she no longer possesses. The mother of the black child responds by hitting her with a pocketbook. "He don't take nobody's pennies!" the black woman shouts (CS 418). Disoriented by the attack, Julian's mother can recover her sense of self only by retreating into a past in which blacks were subservient. She asks for Caroline, the "old darky" who nursed her as a child (CS 409, 420). Julian has told her that "it won't kill you" to "face a few realities," including the loss of her identity (CS 419). In fact, the attack that signals the end of black subservience is the cause of her death.

In "Judgement Day," too, death ends the attempt by a Southerner to maintain an identity dependent on regional assumptions about race. The Southern protagonist in the final story from *Everything That Rises Must Converge* has a Northern residence. Tanner has moved from Corinth, Georgia, to New York City, which he calls "no kind of place" (CS 541). In the North, Tanner is no longer the "somebody" he was "when he was somebody" (CS 532). His identity has been diminished by his distance from the South, where he owed his reputation to the authority he exerted over black workers: "He was known to have a way with niggers." Even before he left the South, however, his identity seemed endangered. "The secret of handling a nigger," from Tanner's perspective, "was to show him his brains didn't have a chance against yours" (CS 536). Having founded his sense of self on this belief in racial "difference," Tanner felt personally threatened by federal efforts to dismantle the racial hierarchy of the region. "You don't have a chance with the government against you," Tanner tells himself in a flashback. Tanner foresees his own defeat in a confrontation with Doctor Foley, the black man who bought the property on which Tanner has been living and operating a still:

> Be prepared, he said to himself, watching him approach, to take something off him, nigger though he be. Be prepared, because you ain't got a thing to hold up to him but the skin you come in, and that's no more use to you now than what a snake would shed. (CS 535)

Foley, who is part black, part Indian, and part white, embodies a racial order that is turning "upside down" as a result of integration. Foley wants to turn Tanner into "a nigger's white nigger," and he delivers the ultimatum that prompts Tanner to leave for New York: "If you want to run the still for me, that's one thing," Foley tells Tanner. "If you don't, you might as well had be packing up." Predicting a day "when the white folks IS going to be working for the colored," Foley informs Tanner that the day has "come for you" (CS 540). Tanner leaves the South, then, to avoid the complete loss of his authority.

The scene in which Tanner wins the loyalty of his black companion, Coleman Parrum, displays his proficiency at "handling a nigger." In this flashback, he upholds the idea of racial "difference" and uses it to his advantage. Confronted by a black stranger who defies his authority as "a white man" (CS 538), Tanner carves a pair of spectacles and tells the stranger to put them on. Tanner then asks him what he sees through the glasses:

> "See a man."
> "What kind of a man?"
> "See the man make theseyer glasses."
> "Is he white or black?"
> "He white!" the Negro said as if only at that moment was his vision sufficiently improved to detect it. "Yessuh, he white!" he said.
> "Well, you treat him like he was white," Tanner said. (CS 539)

In establishing his authority, Tanner initiates a lifelong friendship. After moving to New York, he stays in touch with Coleman by means of postcards; he imagines taking Coleman on a sightseeing tour; and he plans to entrust his remains to Coleman for burial. Their relationship hardly seems representative of a segregated society. But then, the character who advocates racial segregation in "Everything That Rises" boasts of close relations with blacks. "I've always had a great respect for my colored friends," says Julian's mother. "I'd do anything in the world for them." Remembering her black nurse, she says, "There was no better person in the world" (CS 409).

Many Southerners saw no contradiction between interracial friendship and a racial hierarchy. The prospect of reduced social intimacy in a racially integrated society even bothered some Southern integrationists. Despite his opposition to Governor Faubus in the political crisis at Little Rock, Harry Ashmore blamed integration for an "emotional crisis" in the South. If the "peculiar institutions . . . erected around the Negro" were inhibiting, they were also responsible for "a set of conventions accepted by both races and providing the basis for an orderly if uneven social structure." Ashmore held that "there was nothing in the institutions, or the conventions, to proscribe warm relationships between individual whites and Negroes." To support his point, Ashmore contrasted his childhood with that of his daughter:

> As a boy growing up in South Carolina, my experiences were shared with dozens of Negroes – the nurse who tended me until my legs grew long enough to carry me beyond her reach; the cook; the ice man; the grocer's delivery boy; the swarm of Negro children who lived along the dirt streets beyond the white neighborhood; the house servants and the field hands on the cotton farm where I spent the summers. My daughter, growing up in comparable social and economic circumstances in a Southern state, knows only one Negro well enough to call by name – the part-time maid who is regarded as a convenience, not a member of the family.[48]

In "Judgement Day," O'Connor draws the same contrast between generations. Although Tanner's daughter has black neighbors in her apartment building, she has no black friends. "If you have to live next to them," she tells Tanner, "just you mind your business and they'll mind theirs" (CS 543).

When she comes to visit him at the shack in Corinth, she finds Coleman sleeping on a pallet at the foot of his bed. Embarrassed by her suggestion that he "likes to settle in with niggers," Tanner insists on his authority in the relationship with Coleman. "Who you think cooks?" he asks his daughter, indignantly. "Who you think cuts my firewood and empties my slops?" (CS 534, 535). Clearly, the friendship does not conflict with the racial hierarchy. Coleman addresses Tanner as "boss" (CS 542). The friendship still validates Tanner's identity as a man adept at "handling a nigger."[49]

In New York City, he seeks to validate this identity once more by establishing a friendship with a black man. If he could "make a monkey" out of Coleman (CS 539), Tanner assumes, he can do so with the black man who lives next door to his daughter: "He was willing to bet the nigger would like to talk to someone who understood him" (*CS* 543). Unfortunately, Tanner's understanding fails him. He keeps calling the black man a preacher: "It had been his experience that if a Negro tended to be sullen, this title usually cleared up his expression" (*CS* 544). Instead, the man grows exasperated. "I don't take no crap," he tells Tanner, "off no wool-hat red-neck son-of-a-bitch peckerwood old bastard like you." Denying that he is a preacher, the man adds, "There ain't no Jesus and there ain't no God." Tanner responds by falling back on the idea of racial "difference" that served him in the South, in the past: "And you ain't black. . . . And I ain't white!" (*CS* 545). This remark goads the man into slamming Tanner against the wall and shoving him through the door of the apartment. The next time they meet, Tanner again calls the man a preacher; this time, the man shoves him between the spokes of the stair banister, causing his death (*CS* 549).

"Judgement Day" sends mixed signals. The ending, in particular, raises the question of audience response. As the victim of an assault, Tanner invites sympathy on the part of the reader. Like Julian's mother, however, he provokes the attack by insulting a black character. As a defender of individual identity in an urban setting that breeds anonymity, Tanner merits respect. Yet he bases his identity on racist assumptions about authority.

O'Connor certainly disapproved of the gesture that is supposed to put the black woman in her place in "Everything That Rises." The incident in which Julian's mother insults the woman may have been inspired by an incident O'Connor witnessed on a segregated bus. The white driver, addressing his black passengers as "stove-pipe blonds," told them to "git on back ther." At that moment, O'Connor told a correspondent in 1957, "I became an integrationist" (*HB* 253). In her correspondence, however, O'Connor did not articulate a consistent position on racial integration. In 1963, for example, she told a correspondent that she opposed forced busing to create "racially balanced" schools (*HB* 541). On the one hand, the actions of white supremacists appalled her. Recalling a local incident that took place several years before the *Brown* decision, O'Connor belittled segregationists in Milledgeville: "The people who burned the cross couldn't have gone past the fourth grade but, for the time, they were mighty interested in education" (*HB* 195). On the other hand, O'Connor dismissed calls for "racial justice" as "yapping," even when these calls appeared in the Catholic diocesan press (*HB* 499).

One thing did remain consistent: in her correspondence, O'Connor always seemed less concerned with the question of racial justice than with the question of regional identity. After Medgar Evers, the civil rights activist, was murdered in Mississippi in 1963, Eudora Welty wrote

"Where Is the Voice Coming From?" to express her "shock and revolt."[50] O'Connor disliked the story primarily because she read it as an
indictment of the South: "It's the kind of story that the more you think
about it the less satisfactory it gets. What I hate most is its being in the
New Yorker and all the stupid Yankee liberals smacking their lips over
typical life in the dear old dirty Southland" (HB 537).

"Everything That Rises" reflects O'Connor's priorities. The story focuses on the consequences of integration for the white characters, not the
black characters. The "frustrated rage" of the black woman, exploding
"like a piece of machinery that had been given one ounce of pressure too
much" (CS 418), is essentially a plot device for resolving the identity
crisis of the white woman. Julian's mother brings the violence on herself
by giving the penny to the woman's child. Nevertheless, the narrative
encourages the reader to sympathize with Julian's mother. More precisely, it discourages the reader from gloating, as Julian gloats, over "the
lesson she had had." The narrative shows the emotional cruelty that
attends Julian's sense of moral superiority. Taking advantage of his
mother's disorientation, Julian lectures the dying woman:

> "Don't think that was just an uppity Negro woman," he said. "That
> was the whole colored race which will no longer take your condescend-
> ing pennies. That was your black double. She can wear the same hat as
> you, and to be sure," he added gratuitously (because he thought it was
> funny), "it looked better on her than it did on you. What all this
> means," he said, "is that the old world is gone. The old manners are
> obsolete and your graciousness is not worth a damn." (CS 419)

The ending of the story emphasizes the tragic aspect of a woman who
cannot bear the loss of her identity, and who cannot rely on her son for
support when an act of violence forces her to recognize this loss. The
description of her "fiercely distorted" face calls attention to the psychological violence she suffers (CS 420). This suffering separates the mother
from the son who has failed her. Looking at Julian, "trying to determine
his identity," she seems to find "nothing familiar about him" (CS 419).

My point, again, is that racial justice receives less attention than the
impact of integration on white Southerners – its effect in terms of individual and regional identity. "Everything That Rises" adumbrates the
sufferings of black Southerners. The black woman, who might have
diverted sympathy from Julian's mother, disappears immediately after
the assault. The character's sudden departure has troubled at least one
African-American writer. Alice Walker called the story "only half a story" because "O'Connor chose not to say" what happens to the black
woman.[51] The disappearance of the character who has suffered the insult
provides support for the criticism offered by Frederick Crews in his
recent reassessment of O'Connor. Her fiction, he says, never conveys

"any appreciation of the stakes for human dignity at play in the civil rights movement."[52]

"Everything That Rises" ends with a line that translates the narrative conflict from political terms into the theological terms suggested by the title. As Julian runs to get help for his mother, the narration announces "his entry into the world of guilt and sorrow" (CS 420). From its foundation in the rhetoric of Southern identity, the story ascends into the universal – where the specifics of race and region dissolve. Although it deals explicitly with one of the more visible forms of integration – the integration of public transportation – the story communicates no political stance. This is hardly surprising, given the literary standards that O'Connor espoused. "The best American fiction," she declared in 1962, had been produced by regional authors "reading a small history in a universal light" (MM 58). When she criticized Welty's story in a 1963 letter, O'Connor lodged a general complaint against fiction dealing with current social problems. "The topical is poison," she told her correspondent. "I got away with it in 'Everything That Rises' but only because I say a plague on everybody's house as far as the race business goes" (HB 537).

If the "topical" made for bad literature, it also made for risky politics. A regional prohibition of dissent mirrored the national prohibition. The defenders of Southern identity demanded conformity on the issue of segregation; Southerners were expected to support the existing racial order. Mimicking those on the national political scene who compiled lists of "subversive" organizations, a speaker in 1956 named eight organizations that threatened the "Southern way of life."[53] Dissenters from the consensus on segregation could face harassment, or even physical danger.[54] Ministers who advocated integration could be forced to resign their religious positions. "In the South," one observer wrote in 1963, "we have a new class of DP's – displaced parsons."[55] Secular intellectuals were no less vulnerable, according to Harry Ashmore. "The subject of integration in the public schools is off limits for Southern intellectuals," he wrote; "they discuss it only at their peril, and those subject to official reprisal or sensitive to social pressures have been made fully aware of the price they must pay." Throughout the South, it seemed, "the mildest public questioning of the sanctity of segregation brings some degree of condemnation and abuse." Drawing a parallel with the situation before the Civil War, Ashmore observed that the consensus on race forced Southerners to make a choice between allegiance to their region and allegiance to the federal government:

> Today, as in the 1830's, even silence does not afford protection against the fanatics and their uninhibited party press; unless a man goes the whole way with fervid condemnation of the United States Supreme

Court and all its works, he is subject to charges of disloyalty and heresy.[56]

Southern intellectuals occupied a precarious position. As cold warriors on the cultural front, they were supposed to improve the image of the United States abroad – an image tarnished by the institution of segregation at home. As defenders of regional identity, they were expected to support that same institution.

When she rejected her assigned role as an intellectual cold warrior, O'Connor still had to face the moral dilemma of the Southern intellectual. Although her status as a Southern writer gave her a position from which to criticize U.S. society, it enrolled O'Connor in the regional consensus on race. In her paperback edition (1954) of *The Mind of the South* (1941), she marked a passage in which W. J. Cash observed that social and political developments before the Civil War "turned the South toward strait-jacket conformity and made it increasingly intolerant of dissent."[57] O'Connor surely recognized a parallel between the antebellum South and the South of the 1950s. Her attitude toward "the South's instinct to preserve her identity" was ambivalent; a passage from "The Catholic Novelist in the Protestant South" (1963) reveals her mixed feelings:

> The South is traditionally hostile to outsiders, except on her own terms. She is traditionally against intruders, foreigners from Chicago or New Jersey, all those who come from afar with moral energy that increases in direct proportion to the distance from home. It is difficult to separate the virtues of this quality from the narrowness which accompanies and colors it for the outside world. (*MM* 200)

O'Connor dramatizes her dilemma as a Southern intellectual in one of her early stories, which she wrote while away from the South. "The Barber," the second story in the master's thesis she completed at the University of Iowa in 1947, begins with the observation, "It is trying on liberals in Dilton" (*CS* 15). The issue of race in the Democratic white primary sets a liberal intellectual, a college professor, against the barber and his cronies. At the barbershop, everyone except the professor supports Hawkson, the candidate who tells white voters that "he liked niggers fine in their place and if they didn't stay in that place, he had a place to put 'em" (*CS* 17). The barber wants "a man can put these niggers in their places" (*CS* 16). When the professor expresses his support for Darmon, the integrationist candidate, the barber asks him whether he is a "nigger-lover." The story suggests that any deviation from the regional consensus on racial segregation would earn the intellectual this label. There is no middle ground, from the viewpoint of those who support the consensus; the title character, speaking for the majority, insists that "there ain't but two sides now, white and black." The race issue has polarized politics to such an extent that intellectual detachment no longer seems an option. The professor wants to tell the barber, "I am neither a Negro- nor a white-lover," but as another professor has remarked, "That's a poor way to be" (CS 15).

According to Ashmore, writing in 1958, "The great frustration of the intellectual is that, bound by his own regard for facts and logic, he finds it impossible to debate with those who so viciously attack him."[58] In "The Barber," the professor feels frustrated because his kind of "reasoning" (CS 19) proves unpersuasive. "Big words don't do nobody no good," the barber tells him. "They don't take the place of thinkin'." The professor responds angrily: "Thinking!" he shouts. "You call yourself thinking?" (CS 17). His status as an educator does not impress his opponents. From their perspective, the professor simply fails to realize that he, too, has a reason to support the segregationist candidate: "How'd you like a couple of black faces looking at you from the back of your classroom?" (CS 19).

Although the story dramatizes the "professional frustration" that Ashmore would later attribute to the faculties of Southern universities,[59] O'Connor directs her satire against the intellectual himself. The professor, who has the same name as the schoolteacher in *The Violent Bear It Away*, is the prototype of that smug, self-righteous, and ultimately impotent intellectual. Like the Rayber of the novel, the Rayber of the story feels qualified to fight "ignorance" and outmaneuver "fat minds" (CS 21, 25). His own wife recognizes his egotism: "Whenever he mentioned the election, she made it a point to say, 'Just because you teach doesn't mean you know everything'" (CS 22). Although he believes that he has a superior intellect, the professor rarely speaks his mind. At one point, O'Connor writes, "It was time for Rayber to say something but nothing appropriate would come" (CS 16). That night, he rehashes the conversation with the barber, "putting in what he would have said if he'd had an opportunity to prepare himself" (CS 18). Although he believes in his ability to make his opponents "squirm," Rayber knows that he "couldn't open his head in a second like they did. He wished to hell he could" (CS 21). The ending of the story completely discredits the intellectual. Rayber commits the only act of violence: he hits the barber. And he looks ridiculous when he rushes out of the barbershop, with lather dripping from his face and the barber's bib "dangling to his knees" (CS 25).

Despite their racist views, his opponents seem more levelheaded than Rayber. The barber and the other customers have the "horse sense" that Rayber lacks (CS 17). The ease with which they speak their minds also suggests a greater sincerity.[60] Similarly, the portrait of the segregationist mother in "Everything That Rises" is more sympathetic than that of the integrationist son. The story portrays Julian as a spiteful, ungrateful child who imagines himself "participating as a sympathizer in a sit-in demonstration" in order to shock his mother and "teach her a lesson" (CS 414). Crews has noted this aspect of the fiction:

> In story after story, the only white characters who even pretend to care about black emancipation are hypocritical, self-deluded fools who presumably would be better occupied looking out for their own salvation. By default, then, we are left to gather that any active concern to break down the South's apartheid must be a form of vanity.[61]

O'Connor found less to satirize in the position of those who conformed to majority opinion in the South. She adopted this position herself when James Baldwin visited Georgia in 1959. She declined to see the black writer, whose work she admired, because their meeting "would cause the greatest trouble and disturbance and disunion." She told a correspondent, "In New York it would be nice to meet him; here it would not. I observe the traditions of the society I feed on – it's only fair" (HB 329). In the same letter, O'Connor poked fun at Brainard Cheney and his "liberal abolishionist friends" from New York (HB 330).

O'Connor was no racist. The same writer who felt compelled to "observe the traditions" of her society would also challenge the ideological basis of racism. In "The Artificial Nigger" (1955), for instance, she suggests that the ability to recognize racial "difference" is not innate, but the result of training. According to Mr. Head, the white protagonist, "A six-month-old child don't know a nigger from anybody else" (CS 252). The grandson of Mr. Head sees "his first nigger" on a train ride to Atlanta; Nelson, who has grown up in rural seclusion, notices only the gender ("A man"), the weight ("A fat man"), and the age ("An old man") of the black passenger. Mr. Head has to inform him, "That was a nigger." Nelson protests, "You said they were black. . . . You never said they were tan. How do you expect me to know anything when you don't tell me right?" (CS 255). Nelson's literalism calls attention to the artificiality of racial categories.

O'Connor satirized intellectuals who broke with the regional consensus on race because their position seemed to disqualify them as defenders of Southern identity – her primary concern. In spite of her suggestion that racial categories are socially constructed, the author of "The Artificial Nigger" had trouble imagining regional "difference" without the legal institution of racial "difference." She was enmeshed in a rhetoric that defined regional identity by reference to the "Phillipsian doctrine." When she tried to define Southern identity without referring to segregation, her definition proved remarkably vague:

> It is not made from the mean average or the typical, but from the hidden and often the most extreme. It is not made from what passes, but from

those qualities that endure, regardless of what passes, because they are related to truth. It lies very deep. In its entirety, it is known only to God, but of those who look for it, none gets so close as the artist. (*MM* 58)

As an artist, O'Connor accepted a role at the regional level that she rejected at the national level: the role of cultural defender. While she refused to provide the nationalistic affirmation demanded by *Life* and *Partisan Review,* she maintained that "the Georgia part of being a Georgia writer has some positive significance" at a time when Southern identity seemed "in doubt" (*MM* 57). Consequently, regional dissent from a national consensus took priority over protest against a regional consensus. O'Connor felt that such protest could only work against the "serious" Southern writer, "who is a part of what he writes about and is recognized as such" (*MM* 56). Dissent from the regional consensus on race would have cut her off from the cohesive society that she considered necessary to the writer. "Unless the novelist has gone utterly out of his mind," O'Connor said in 1962, "his aim is still communication, and communication suggests talking inside a community" (*MM* 53). It was, after all, the South to which the Southern writer had to answer: "His true audience, the audience he checks himself by, is at home" (*MM* 54).

5

The Invisible Country

Southerners were not the only Americans who feared a nationally homogeneous culture or who feared for the survival of individuality in such a culture. The defenders of Southern identity shared these concerns with social observers outside the region. To this extent, O'Connor fell in line with other American intellectuals after World War II. Her fiction reflects the widespread tendency to perceive conformity as a defining characteristic of postwar society.[1]

Her unflattering portrait of Rayber, the schoolteacher who preaches conformity in *The Violent Bear It Away*, has its counterpart in contemporary works of nonfiction. For example, the personality tests administered by Rayber are among the "constrictions on the individual" attacked by William H. Whyte.[2] In *The Organization Man* (1956), which has been called "the locus classicus of the 1950s critique of conformity,"[3] Whyte devoted a chapter to "The Organization Children" and their education in the public schools of Park Forest, a suburban community located south of Chicago. At school, Whyte reported, "the concept of adjustment has been dominant." The professional goal that motivates Rayber in O'Connor's novel is the goal the parents of Park Forest assigned to education: "The primary job of the high school, they wrote, should be to teach students how to be citizens and how to get along with other people."[4] This view of teaching also caught the attention of David Riesman, a sociologist who focused on "modes of conformity." In *The Lonely Crowd* (1950), Riesman observed that college graduates entering the profession "have been taught to be more concerned with the child's social and psychological adjustment than with his academic progress – indeed, to scan the intellectual performance for signs of social maladjustment." To Riesman, the idea of "progressive education" carried a certain irony in postwar America: "Educational methods that were once liberating may even tend to thwart individuality rather than advance and protect it."[5]

The social paradigm with the widest intellectual currency during the

Cold War era tied conformity to mass consumption.[6] The paradigm encouraged hyperbole among Cold War intellectuals, to whom the Soviet Union represented mass society at its worst. In the 1952 *Partisan Review* symposium, Louis Kronenberger treated Soviet totalitarianism and American "mass culture" as parallel threats to individuality. He wrote, "In the exact same way that we oppose regimentation of thought on political grounds, we must oppose regimentation of taste on cultural ones." The symposium editors blamed mass culture for the problems encountered by the group that upheld "the tradition of critical non-conformism" in the United States: "the intellectual minority." In fact, the editors hoped that the symposium would yield an appropriate intellectual response to mass culture. They asked the contributors, "Must the American intellectual and writer adapt himself to mass culture?" Newton Arvin spoke for most of the respondents when he urged intellectuals "to master and to fertilize it."[7]

In *The Mechanical Bride,* published the year before the symposium, Marshall McLuhan proposed another strategy for dealing with consumer culture, "a method for reversing the process" by which "commercial education" brought about "public helplessness." In short, McLuhan analyzed the very advertising that was supposed to "keep everybody in the helpless state." He asked, "Why not use the new commercial education as a means to enlightening its intended prey? Why not assist the public to observe consciously the drama which is intended to operate upon it unconsciously?" Like Kronenberger, McLuhan thought that mass consumption threatened individuality. "When men and women . . . have become accustomed to the consumption of uniform products," McLuhan wrote, "it is hard to see where any individualism remains."[8]

Through her fiction, O'Connor expresses the same anxiety over the status of the individual in consumer society. Her first novel, in particular, depicts a society pervaded by advertising messages. Past analyses of *Wise Blood* have failed to mention the proliferation of advertising and marketing techniques in the novel. Electric signs that "moved up and down or blinked frantically" define the boundaries of the urban setting, Taulkinham; the signs for "PEANUTS, WESTERN UNION, AJAX, TAXI, HOTEL, CANDY" inform Hazel Motes that he has reached the city (*WB* 29). The window displays in the downtown business district captivate shoppers: "No one was paying any attention to the sky. The stores in Taulkinham stayed open on Thursday nights so that people could have an extra opportunity to see what was for sale" (*WB* 37). In this commercial setting, the man who sells potato peelers has built an "altar" to his product, a pyramid of green cardboard boxes atop a card table (*WB* 38). When Hazel visits the city park in which Enoch Emery works, Enoch takes him to a hot dog stand whose very structure advertises a product. The Frosty

THE CRANBERRY BOTTLE,
ONSET, MASSACHUSETTS, ON ROUTES 6 AND 28 TO CAPE COD

When O'Connor describes the Frosty Bottle in *Wise Blood*, she points to a tradition of "mimetic" commercial architecture – a tradition illustrated by the Cranberry Bottle, built in the early 1930s. Like the Frosty Bottle, the Cranberry Bottle advertised a brand of soft drink by mimicking the container in which the drink was sold. Courtesy of the Lake County Museum, Curt Teich Postcard Archives, Wauconda, Illinois.

Bottle is "in the shape of an Orange Crush with frost painted in blue around the top of it" (*WB* 82). Inside the stand, "there was a large advertisement for ice cream, showing a cow dressed up like a housewife" (*WB* 88). Even the rural countryside, which Enoch and Hazel have left for the city, contains advertising messages. "CCC snuff ads" are pasted on deserted farm buildings (*WB* 12–13, 207).

Beyond their scenic function, the techniques of advertising and marketing that appear in the novel have significance for individual identity. O'Connor first suggests this by placing Enoch in front of a Walgreen's window, "against a background of alarm clocks, toilet waters, candies, sanitary pads, fountain pens, and pocket flashlights, displayed in all colors to twice his height" (*WB* 135). Enoch is the character most closely identified with consumerism, the character whose "fondness for Supermarkets" leads him "to spend an hour or so in one every afternoon . . . browsing around among the canned goods and reading the cereal stories" (*WB* 130). At home, he spends time looking at the commercial illustrations that hang on his walls: "They were over calendars and had been sent him by the Hilltop Funeral Home and the American Rubber Tire Company" (*WB* 133).

As a consumer, Enoch exemplifies the "public helplessness" that McLuhan hoped to remedy by analyzing advertising. Enoch is pathetically vulnerable to advertising messages. Outside a movie theater, he sees "a large illustration of a monster stuffing a young woman into an incinerator." He cannot fight the impulse to watch something he is afraid to watch:

> I ain't going in no picture show like that, he said, giving it a nervous look. I'm going home. I ain't going to wait around in no picture show. I ain't got the money to buy a ticket, he said, taking out his purse again. I ain't even going to count thisyer change.
>
> It ain't but forty-three cent here, he said, that ain't enough. A sign said the price of a ticket for adults was forty-five cents, balcony, thirty-five. I ain't going to sit in no balcony, he said, buying a thirty-five cent ticket.
>
> I ain't going in, he said.
>
> Two doors flew open and he found himself moving down a long red foyer and then up a darker tunnel and then up a higher, still darker tunnel. (*WB* 138)

Enoch ends up watching a triple feature. He might blame his "wise blood" for making him act against his will, but the movie poster is the immediate impetus. Clearly, Enoch is motivated by an internal compulsion he does not understand. He feels he is "always having to do something that something else wanted him to do," and this inner drive places even his purchases beyond his control; since the "new jesus" requires a "tabernacle," Enoch has "to spend all his money on drapes and gilt" for its decoration (*WB* 135, 137, 174, 175). At the same time, however, the external stimulus of advertising determines the particular manner in which his internal compulsion will be expressed.[9]

The advertising image that dominates the interior of the Frosty Bottle in *Wise Blood* is the figure of Elsie Borden. One of the more successful corporate symbols, Elsie gained tremendous popularity by fusing the pastoral and domestic ideals. In this illustration from a 1949 Borden ad, she appears with her husband, Elmer, and their second child, Beauregard. ("Elsie" and the characters "Elsie," "Elmer," and "Beauregard" are trademarks and are used with the permission of Borden, Inc.)

In the twelfth chapter of the novel, Enoch experiences an "awakening" (*WB* 194). He suddenly understands how he will be "rewarded" for following the dictates of his blood (*WB* 191), and his recompense, he thinks, will involve an advertising gimmick. "I know what I want,"

Enoch murmurs after reading a newspaper advertisement for a movie and its star, "Gonga, Giant Jungle Monarch," whose publicity tour of local theaters will end that evening at the Victory on 57th Street (*WB* 193, 194). The promotional tour consists of a man in an ape suit shaking hands with moviegoers. Impressed by the example of Gonga, who can attract a crowd of young fans, Enoch longs for the same kind of public attention: "He wanted, some day, to see a line of people waiting to shake his hand" (*WB* 191).

Enoch hopes to realize the promise conveyed by the advertising he has seen, the promise of personal distinction. He aspires "to be THE young man of the future, like the ones in the insurance ads" (*WB* 191). The statement yokes together contradictory desires: to stand out, to fit in. It is the contradiction that McLuhan located at "the center of the drama of a consumer economy." In this drama, the individual is "torn between the fear of being a misfit and the passion for the distinction conferred by purchasing a mass-produced item." In *The Mechanical Bride*, McLuhan analyzed an advertisement implying that men who consumed Lord Calvert Whiskey were "distinct from the herd." McLuhan intended for his readers to reject "the notion of distinction and culture as being a matter of consumption rather than the possession of discriminating perception and judgment."[10] Enoch misses the irony to which McLuhan directed attention – the irony of basing personal distinction on the commercial imagery used to promote consumption. By appropriating that imagery, Enoch believes, he can emerge "as an entirely new man, with an even better personality than he had now" (*WB* 175). Specifically, Enoch hopes to gain distinction by stealing the promotional gimmick, the ape suit, and wearing it himself.

Helpless to resist the appeal of a movie poster, he is likewise vulnerable to the ways in which advertising validates personal identity or withholds validation. Enoch will change "the way I am" to fit the model of individual distinction that he has seen in front of the movie theater: "a successful ape" shaking the hands of his fans (*WB* 178, 194). This role model has suggested that Enoch's own identity, grounded in his own experience, is unimportant. Enoch greets Gonga by identifying himself and recounting the facts of his life. "My name is Enoch Emery," he says. "I attended the Rodemill Boys' Bible Academy. I work at the city zoo. . . . I'm only eighteen year old but I already work for the city." Gonga responds by humiliating the young man who has seen two of the movies in the Gonga series. "The star" tells the movie consumer to "go to hell" (*WB* 182).

Impelled by the "envy" he feels when he watches other moviegoers line up to meet Gonga (*WB* 195), Enoch overpowers the man in the ape suit. Then, "burning with the intensest kind of happiness," he digs a hole and buries his clothes; the narrator suggests an analogy with "burying his

This 1947 advertisement reappeared in *The Mechanical Bride* by Marshall McLuhan. Analyzing the ad, McLuhan noted the implicit equation between consumption and individual distinction. Courtesy of Jim Beam Brands Co.

The gimmick used to promote "Gonga, Giant Jungle Monarch" has a
clear precedent in the publicity campaign for *Mighty Joe Young* (1949).
On the day the film opened in New York City, a man wearing an ape
suit appeared outside the Criterion Theater. The stunt made the pages
of *Newsweek*, which ran a photograph of the man – dangling from a line
stretched across Broadway – in its edition of 8 August. At the time of
the stunt, O'Connor was living in Manhattan and working on *Wise
Blood*. Her novel reveals her familiarity with the film and its simian
hero: when she describes one of the movies that Enoch sees, a movie
"about a baboon named Lonnie who rescued attractive children from a
burning orphanage" (*WB* 139), O'Connor lifts the grand finale of
Mighty Joe Young. Copyright © 1949 RKO Pictures, Inc. All rights
reserved. Used courtesy of Turner Entertainment Co.

Want To Win Movie Pass? Shake Hands With Live Gorilla

The immediate inspiration for the "Gonga" publicity stunt was a *Union-
Recorder* article promoting *Mark of the Gorilla*, a 1950 entry in the "Jungle Jim" movie series. The article announced that a gorilla named Con-
go would appear "in person" outside a Milledgeville theater; at each
showing, free passes would go to the first ten children who were "brave
enough" to shake hands with him. Headline reprinted from the Milledgeville *Union-Recorder*, 14 Sept. 1950.

former self" (*WB* 196). Donning the ape suit, Enoch anticipates a new and improved self. The narrative, however, shows only the loss of individual identity. Enoch will be obscured, not improved, by the commercial image. He disappears, leg by leg, arm by arm, into the ape suit: "A black heavier shaggier figure replaced his." The narrative no longer refers to Enoch by name. He becomes a two-headed, then a one-headed "it" (*WB* 197).

The appropriation of commercial imagery does not bring Enoch the distinction he expects. Dressed as Gonga, he extends his hand to a man and a woman. They do not shake his hand; instead, they flee from the "hideous" gorilla (*WB* 198). Critical readings of this scene usually interpret Enoch's transformation as a descent from the human to the bestial – an illustration of O'Connor's "grotesque" diminution of human stature.[11] But his transformation into a gorilla has less to do with animal nature than with consumer culture. In *Wise Blood*, forms of advertising and marketing envelop the self, submerging it in a world of salable objects. The scene that takes place at the Walgreen's drugstore foreshadows Enoch's submersion in the commercial image of Gonga. O'Connor describes a young woman who has become an inextricable element of a commercial display:

> The fountain counter was pink and green marble linoleum and behind it there was a red-headed waitress in a lime-colored uniform and a pink apron. She had green eyes set in pink and they resembled a picture behind her of a Lime-Cherry Surprise, a special that day for ten cents. (*WB* 136)

The description suggests more than the suppression of personality in the commercial setting. The waitress can take off the uniform and the apron after work, but her eyes will remain green and pink. Her identity has been assimilated into the presentation of the product, the fountain drink she pushes so aggressively: "Enoch couldn't decide which of several concoctions was the one for him to have until she ended it by moving one arm under the counter and bringing out a Lime-Cherry Surprise." When Enoch ignores her, she prepares a second Surprise and tries to force that on him (*WB* 137).

The idea that a salesperson would have to identify herself with the product being sold found expression in the contemporary critique of consumerism. The idea first took shape in *White Collar*, a sociological study published a year before *Wise Blood*. The author, C. Wright Mills, noted the rise of a "personality market" in which the "personal or even intimate traits of the employee are drawn into the sphere of exchange and become of commercial relevance." These traits, he added, "become commodities in the labor market." The situation of the waitress in *Wise Blood* is analogous, then, to the situation of a salesgirl described by Mills:

> The one area of her occupational life in which she might be "free to act," the area of her own personality, must now also be managed, must become the alert yet obsequious instrument by which goods are distributed.
>
> In the normal course of her work, because her personality becomes the instrument of an alien purpose, the salesgirl becomes self-alienated.[12]

The waitress with the eyes of green and pink appears only briefly in *Wise Blood*. Solace Layfield is the more prominent figure of self-alienation in the novel. The sales strategy most important to the plot is his impersonation of Hazel Motes. After Hazel refuses to work with Hoover Shoats and turn the Church Without Christ into a moneymaking venture, Hoover hires Solace and turns him into a sales instrument. Submerging his identity in that of Hazel, Solace becomes an "illusion." Solace, like Hazel, wears a "glare-blue" suit and a white hat; the "other Prophet," like the original, preaches from the hood of a "rat-colored" car (*WB* 166, 167, 204). The submersion of identity is not just a matter of physical appearance. In pretending to be Hazel, Solace has to deny his own Christian faith. Hazel recognizes that Solace is not being "true" to himself: "What do you get up on top of a car and say you don't believe in what you do believe in for?" (*WB* 203).

If Solace "ain't true," he also "mocks what is" (*WB* 204). Hazel suffers his own episode of self-alienation when he first sees Solace: "He had never pictured himself that way before." In effect, Hazel's identity is submerged in Hoover's reconception of the "True Prophet" (*WB* 167). Hazel regains his sense of self by forcing Solace to undress and by hitting the impostor with the rat-colored Essex: "The man didn't look so much like Haze, lying on the ground on his face without his hat or suit on" (*WB* 204).

Hazel uses his car to kill his impersonator, but the value he places on the Essex shows that Hazel himself has succumbed to a way of thinking promoted by consumer society. He links his identity with a product of U.S. industry, a car "that ain't been built by a bunch of foreigners" (*WB* 126). As a place that Hazel "can always get away in," the Essex seems to confirm his self-conception as a totally free individual.[13] Praising his Essex, Hazel claims that "I knew when I first saw it that it was the car for me" (*WB* 115). His assertion resembles a promise made in advertising copy for Buick: "It makes you feel like the man you are." The author of a widely read study of advertising cited this copy to show how Madison Avenue encouraged consumers to view car ownership as a mode of self-expression. In *The Hidden Persuaders* (1957), Vance Packard observed that

"American consumers were becoming self-image buyers." Drawing on the findings of motivational research, merchandisers had found it lucrative to "help people buy a projection of themselves." Packard conjectured that "the most spectacularly successful image building has been done by the automobile industry." In fact, a study commissioned by the *Chicago Tribune* reported that Americans valued automobiles because they "provide avenues for the expression . . . of the character, temperament and self concept of the owner and driver."[14]

O'Connor suggests that consumer society reneges on the advertised promise of self-expression. Consumers who identify themselves with products, or with the imagery used to advertise these products, will be disappointed and betrayed in their search for self-realization. As the image of Gonga fails to bring Enoch the distinction he desires, so the Essex fails Hazel. The car falls to pieces after a highway patrolman pushes it down a hill. The destruction of the product with which he has identified himself forces Hazel to consider the possibility of some reality other than the material. As Hazel looks out over the pasture in which his wrecked car lies, his face seems "to reflect the entire distance across the clearing and on beyond, the entire distance that extended from his eyes to the blank gray sky that went on, depth after depth, into space" (*WB* 209). The new worldview implicit in the description of a face "concentrated on space" (*WB* 210) has a fairly short duration within the novel. Hazel gains his new perspective in the penultimate chapter; in the final chapter, he dies. For the most part, materialism defines the lives of Hazel and the other characters. Their experiences are circumscribed by the material world, understood in two ways – as a world in which the spiritual has no place and as one in which everything is for sale.

In *Wise Blood,* religion itself becomes a commodity. Charging a dollar for each new membership in the Holy Church of Christ Without Christ, Hoover Shoats urges his listeners "to take advantage of this church" (*WB* 154). The idea of the "new jesus" strikes Hoover as a lucrative one. "All it would need is a little promotion," says the self-proclaimed "radio star" (*WB* 156, 157). When Hazel refuses to make Hoover his partner, Hoover threatens him: "You watch out, friend. I'm going to run you out of business. I can get my own new jesus and I can get Prophets for peanuts, you hear?" Hoover will distort religious doctrine to suit his audience, but he adheres to one of the central tenets of capitalist society. "What you need," he tells Hazel, "is a little competition" (*WB* 159).

The world of *Wise Blood* resembles the "new society" that Mills described in *White Collar,* the society in which "selling is a pervasive activity, unlimited in scope and ruthless in its choice of technique and manner." To postwar Americans, Mills wrote, salesmanship represented the social norm:

> The salesman's world has now become everybody's world, and, in some part, everybody has become a salesman. . . . The market now reaches into every institution and every relation. The bargaining manner, the huckstering animus, the memorized theology of pep, the commercialized evaluation of personal traits – they are all around us; in public and in private there is the tang and feel of salesmanship.[15]

In her second novel, O'Connor makes salesmen the representatives of the social norm; they form the social background against which her main characters wage their battle over religion. The normative concept of the "real world" in *The Violent Bear It Away* originates with Rayber's father, a salesman who calls himself "a prophet of life insurance." He is indifferent to the question of salvation that will set his son at odds with the two Tarwaters: "When you told him his soul was in danger, he offered to sell you a policy against any contingency" (*VBA* 59). When he retrieves his son from Powderhead, where the seven-year-old Rayber claims to have been "born again," he tells Rayber they are going "back to the real world. And that's me." The insurance salesman dismisses the announcement of a religious conversion. "Who cares?" he says, and he predicts, accurately, that Rayber will lose the faith instilled by old Tarwater: "You'll find out soon enough" (*VBA* 128).

T. Fawcett Meeks, the other salesman in the novel, also disregards values that traditionally lie outside the commercial sphere. Grief affects him only to the extent that it affects the sale of copper flues. Meeks, a manufacturer's representative, keeps a book in which he records the ailments suffered by the members of each customer's family:

> A man's wife had cancer, he put her name down in the book and wrote *cancer* after it and inquired about her every time he went to that man's hardware store until she died; then he scratched out the word *cancer* and wrote *dead* there. "And I say thank God when they're dead," the salesman said; "that's one less to remember." (*VBA* 51)

Meeks reduces the ideal of love to a sales tool: "The salesman said that it had been his personal experience that you couldn't sell a copper flue to a man you didn't love. . . . He said love was the only policy that worked 95% of the time." He feigns altruism by giving Tarwater "the best advice he could give any young fellow setting out to find himself a place in the world" (*VBA* 50–1). In actuality, Meeks plans to exploit Tarwater. What he wants is "a very ignorant energetic boy to work for him" (*VBA* 54).

The only middle ground between the "equal and opposite" passions of the main characters, between the extremes of religious "madness" and atheistic "emptiness," is the "policy" of manipulation espoused by the copper-flue salesman (*VBA* 34, 115). In *The Violent Bear It Away*, O'Connor makes the social norm decidedly offensive. Indeed, her attitude toward consumer society was more negative than that of most Cold War intellectuals. By refusing to limit her cultural criticism to matters of taste, O'Connor set herself apart from others who viewed mass consumption as a threat to individuality. She told a correspondent in 1959 that "some revolt against our exaggerated materialism is long overdue" (*HB* 336). For the majority of intellectuals, the object of criticism was not materialism per se. After all, material prosperity was supposed to show the superiority of U.S. capitalism to Soviet Communism. When Kronenberger drew his analogy between "regimentation of thought" and "regimentation of taste" in the *Partisan Review* symposium, he made it clear that he considered the first a foreign development, the second a domestic one. In other words, the problems arising from *within* American society were aesthetic, not ideological. Most Cold War intellectuals made the same distinction. Preferring the topic that was safer politically, the bogeyman of homogenized "taste," they neglected to criticize the modes of collective "thought" enforced by U.S. consumer society. In their attacks on conformity, intellectual cold warriors tacitly confirmed Whyte's criticism of the organization man who lived according to "a belief in 'belongingness' as the ultimate need of the individual."[16] But the warriors themselves wanted "to be a part of American life," in the words of the *Partisan Review* editors. Mass culture merited attack primarily because it kept intellectuals from achieving this goal; it separated them from their "natural audience."[17]

To O'Connor, taste was a superficial concern. Her position was closer to that of Mills, a dissenting voice in the *Partisan Review* symposium, and to that of McLuhan. In *White Collar*, Mills criticized not merely the "style of life," but the very "ideology" of "a society that has turned itself into a fabulous salesroom."[18] In *The Mechanical Bride*, McLuhan tried to untie the "mental strait jackets" employed by consumer culture.[19] O'Connor likewise opposed the ways of thinking promoted by consumerism. She specifically rejected the ideology that tied consumption to individuality – an ideology evident not only in advertising, but also in political rhetoric. Nixon, for example, made this argument in his 1959 "kitchen debate" with Khrushchev.[20] O'Connor connected advertising and political affirmation in "The Fiction Writer and His Country." She damned the advertising agencies with faint praise when she answered the question posed by the 1955 *Life* editorial, "Who speaks for America today?" The agencies, she wrote, were best suited to the role: "They are entirely capable of showing us our unparalleled prosperity and our almost classless society" (*MM* 34).

While other intellectuals contended that their task should be to educate the taste of American consumers,[21] O'Connor, McLuhan, and Mills expressed a desire to resist a consumerist ideology that dovetailed with the reigning political consensus. Lamenting a culture in which "the capital of individual resistance and autonomous existence is being used up at a very visible rate," McLuhan suggested that "we would do well to strengthen those inner resources, which we still undoubtedly exert, to resist the mechanism of mass delirium and collective irrationalism." From his perspective, would-be resisters faced two problems: the combined power of the institutions they challenged and a weak understanding of the form their challenge should take. McLuhan pointed to "the increasingly numerous mechanisms for anticipating and controlling the thoughts and feelings of many millions." Resisters were up against "the unofficial nation-wide agencies of education, production, distribution, entertainment, and advertisement." To overcome the odds, resisters needed a clear strategy. Without "workable standards of securely civilized judgment," their challenge could prove ineffectual. Unfortunately, McLuhan remarked, "there are no accepted standards of submission or resistance to commercially sponsored appeals."[22] Resistance to consumer society seemed a rather vague proposition.

The question of strategy vexed O'Connor. One possibility was resistance organized along regional lines. In the political realm, of course, her home state of Georgia had announced a policy of "massive resistance" to federally mandated integration. Before World War II, the Agrarians had united to resist the "American industrial ideal." But these examples of organized regional opposition did not impress O'Connor. Several of her stories, including "Everything That Rises" and "Judgement Day," suggest that racial integration is inevitable; though she sympathized with the Agrarians, she felt their challenge to industrialism had been doomed to failure. When O'Connor read *I'll Take My Stand* for the first time, she found it "interesting" but "futile of course." She likened the social and economic manifesto to a quaint poetic injunction: "Woodman, spare that tree" (*HB* 566).

She thought it equally futile to resist the postwar "Bulldozer Revolution" identified by C. Vann Woodward – the transformation of the rural South into urban and suburban areas.[23] Where the Agrarians had seen the intrusion of the factory into the Southern landscape, O'Connor saw the extension of the commercial strip. A story from her second collection, "A View of the Woods" (1957), conveys her sense of inevitable transformation. As the story opens, a construction project is under way; a steam shovel digs the foundation for a fishing club. The main characters, Mark Fortune and his granddaughter, watch "while the machine systematically ate a square red hole in what had once been a cow pasture." O'Connor expresses her distaste for commercial development in the rural South by giving such "progress" the shape of "the big disembodied gullet" that will constantly "gorge itself on the clay" of the construction site (*CS*

335). The story ends with the same image: "one huge yellow monster . . . gorging itself on clay" (*CS* 356). The advocate of "progress," Mr. Fortune, may die at the end of the story, but progress itself continues unabated. The Southern countryside will come to resemble his vision of it: a new setting for consumer activity, a strip like any other, complete with a supermarket, a gas station, a motel, and a drive-in movie theater (*CS* 337).

Another story from *Everything That Rises* suggests an additional link between consumerism and the loss of Southern regional identity. "Revelation" (1964) places the kind of "stratification" discussed by McLuhan, the "consumer ratings" of "low, middle, and high," in conflict with the racial hierarchy that supposedly made the South unique. Like the media pundits who divided consumers into "middle-brow Midwestern dentist, or low-brow Eastern salesman, or high-brow Southern agrarian," the main character in the story by O'Connor applies "a set of social and intellectual distinctions in accordance with consumer goods."[24] The most significant goods, from the perspective of Ruby Turpin, are shoes:

> Without appearing to, Mrs. Turpin always noticed people's feet. The well-dressed lady had on red and gray suede shoes to match her dress. Mrs. Turpin had on her good black patent leather pumps. The ugly girl had on Girl Scout shoes and heavy socks. The old woman had on tennis shoes and the white-trashy mother had on what appeared to be bedroom slippers,. black straw with gold braid threaded through them – exactly what you would have expected her to have on. (*CS* 490–1)

In a society where everyone shops with "green stamps" (*CS* 492), it comes as no surprise that consumerist values dictate the judgments Ruby passes on people. Such values, however, are displacing more traditional judgments based on race. A "colored dentist" who owns "two red Lincolns" does not fit into the social structure that Ruby has inherited as a Southerner:

> On the bottom of the heap were most colored people, not the kind she would have been if she had been one, but most of them; then next to them – not above, just away from – were the white-trash; then above them were the home-owners, and above them the home-and-land owners, to which she and Claud belonged. Above she and Claud were people with a lot of money and much bigger houses and much more land.

Consumerist values account for the "complexity" that bedevils Ruby when she tries mentally to uphold the status quo (*CS* 491).

If Southerners could not prevent social and economic change, Southern artists, at least, could organize to preserve regional distinctiveness in the realm of culture. In "The Regional Writer," O'Connor mentioned one form of cultural organization: "Today, every self-respecting Southern college has itself an arts festival where Southern writers can be heard and where they are actually read and commented upon." Although her status as a Southern writer gave O'Connor a position from which to criticize consumer society, she did not place much faith in the organized efforts of the Southern literary community. "All this sounds fine," she said in her lecture, "but while it has been happening, other ground has been shifting under our feet." Efforts to preserve and promote regional culture ran up against the homogenizing power of the national media, specifically the medium of television. Evaluating the stories she had read at the 1957 Southern Writers' Conference, O'Connor complained that they had been influenced "only by the television" (*MM* 56). She expanded on this point in her correspondence, blaming television for displacing a regional idiom from Southern fiction. Participants in the conference had produced "television stories written in television language for the television world. The old souls don't know the South exists" (*HB* 234). O'Connor elsewhere disparaged the conference held in Athens, Georgia, for being "about as Southern as the southern part of Madison Avenue" (*C* 59). If Southern writers were "anguished" by the prospect of a South "more and more like the rest of the country" (*MM* 28–9), their writing itself was threatened by the language of television and advertising.[25]

O'Connor saw her own writing distorted by the conventions of television. She had misgivings about the sale of the television rights to "The Life You Save May Be Your Own." After she sold the rights in 1956, O'Connor predicted that the producers would add a happy ending, an ending that would include a plug for one of the network sponsors: "Mr. Shiftlet and the idiot daughter will no doubt go off in a Chrysler and live happily ever after" (*HB* 174). The producers did not, in fact, "make a musical out of it" (*HB* 186), but the version of the story that aired on CBS in early 1957 did feature a musical film star, Gene Kelly, as Tom T. Shiftlet. Publicity regarding the *Schlitz Playhouse* adaptation suggested that it owed more to Hollywood versions of Southern life than to the short story by O'Connor. In her correspondence, she quoted an announcement describing it as a "backwoods love story" and a statement by Kelly himself, who said, "It's a kind of hillbilly thing in which I play a guy who *befriends* a deaf-mute girl in the hills of Kentucky" (*HB* 191). O'Connor added the emphasis to indicate the discrepancy she saw between her story and the adaptation. "I didn't recognize the television version," she told an interviewer in 1962. The producers did as she had predicted: "They changed the ending just a bit by having Shiftlet suddenly get a conscience and come back for the girl."[26]

O'Connor felt that any regional resistance to the national consumer culture would be ambivalent at best. Southerners themselves appeared to

Tonight! **GENE KELLY**

(soon to appear in MGM's hilarious comedy "The Happy Road")

MAKES HIS

Tv Debut

IN

"The Life You Save"

on the

SCHLITZ PLAYHOUSE

10:00 P. M. Channel 5

© 1957 Jos. Schlitz Brewing Co., Milwaukee, Wis., Brooklyn, N. Y., Los Angeles, Cal., Kansas City, Mo.

22 12 8 SCHLITZ PLAYHOUSE "The Life You Save." Tom T. Triplet is an engaging one-armed tramp, a man who has been to a lot of places and seen a lot of things. But never before has he seen anyone like Lucynell Crater, a deaf-mute of angelic innocence. Marriage was the furthest thing from his mind as he made his rounds through an impoverished section of the South. Lucy's mother, however, tries to sell Tom on the idea of marrying a woman who can't talk back! Gene Kelly, Janice Rule and Agnes Moorehead are starred.

As these program announcements suggest, the 1957 adaptation of "The Life You Save May Be Your Own" demonstrated the homogenizing power of television. Influenced, no doubt, by the image of Gene Kelly and the wishes of the corporate sponsor, the producers adhered to the conventions of "hillbilly" comedy – confirming national stereotypes about regional culture. Advertisement courtesy of the Stroh Brewery Company. Program listing reprinted with permission from *TV Guide* ® Magazine. Copyright © 1957 by News America Publications, Inc.

favor assimilation with the rest of the country. In her 1963 lecture, "The Catholic Novelist in the Protestant South," O'Connor noted a contradiction between "the South's instinct to preserve her identity" and "her equal instinct to fall eager victim to every poisonous breath from Hollywood or Madison Avenue" (*MM* 200). The attraction of consumer goods seemed overwhelming. In a joint interview with Robert Penn Warren, conducted in 1959, O'Connor maintained that Southerners were losing their "regional sense" primarily "because everybody wants the good things of life, like supermarkets."[27]

In her fiction, O'Connor uses one particular brand of consumer item to indicate the reach of American consumer culture within the region: Coca-Cola. A young Southern girl drinks a bottle of the soda pop in a scene from "The Partridge Festival." Like the waitress and the Lime-Cherry Surprise in *Wise Blood,* the person and the product in this scene bear a noticeable similarity: "Her eyes were the same green as the bottle" (*CS* 428). The family in "A Good Man Is Hard to Find" also drinks "Co'-Colas" (*CS* 122). The grandmother, in her youth, had been courted

Cover, *Time*, 15 May 1950. Copyright © 1950 Time, Inc. Reprinted by permission. Illustrator: Boris Artzybasheff.

by a man whom the Agrarians would have resented as a representative of the New South, a Georgian who "had bought Coca-Cola stock when it first came out" (*CS* 120). As the emblem of a dominant national culture, Coca-Cola takes a prominent place in "A Late Encounter with the Enemy." The story ends with the corpse of its protagonist stranded "in the long line at the Coca-Cola machine" (*CS* 144). General Sash belongs here, O'Connor implies, because he is a Southerner who prefers the "nashnul" to the "local," a Southerner who places little value on Southern identity, despite his yearly service as a symbol of the "old traditions" (*CS* 135, 136, 142).

In the last scene, O'Connor plays up the irony that attended the phenomenal success of Coca-Cola. The company that produced the drink had its headquarters in a "local" setting, Atlanta, but the drink itself came to represent the United States. When O'Connor mentions the green of the Coke bottle in "The Partridge Festival" and the red of the Coke machine in "A Late Encounter" (*CS* 141), she alludes to a form of cultural imperialism noted by her contemporaries. After World War II, the colors used in the distribution of the soft drink came to signify the spread of American consumer culture throughout the world. A *Time* cover story in 1950 suggested that the colors functioned as a form of camouflage, making possible an American cultural invasion: "In most places Coke has blended into the local scene as if the brown-green of its bottles and the fire-brigade red of its advertising were some kind of protective coloring." As a matter of fact, the establishment of the "Cokempire" had been facilitated by an actual military invasion. During World War II, *Time* reported, the company supplied U.S. soldiers with nickel bottles of the drink: "The Coke bottling plants which moved along with the invading U.S. armies . . . were actually the biggest impetus of Coca-Cola's present international boom." Although *Time* observed that the Coca-Cola Company was "not specifically trying to spread the American way of life," the cover story gave a description of Coke as the "sublimated essence of all America stands for." The spread of the American "essence" seemed irreversible: "Coke's peaceful near-conquest of the world" continued in spite of "Communist mouthpieces" who denounced it as an "imperialistic" drink.[28]

O'Connor saw the same kind of imperialism at work in the South. Regional culture, like the national cultures of Western Europe and the Third World, seemed to be losing to American consumerism. Regional resistance seemed futile. O'Connor herself considered investing in Coca-Cola stock. "I keep wondering," she wrote a correspondent in 1960, "if Coca-Cola will be good for eternity" (*HB* 416).

Her use of the word "eternity" in conjunction with a brand of soft drink is uncharacteristically facetious. As a Christian writer, O'Connor identified the "eternal and absolute" as her primary concern, her "true country" (*MM* 27). In these terms, in this "territory," resistance would be viable – more so than resistance based on regional identity. O'Connor saw a deeper philosophical division between consumerism and Catholicism than between consumer society and the South. Here again, one of her comments about her religious position is instructive: "Catholicism is opposed to the bourgeois mind" (*CW* 862). Consequently, a religious challenge to consumerist values would be less ambivalent than any regional defiance.

The form of religious resistance that O'Connor valorizes is withdrawal. She explores the possibility of "inner resistance" to the agencies of manipulation – the possibility that McLuhan, himself a Catholic, mentioned in *The Mechanical Bride*.[29] In her fiction, such withdrawal is clearly problematic. Only his own death can remove Hazel Motes from a world pervaded by advertising. At the end of *Wise Blood*, O'Connor leaves him "moving farther and farther away, farther and farther into the darkness" (*WB* 232). But if *Wise Blood* ties withdrawal to death, *The Violent Bear It Away* suggests that a hermitage in this life is possible. Powderhead, the clearing in "the farthest part of the backwoods," furnishes a place of retreat from the consumer society to which Rayber will introduce young Tarwater on their tour of supermarkets, department stores, and movie theaters (*VBA* 5, 108).

Old Tarwater, who holds the title to Powderhead, has learned that the "real world" will not tolerate dissent and that it has the institutional power to enforce its version of reality. His attempts to convert his sister, the wife of the insurance salesman, lead to his own incarceration. Tired of hearing her brother prophesy outside her suburban home, she "worked a perfidy on him" (*VBA* 60) by having him committed to an insane asylum. By declaring him "not only crazy but dangerous" (*VBA* 61–2), the psychiatrist who signs the commitment papers invalidates the religious worldview of old Tarwater. Years later, after Rayber invalidates this worldview in print, in a "schoolteacher magazine" (*VBA* 4), old Tarwater kidnaps young Tarwater and brings the boy to Powderhead. Here, in rural seclusion, young Tarwater receives the religious training that the "real world" disallows: "The Lord had seen fit to guarantee the purity of his up-bringing, to preserve him from contamination, to preserve him as His elect servant, trained by a prophet for prophesy [*sic*]" (*VBA* 17).

Although Powderhead is a hermitage, a place of retreat, it is also something more. The author who refused to evade ideological issues by escaping into a realm of aesthetic concerns – as other intellectuals had done – would hardly have accepted peaceful coexistence with consumer society. Powderhead conveys her vision of a religious alternative to the consumerist values she found so debilitating to the individual. Despite the fundamentalist idiom in which old Tarwater delivers his religious witness, the religious alternative is Catholic. "As a prophet," O'Connor wrote in her correspondence, old Tarwater "has to be a natural Catholic" (*HB* 407). At Powderhead, her "crypto-Catholic" prophet (*HB* 517) establishes a stronghold of individualism. From her perspective, the Catholic Church is the locus of cultural resistance.

If Tarwater's education at Powderhead is private, with all the benefits attributed to private schools in the rhetoric of Southern identity, it is also parochial. As such, it calls to mind a perceived connection between religious education and cultural resistance, dating back to the early years of the Cold War. In the anti-Catholic literature that appeared after World War II, parochial education was a prime target. Writing for the *Nation* in November 1947, Paul Blanshard noted "a tremendous revival of anti-Catholic feeling in the United States in recent months," and he said that "its focal point is unquestionably the educational policy of the church."[30] The same critics who cast the Church as a totalitarian threat to the United States attacked the withdrawal of Catholic students from the public schools; according to Blanshard and other anti-Catholic writers, this withdrawal advanced the Catholic subversion of U.S. democracy. Withdrawal could only mean subversion, given the value the critics attached to public education. Blanshard wrote in 1948 that "the outcome of the struggle between American democracy and the Catholic hierarchy depends upon the survival and expansion of the public school."[31] According to Bishop Oxnam, writing in 1949, "The American public school has been and is a bulwark of democracy."

The critics of the Church were especially disturbed by what they considered to be a Catholic effort "to reach the public treasury" and gain state funding for parochial education.[32] Many were scandalized when the U.S. Supreme Court ruled that public funds could be used to provide transportation for students in parochial schools. Criticizing the decision in *Everson v. Board of Education* (1947), they warned that the Catholic hierarchy sought ultimately to breach the wall of separation between church and state. An essayist in the *Christian Century* argued that the "ultimate aim" of the Church was to obtain "the complete support of its parochial schools with money derived from taxes levied on all citizens." Having achieved its aim, the Church would withdraw all Catholic children from the public schools, and a "cultural fission" would result: "Two school systems operating side by side, both financed by public funds, each suspecting if not hostile to the other, would mark nothing less than a breach in the cultural foundation upon which a democratic state can be erected."[33]

In 1964 a Catholic literary figure defended parochial education for the very reason that the *Christian Century* writer attacked it. The novelist

Wilfrid Sheed assigned a "necessarily divisive mission" to the parochial school, which he praised as the foe of ideological consensus:

> The parochial school is one of the few surviving objects of cultural diversity. To my mind, it already mimes the public school much too closely; but it is different enough to preserve a certain openness in an increasingly stuffy society. Modern American life maintains a consensus not only of opinion but of intellectual style probably more overpowering than that of any other civilized country. The consensus is so all-encompassing that many of us are not even aware of its existence. As far as we are concerned, it is simply the only way to think.

Answering those who called for its "abolition," Sheed recommended the parochial school as an "educational alternative."[34]

In *The Violent Bear It Away*, O'Connor attaches a similar value to the education that young Tarwater receives at Powderhead. Trained by the prophet who took him away from suburbia, the boy learns to distrust "reality" as consumer society defines the term (*VBA* 125). O'Connor presents withdrawal as a strategic move – the first step in a necessary process of estrangement. Tarwater must be "rescued" from the dominant culture (*VBA* 41), and raised according to standards that consumer society does not recognize, if he is to accomplish his prophetic mission.

Withdrawal is only the first step for Tarwater. Although Powderhead is the site of his training "according to the truth," the mission itself will be accomplished elsewhere: "It was to the city that the prophets came" (*VBA* 27, 41). They come, specifically, as a reproach to the society that would define them out of existence. Estrangement translates into resistance. His indoctrination into "unreality" at Powderhead (*VBA* 125) prepares Tarwater for his confrontation with the "real world." Expanding on the idea of withdrawal, O'Connor imagines an alternative society, an "invisible country" of the faithful (*VBA* 160). What unites them is the spiritual "hunger" that Tarwater cannot satisfy by eating packaged "city food" (*VBA* 161). After several failed attempts to satisfy this hunger, Tarwater realizes its significance:

> He felt it rising in himself through time and darkness, rising through the centuries, and he knew that it rose in a line of men whose lives were chosen to sustain it, who would wander in the world, strangers from that violent country where the silence is never broken except to shout the truth. (*VBA* 242)

Undoubtedly, the "invisible country" has roots in the theological tradition of the Church Invisible, which O'Connor mentions in her nonfiction (*MM* 207). But the "silent country" of religious prophets (*VBA* 160) also has a meaning specific to her historical moment – a moment characterized, for many, by the silencing of dissent. According to John Marion, who wrote on Christian ethics at a time when any form of social protest could earn the protester the "pro-Communist" label, American Christians were justified in "waging important spiritual battles by so-called 'underground' means."[35] In *The Violent Bear It Away*, the "real world" drives dissenters underground. It will give old Tarwater his freedom only if he silences himself. After four years in the insane asylum, he realizes that "the way for him to get out was to stop prophesying on the ward." Old Tarwater does not give up his mission. He simply changes his tactics: "In the asylum the old man had learned caution and when he got out, he put everything he had learned to the service of his cause." He comes to understand that his resistance must be clandestine: "He proceeded about the Lord's business like an experienced crook" (*VBA* 62). His first act as a "crook" is his abduction of Rayber, whom he urges to lead "a secret life in Jesus" (*VBA* 64).

Although Rayber disappoints him, the next abducted child will follow his example. The mission on which young Tarwater sets out, at the end of the novel, will be fundamentally subversive. Young Tarwater will use the silence demanded by the "real world" to carry out his resistance. He will "shout the truth" when the time is right, but he must remain separate – a stranger to the audience he would turn against the "real world." Within the city, "where the children of God lay sleeping," he must preserve his "backwoods" independence (*VBA* 100, 243).

In her 1963 lecture, O'Connor identified "underground religious affinities" between "backwoods prophets" and the Catholic writer. As a member of "the invisible Church," Tarwater can claim a "kinship" with the literary representative of "the visible Catholic Church" (*MM* 207, 209). Like Tarwater, the novelist described by O'Connor speaks for a religious community that is estranged from the surrounding culture. The Catholic novelist, like Tarwater, considers this estrangement necessary; the Catholic Church cannot accommodate itself to a society defined by materialism. Unfortunately, O'Connor observed, the consumer culture that "understands us less and less" weakens the ties that "bind us together as Catholics." Where Catholics abound in the United States, "they usually blend almost imperceptibly into the general materialistic background" (*MM* 201).

The desire for "the good things of life" worked against religious resistance, just as it worked against regional resistance; Catholics in the United States were no more immune to the desire than Southerners. This perception kept O'Connor from exaggerating the cultural impact that religious resistance would have. She never suggested, for instance, that the American Catholic could eradicate materialism and reshape American culture "in his image" (*MM* 200). Tarwater, the Catholic's fictional counterpart in *The Violent Bear It Away*, will have little impact. Discussing the novel in a letter, O'Connor said she did not consider "prophets like Tarwater" to be "God's solution for the problems of our particular world." Indeed, she predicted that "Tarwater's future" in the city will be inauspicious: "The children of God I daresay will dispatch him pretty quick" (*HB* 342). Within the novel, O'Connor makes it clear that religious resistance can result in martyrdom. Young Tarwater, succeeding old Tarwater, can expect to be "spit on and snickered at" and "beaten and tied up" (*VBA* 20).

Nevertheless, O'Connor affirmed religious resistance. It was the Catholic writer, not the Southern writer, to whom she attributed an "ability to resist the dissolution of belief." If the "best traditions" of her religion and her region were "the same," the writer guided by "the teachings of the Church" could "bolster" these traditions more effectively (*MM* 202, 208). O'Connor looked to the Church to provide the counterforce to American consumerism. In doing so, she exemplified a phenomenon noted by the historian Jackson Lears. Applying the concept of "cultural hegemony" to postwar consumer society, Lears has suggested that religious bodies, among other "mediating institutions," helped the individual to escape "absorption by the all-encompassing system."[36] As her concept of the "invisible country" demonstrates, O'Connor was sensitive to a parallel phenomenon noted by Lears: the fact that many subcultures, however vital, "were rendered marginal or even invisible to the wider public culture."[37] Under these circumstances, the ability to break the silence, "to shout the truth" and be heard, seemed a victory in itself. Catholicism might not reform American culture, but as a stronghold of individualism, it would militate against the unanimous celebration of that culture.

Epilogue

As I have portrayed her, Flannery O'Connor was an advocate of cultural resistance at a time when such resistance carried specific political implications. Why, then, does this O'Connor seem so different from the one who has gained canonical status? If she envisioned herself as a critic of Cold War culture, why has her criticism gone unremarked?

The answer lies partly in the nature of the resistance she advocated. Ironically, her reputation as an apolitical writer testifies to the success of her attempt to project a religious alternative. Her "invisible country" of Catholic faith proved fascinating enough, in its own terms, to monopolize the attention of her readers. They could see little else, primarily because her religious worldview seemed so fully realized. As one admirer of her "imagined world" insisted, "There is no need, no temptation, to look outside that world for explanation or completion."[1]

Indeed, the "completeness" of her fictive world had become a critical truism by the time her second collection of short stories appeared in 1965. Few of the critics who reviewed *Everything That Rises* felt they could pigeonhole O'Connor as easily as some readers of her first collection had done. A columnist reviewing *A Good Man* in 1956 found nothing that distinguished its "Made-to-Order Stories" from the general run of "Southern Gothic" fiction; another critic, writing the same year, dismissed O'Connor as a literary conformist who provided "academic intellectuals" with "a little sprinkling of fake old magnolia blossoms."[2] Over the next decade, the critical emphasis shifted from her perceived similarities with established Southern writers, such as Erskine Caldwell, Truman Capote, and Carson McCullers, to her distinctiveness as an author.[3] More and more, her critics framed their analyses in terms adopted from her fiction. One review of *Everything That Rises* illustrates this tendency. To describe O'Connor and her last stories, the reviewer borrowed the language O'Connor used to characterize old and young Tarwater in her last novel. Calling the novelist "a young prophetess of doom," Robert Kiely observed that "even prophecies of doom imply an alternative which chaos cannot provide."[4]

In 1961 this sense of an alternative prompted Joseph Waldmeir to group her with postwar American novelists who were "not social critics in the traditional sense" but who offered "a challenge, an accusation and a demand for change." It was only in passing, however, that Waldmeir referred to O'Connor.[5] The occasional references to O'Connor as a social critic were always brief, indicating that the primary interest for her readers lay elsewhere – in the spiritual dimensions of the proposed alternative. Although "Southern Gothic" no longer seemed an appropriate label for her, she still seemed accessible in only one way. The same critics who retrieved O'Connor from her Gothic niche, by emphasizing her distinctiveness or completeness, placed O'Connor in another literary pigeonhole – that of the religious writer. According to a *Christian Century* columnist, eulogizing O'Connor in 1964, "Her unique achievement . . . was her depiction of the world in terms that were entirely those of the orthodox Christian."[6] A *Nation* columnist described her worldview similarly, if less sympathetically, in a 1965 review of *Everything That Rises*. "Based on the most depressing features of Christianity," he wrote, "her stories created a small universe."[7]

Once they had categorized O'Connor as a religious writer, readers both sympathetic and unsympathetic to her worldview could overlook the political dimensions of her art. During her career, after all, American religion seemed political only to the extent that it valorized and reinforced the Cold War consensus. Although there were significant exceptions,[8] the adoption of a religious voice usually signaled political quietism or superpatriotism. The superpatriotism of Catholic leaders, in particular, appeared to rule out any alliance between religious faith and cultural resistance. However clear it seemed to O'Connor, her choice of Catholicism as the site of resistance obscured her cultural critique, which readers viewed simply as an attack on secular values.

O'Connor compounded the problem by keeping her resistance contained within the realm of literary discourse. Her criticism of Cold War culture has gone unremarked not only because readers focused on her religious message, but also because O'Connor hesitated to make political statements through forms of discourse less ambiguous than fiction. As "a veteran of Yaddo" (*HB* 538), she could have spoken with authority about investigations into political subversiveness and about demands for political orthodoxy on the part of writers. She never did so. The writer who felt compelled to "shout" in her stories and novels (*MM* 34) believed that other forms of public statement required greater circumspection. Even when the mode of expression was a book review, O'Connor preferred a guarded approach, thinking it "better to be a combination of cautious

and polite." In a letter to her friend "A," she admitted her disappointment with the short stories that appeared in *The Presence of Grace* (1956)
by J. F. Powers: "Nothing in this present collection," she wrote, "equals
the best in the first." At the same time, O'Connor admitted that she
would not express her disappointment "in public." Explaining her reti-
cence as a reviewer, she told her friend, "These are the only reviews I
have ever written and I make the discovery that they are not the place for
that kind of absolute honesty" (*HB* 152).

Public appearances occasioned a comparable anxiety. Judging from her
private correspondence, O'Connor would gladly have avoided the "hideous talks" in which she discussed her fiction (*HB* 368). When she told
another friend about a "Public Lecture" she had delivered at Notre Dame
in 1957, she referred to the lecture fee as compensation "for any damage
that may have been done to my nervous system" (*HB* 215).

O'Connor expected other writers to be equally "cautious and polite"
outside the realm of literary discourse. She disapproved of literary contemporaries who used their lives, as well as their writings, to make a
point. Her disapproval did not hinge on the point being made; she specifically criticized a group of writers, the Beats, who shared many of her
cultural concerns. She sensed a kinship with the group, which included
the novelist Jack Kerouac and the poet Allen Ginsberg, because its members seemed "to know a good many of the right things to run away
from." By articulating this knowledge, O'Connor wrote, the Beats offered Americans something "long overdue," a "revolt against our exaggerated materialism" (*HB* 336). Kerouac himself made an explicit connection between the "Beat Generation" and Catholicism; in a 1959 essay,
he recalled a visit to a Catholic church, where he experienced "a vision of
what I must have really meant with 'Beat' anyhow . . . the vision of the
word Beat as being to mean beatific."[9] Even as she acknowledged such
aspirations to "holiness," however, O'Connor dismissed the literary efforts of the Beats. "You can't trust them as poets," she told a correspondent in 1959, "because they are too busy acting like poets." She objected,
on principle, to writers who called attention to their way of life: "These
boys have to look, act, and apparently smell like poets." Their way of
life, as much as their poetry, may have embodied the Beats' alternative to
the American way, but O'Connor upheld a model of the literary artist
that suppressed the extraliterary. "The true poet is anonymous, as to his
habits," she wrote (*HB* 336, 337).

Her adherence to the ideal of the "anonymous" poet distinguished
O'Connor from many Catholic literary figures. On the Right there were
vocal anti-Communists, like the novelist she judged "a bit short" in her
occasional prose: Francis Cardinal Spellman (*MM* 175).[10] On the Left
there was a tradition of activism closely identified with the *Catholic Work-*

er, a publication that irritated O'Connor "considerably" because she did not "go for the pacifist-anarchist business" (*HB* 173). On either side, then, Catholic writers did what O'Connor declined to do. Presenting themselves as political actors with specific positions vis-à-vis the Cold War consensus, they explicitly politicized the Catholic moral witness.

The new forms taken by the tradition of Catholic activism as it evolved during the 1960s provide the most telling contrast with the Catholic witness of O'Connor.[11] One literary figure, more than any other, personified the changing nature of Catholic activism in the third decade of the Cold War. Daniel Berrigan enjoyed considerable recognition as a poet. His first collection, published in 1957, had been nominated for a National Book Award. In 1970, a year before the fiction award went to *The Complete Stories* of O'Connor, Berrigan received his third nomination. By that time, however, Americans knew him better as a Jesuit priest who denounced the war in Vietnam. He had cofounded the Catholic Peace Fellowship in 1964, along with his brother Philip, a priest in the order of Saint Joseph, and Thomas Merton, a Trappist monk who admired O'Connor. In 1967 Berrigan went to jail for participating in a massive antiwar demonstration at the Pentagon. The following year, he and his brother led a raid on a Selective Service office in Catonsville, Maryland; the raiders, who came to be known as the Catonsville Nine, stole three hundred draft files and burned them in the parking lot outside, "amid prayers and the whir of television cameras." For his part in the raid, Daniel Berrigan received a sentence of three years in federal prison – a sentence he refused to serve after the Supreme Court rejected his appeal. In 1970 he spent four months eluding FBI agents.[12]

The letters he wrote during these months show that his continuing protest against the Vietnam War was also a protest against the leading institutions of Cold War America. Repelled by "an atmosphere of cold war competitiveness, consumer economics, and progressive militarization," Berrigan felt a bond with "the student resisters, for whom the war [in Vietnam] has provided an occasion for a profound revulsion against national absurdity." Like them, he was reacting to "the enormous cultural ferment and the long genetic period of the cold war."[13]

Clearly, Berrigan took cultural resistance beyond the bounds of literary discourse – thus violating O'Connor's principle of the "anonymous" poet. Nevertheless, his challenge to the dominant values of Cold War America linked Berrigan with O'Connor. His activism had a "highly symbolic character," as one commentator noted, and his strategy of "creating pictorial images that are uncomfortably difficult to erase from our minds" paralleled the fictional strategy favored by O'Connor. The phrasing used by the commentator, an acquaintance of Daniel and Philip

Berrigan, suggests this parallel: "If their action at Catonsville seemed 'grotesque' to some, it also served to dramatize, in unforgettable fashion, the grotesque moral priorities that have been erected in our country."[14]

Like O'Connor, Berrigan invalidated the American way of life as a cultural ideal. He called this construct "the most euphemistic and deceptive of phrases" because it masked the "dark obsessions" of "militarized consumer-technology." The material prosperity that followed World War II, the "consumer cornucopia" that seemed to demonstrate U.S. cultural superiority, reinforced the Cold War consensus by distracting Americans with goods and services: "They are pressurized and processed and finally anesthetized against moral choice or movement." For most Americans, Berrigan lamented, "distraction as a way of life" had become the norm.

In one of his poems, the Jesuit priest invited Americans to imagine a life transformed, a life of "holiness" and "wholeness." To affirm the possibility as well as the necessity of change, Berrigan employed the scenario of the fortunate invasion. A flying saucer, he wrote, "floats downward . . . in the macadam back yard where one paradise tree   a hardy weed   sends up its signal flare." Berrigan underscored the religious significance of the saucer, which he urged his readers to "fly" themselves: "This disk like manna   miraculous loaves and fishes / exists to be multiplied   savored   shared."

His vision of a Catholic alternative to the American way of life mirrored O'Connor's vision, just as the title of his poem, "America Is Hard to Find," recalled the title of her first fiction collection. Berrigan wrote the poem in 1970, shortly before he and his brother decided to avoid incarceration in "the NATIONALLY ENDOWED ELECTRONICALLY INESCAPABLE ZOO."[15] As a fugitive from federal authorities, Berrigan realized in action the alternative that O'Connor adumbrated in her fiction. More precisely, he realized the "invisible country" to which the prophets belong in *The Violent Bear It Away*. Berrigan, who seemed "prophetic" to many American Catholics,[16] described himself as an "invisible man" in 1970. Acting on his desire "to bring a larger community of resistance into being," he carried his moral witness into a radical underground composed mostly of Catholics. By remaining "at large," Berrigan wrote, he could "shout the truth" that the U.S. government wanted to silence. The underground itself, he suggested, could provide something more than a hiding place for fugitives:

> Instead of thinking of the underground as temporary, exotic, abnormal, perhaps we should start thinking of its implication as an entirely self-sufficient, mobile, internal revival community; the underground as a definition of our future.

Berrigan and his brother chose "to be exiles in our own land,"[17] but like the prophets of O'Connor, they considered this choice a preliminary step in the anticipated transformation of society.

The similarities between the language used by O'Connor, in describing her prophetic characters, and the language used by Berrigan, in explaining his own actions, reveal a common debt to a shared religious heritage. Obviously, the "loaves and fishes" mentioned in Berrigan's poem and O'Connor's novel (*VBA* 21, 241) have their source in a single, sacred text. But the similarities do not end with the incorporation of Scripture. Both writers took transcendent concerns, as defined by Scripture, and brought them to bear on contemporary American culture. In doing so, they demonstrated the multiplicity of the religious voice. However monolithic the Catholic Church seemed, its traditions gave Berrigan and O'Connor a position from which to deliver their cultural criticism. Acting on beliefs that antedated the ideological struggle between capitalism and Communism, Berrigan broke with the members of the American hierarchy who had allied the Church with the Cold War consensus. For this reason alone, many Catholics felt, he and his brother Philip deserved thanks. One admirer wrote, "I can feel the relief of a liberal Catholic who finally has some public heroes to belie the Cardinal Spellman stereotype of American Catholicism."[18] O'Connor belied the same stereotype through her fiction. Refusing to serve the Cold War consensus, she dramatized a faith whose claims on its adherents were more primal than those of political orthodoxy and cultural celebration. In this respect, her fiction encourages a view of religious writers that does not presuppose their indifference to politics or their commitment to the status quo. Far from providing metaphysical escapism, such writers may offer a range of alternatives to a culture that seems intent on homogeneity.

Notes

Introduction

1 I cite multiple sources in a single footnote whenever I provide a summary of historical events. The information included in the present summary comes from the following sources: Robert Donner, "She Writes Powerful Fiction," in *Conversations with Flannery O'Connor*, ed. Rosemary M. Magee (Jackson: University Press of Mississippi, 1987), 44, 47; Nikita Khrushchev, "Excerpts from Premier Khrushchev's Remarks on U.S. Jet Downed in Soviet," *New York Times*, 8 May 1960, late ed., 24; Peter Lyon, *Eisenhower: Portrait of the Hero* (Boston: Little, Brown, 1974), 809–15; Francis Gary Powers and Curt Gentry, *Operation Overflight: The U-2 Spy Pilot Tells His Story for the First Time* (New York: Holt, Rinehart & Winston, 1970), 195, 199.

2 Donner, "She Writes Powerful Fiction," 44.

3 According to Michael Bess, the major participants in this historical debate include Gar Alperovitz, Herbert Feis, John Lewis Gaddis, Gabriel Kolko, Walter LaFeber, Charles S. Maier, Ronald Steel, Adam B. Ulam, and William Appleman Williams. Bess, an assistant professor of history at Vanderbilt University, gave me this list during a conversation in September 1991.

4 Everette E. Dennis, George Gerbner, and Yassen N. Zassoursky, eds., *Beyond the Cold War: Soviet and American Media Images* (Newbury Park, Calif.: Sage, 1991), 2.

5 Todd Gitlin, *The Sixties: Years of Hope, Days of Rage* (Toronto: Bantam, 1987), 269.

6 Donald E. Pease, in his analysis of *Moby-Dick*, and Michael Paul Rogin, in his discussion of *Kiss Me Deadly* and other Hollywood films, have taken this approach. According to Pease, the reading of *Moby-Dick* that gained canonical status after World War II reflected the ideological assumptions of the Cold War consensus. See *Visionary Compacts: American Renaissance Writings in Cultural Context* (Madison: University of Wisconsin Press, 1987), 243–75. In analyzing film, Rogin explains, "I am trying, against dominant tendencies in the study and practice of American politics, to use cultural documents to connect political action to its makers and its meanings." See his *Ronald Reagan, the Movie and Other*

Episodes in Political Demonology (Berkeley and Los Angeles: University of California Press, 1987), xx.

7 Quoted in Clifford Geertz, "Blurred Genres: The Refiguration of Social Thought," in *Critical Theory Since 1965,* ed. Hazard Adams and Leroy Searle (Tallahassee: Florida State University Press, 1986), 521.

8 David Riesman, "The Nylon War: Epilogue (1962)," in *Abundance for What? and Other Essays* (Garden City, N.Y.: Anchor-Doubleday, 1965), 73.

9 Stephen J. Whitfield provides an excellent, wide-ranging analysis of this "interpenetration," and he also quotes the passage from Riesman. See *The Culture of the Cold War* (Baltimore: Johns Hopkins University Press, 1991), 10, 72.

10 The journalist, Agnes Smedley, openly supported the Chinese Communists. Although she never belonged to the U.S. Communist Party, she had applied – unsuccessfully – for membership in the Chinese Communist Party in 1937. See Janice R. MacKinnon and Stephen R. MacKinnon, *Agnes Smedley: The Life and Times of an American Radical* (Berkeley and Los Angeles: University of California Press, 1988), 186, 300, 302.

11 Ihab Hassan, *Radical Innocence: Studies in the Contemporary American Novel* (Princeton, N.J.: Princeton University Press, 1961), 3.

12 Miles Orvell, *Invisible Parade: The Fiction of Flannery O'Connor* (Philadelphia: Temple University Press, 1972), 10.

13 Gitlin, *The Sixties,* 256.

14 Marion Montgomery, "In Defense of Flannery O'Connor's Dragon," *Georgia Review* 25 (1971): 304, 309, 310.

15 See Louise Westling, *Sacred Groves and Ravaged Gardens: The Fiction of Eudora Welty, Carson McCullers, and Flannery O'Connor* (Athens: University of Georgia Press, 1985); James M. Mellard, "Flannery O'Connor's *Others:* Freud, Lacan, and the Unconscious," *American Literature* 61 (1989): 625–43; and Robert H. Brinkmeyer, Jr., *The Art and Vision of Flannery O'Connor* (Baton Rouge: Louisiana State University Press, 1989).

16 See John Hawkes, "Flannery O'Connor's Devil," in *Critical Essays on Flannery O'Connor,* ed. Melvin J. Friedman and Beverly Lyon Clark (Boston: G. K. Hall, 1985), 92–100. See also André Bleikasten, "The Heresy of Flannery O'Connor," in ibid., 138–58.

17 Thomas Hill Schaub is one of the few critics to include O'Connor in such a discussion. See *American Fiction in the Cold War* (Madison: University of Wisconsin Press, 1991), 116–36. Jan Nordby Gretlund discusses the "social sensibility" evident in the fiction but considers O'Connor in isolation; Gretlund makes no effort to connect her "sympathies" with those of other American writers. See "The Side of the Road: Flannery O'Connor's Social Sensibility," in *Realist of Distances: Flannery O'Connor Revisited,* ed. Karl-Heinz Westarp and Jan Nordby Gretlund (Aarhus, Denmark: Aarhus University Press, 1987), 197.

18 Frederick Crews, "The Power of Flannery O'Connor," *New York Review of Books,* 26 Apr. 1990, 49.

19 See, e.g., H. Richard Niebuhr, *The Social Sources of Denominationalism* (New York: Holt, 1929).

20 One example of this critical reorientation is a volume of essays, *Southern*

Literature and Literary Theory, ed. Jefferson Humphries (Athens: University of Georgia Press, 1990). The contributors to this "heterodox" volume break with the previous generation of Southern scholars, whose unofficial head is Louis D. Rubin, by rejecting "the transparency and organic Truth, the immediacy, of literary language" and by applying poststructuralist theory to Southern literature. According to the editor, the contributors share "the basic assumption that the meaning and significance of literature is not in the immanence of the literary object, or in history, but in the complex ways in which the literary, the historical, and all the 'human sciences' that study both, are interrelated" (ibid., viii, xv, xvii).

21 Louis A. Montrose, "Professing the Renaissance: The Poetics and Politics of Culture," in *The New Historicism,* ed. H. Aram Veeser (New York: Routledge, 1989), 23.

22 Brian Abel Ragen notes O'Connor's interest in popular culture, her admiration for *The Mechanical Bride,* and the relevance of its insights to her fiction. But he confines his analysis to her use of the automobile as a thematic device. And though he occasionally places O'Connor in her immediate historical context, Ragen discusses her primarily in relation to "the image of the free and unrooted individual that has grown up in American literature over the last two centuries." See *A Wreck on the Road to Damascus: Innocence, Guilt, and Conversion in Flannery O'Connor* (Chicago: Loyola University Press, 1989), 60–1, 67.

23 Marshall McLuhan, *The Mechanical Bride: Folklore of Industrial Man* (Boston: Beacon, 1967), 59, 152.

1. The Invaded Pastoral

1 Orvell notes the pattern of intrusion, but he does not relate it specifically to the pastoral. Setting is incidental in his discussion, which groups stories located on farms with stories located elsewhere. See *Invisible Parade,* 126–72.

2 Donner, "She Writes Powerful Fiction," 49.

3 For a discussion of the Cold War narrative as an instance of "cultural persuasion," see Pease, *Visionary Compacts,* 243–8.

4 Elaine Tyler May, *Homeward Bound: American Families in the Cold War Era* (New York: Basic Books, 1988), 13–14; Andrew Ross, *No Respect: Intellectuals and Popular Culture* (New York: Routledge, 1989), 45–7.

5 "Communism in Agriculture," *American Legion Firing Line* 4 (1955): 46.

6 "The Green Thing!" in *The Complete Weird Fantasy* (West Plains, Mo.: Russ Cochran, 1980), 3: 2. Joe Orlando illustrated "The Green Thing!" and three other stories from 1952 that feature aliens invading the pastoral setting: "Say Your Prayers," "Don't Count Your Chickens . . . ," and "Chewed Out!" Reprints appear in *The Complete Weird Fantasy,* vol. 3, and in *The Complete Weird Science,* 2d ed. (West Plains, Mo.: Russ Cochran, 1980), vol. 3. Each story has separate page numbers.

7 Al Feldstein, "It Was the Monster from the Fourth Dimension," in *The Complete Weird Science,* 2: 2.

8 Ibid., 4.

9 Ibid., 3, 5.

10 Ibid., 8.

11 Ibid.

12 Patrick Lucanio, *Them or Us: Archetypal Interpretations of Fifties Alien Invasion Films* (Bloomington: Indiana University Press, 1987), 44.

13 *Earth vs. the Flying Saucers,* dir. Fred F. Sears, Columbia, 1956.

14 *This Island Earth,* dir. Joseph Newman, Universal-International, 1955; *The War of the Worlds,* dir. Byron Haskin, Paramount, 1953; *The Blob,* dir. Irvin S. Yeaworth, Jr., Paramount, 1958; *Invasion of the Body Snatchers,* dir. Don Siegel, Allied Artists, 1956.

15 Henry Nash Smith, "Can 'American Studies' Develop a Method?" *American Quarterly* 9 (1957): 202.

16 Leo Marx, *The Machine in the Garden: Technology and the Pastoral Ideal in America* (New York: Oxford University Press, 1964), 15, 26.

17 Ibid., 15–16.

18 Frederic I. Carpenter, "'The American Myth': Paradise (To Be) Regained," *PMLA* 74 (1959): 599.

19 Henry Nash Smith, *Virgin Land: The American West as Symbol and Myth* (Cambridge, Mass.: Harvard University Press, 1950), 123–4, 259.

20 Marx, *The Machine in the Garden,* 3, 4, 141.

21 R. W. B. Lewis, *The American Adam: Innocence, Tragedy, and Tradition in the Nineteenth Century* (Chicago: University of Chicago Press, 1955), 1.

22 Smith, *Virgin Land,* 124, 159.

23 Henry Nash Smith, "The West as an Image of the American Past," *University of Kansas City Review* 18 (1951): 29.

24 Lewis, *The American Adam,* 196.

25 Ernesto G. Laura, review of *Invasion of the Body Snatchers,* in *Invasion of the Body Snatchers,* ed. Al LaValley (New Brunswick, N.J.: Rutgers University Press, 1989), 182.

26 *I Married a Monster from Outer Space,* dir. Gene Fowler, Jr., Paramount, 1958; *I Married a Communist,* dir. Robert Stevenson, RKO, 1949; *The Day the Earth Stood Still,* dir. Robert Wise, Twentieth Century-Fox, 1951. Lucanio mentions the double bill in *Them or Us,* 155.

27 For examples of this rhetoric, see Ross, *No Respect,* 45.

28 Rogin, *Ronald Reagan,* xiii, 3.

29 Richard Ginder, "Red Fascism Confronts Religious America," *Catholic World* 162 (1946): 491.

30 *Saboteur,* dir. Alfred Hitchcock, Universal, 1942.

31 Color reproductions of *Stone City, Arbor Day,* and other works to be discussed can be found in Wanda M. Corn, *Grant Wood: The Regionalist Vision* (New Haven: Yale University Press, 1983), 73, 81, 91, 92, 105, 128.

32 James M. Dennis, *Grant Wood: A Study in American Art and Culture* (New York: Viking, 1975), 168.

33 John Crowe Ransom, "Reconstructed but Unregenerate," in *I'll Take My Stand: The South and the Agrarian Tradition* (New York: Harper and Brothers, 1930), 19–20.

34 Grant Wood, "Revolt Against the City," in Dennis, *Grant Wood*, 234.

35 See, e.g., Kathleen Feeley, *Flannery O'Connor: Voice of the Peacock*, 2d ed. (New York: Fordham University Press, 1982), 112–39; and Carter Martin, "'The Meanest of Them Sparkled': Beauty and Landscape in Flannery O'Connor's Fiction," in *Realist of Distances*, ed. Westarp and Gretlund, 147–59.

36 Wood, "Revolt Against the City," 229.

37 Ibid., 233.

38 These works appear in Patricia Hills, *Social Concern and Urban Realism: American Painting of the 1930s* (Boston: Boston University Art Gallery, 1983), 21, 50, 58, 80, 84.

39 Ransom, "Reconstructed but Unregenerate," 20.

40 See Hills, *Social Concern and Urban Realism*, 32–3.

41 See Corn, *Grant Wood*, 80–2.

42 Peyton Boswell, "The Grant Wood Controversy," *Art Digest*, 1 Dec. 1942, 3. Boswell counted himself among Wood's admirers; he was referring to critics like Fritzi Weisenborn, who called Wood's oeuvre "a culmination of a trend of escapist and isolationist thought and action which was popular with some groups yesterday, but which is definitely obsolete today." See "Knocking Wood," *Art Digest*, 1 Dec. 1942, 12. For examples of paintings in which the regionalists addressed the subjects of fascism and war, see Cécile Whiting, *Antifascism in American Art* (New Haven: Yale University Press, 1989), 98–132.

43 Franklin D. Roosevelt, address, 10 June 1940, in U.S. Dept. of State, *Peace and War: United States Foreign Policy, 1931–1941* (Washington, D.C.: U.S. Government Printing Office, 1943), 546–7.

44 John Foster Dulles, "A Policy of Boldness," *Life*, 19 May 1952, 146, 152, 154.

45 Serge Guilbaut, *How New York Stole the Idea of Modern Art: Abstract Expressionism, Freedom, and the Cold War*, trans. Arthur Goldhammer (Chicago: University of Chicago Press, 1983), 142–3.

46 Quoted in Steven Naifeh and Gregory White Smith, *Jackson Pollock: An American Saga* (New York: Clarkson N. Potter, 1989), 473.

47 To the many viewers who have asked him about *Christina's World*, "wanting to know what she's doing," Wyeth has offered little additional information. "Actually," Wyeth once said, "there isn't any definite story." This statement accompanies a color reproduction of *Christina's World* in Wanda M. Corn, *The Art of Andrew Wyeth* (Greenwich, Conn.: New York Graphic Society, 1973), 38–9. A color reproduction of *Winter 1946* also appears in ibid., 59. *April Wind* appears, in black and white, in *Andrew Wyeth: Temperas, Water Colors and Drawings* (Buffalo, N.Y.: Albright-Knox Art Gallery, 1962), 29.

48 Such works fall under the heading of "suspended genre scenes," as defined by Vivien Green Fryd, an associate professor of art history at Vanderbilt University. Fryd used the phrase during a February 1990 lecture in her course on twentieth-century American art.

49 Color reproductions of these paintings appear in Gail Levin, *Edward Hopper: The Art and the Artist* (New York: Norton, 1980), 217, 259, 260, 296, 297.

50 The *Sounds in the Grass* series includes *The Blue Unconscious, The Dancers,*

Something of the Past, Croaking Movement, Eyes in the Heat, Earth Worms, and *Shimmering Substance.* Ellen H. Johnson notes that Pollock himself named the series and that he later named the two numbered paintings. See her *Modern Art and the Object: A Century of Changing Attitudes* (New York: Harper & Row, 1976), 114. Color reproductions of the works under discussion can be found in Ellen G. Landau, *Jackson Pollock* (New York: Abrams, 1989), 37, 38, 87, 97, 201–2, 204–5, 212.

51 The first quoted phrase appears in Elizabeth Frank, *Jackson Pollock* (New York: Abbeville, 1983), 110. The second appears in Landau, *Jackson Pollock,* 159.

52 Interview with Betty Parsons in "Who Was Jackson Pollock?" ed. Francine du Plessix and Cleve Gray, *Art in America* (May–June 1967): 55.

53 Paul Boyer, *By the Bomb's Early Light: American Thought and Culture at the Dawn of the Atomic Age* (New York: Pantheon, 1985), xviii, 275.

54 Quoted in Landau, *Jackson Pollock,* 254.

55 Quoted in Erika Doss, *Benton, Pollock, and the Politics of Modernism: From Regionalism to Abstract Expressionism* (Chicago: University of Chicago Press, 1991), 331.

56 Quoted in Boyer, *By the Bomb's Early Light,* 311.

57 Quoted in ibid., 323.

58 Quoted in Charles Grutzner, "City Folk's Fear of Bombs Aids Boom in Rural Realty," *New York Times,* 27 Aug. 1950, late ed., 42. John Cheever parodied this phenomenon in his short story "The Brigadier and the Golf Widow" (1961). The Flannagans have left New York because "Mr. Flannagan thought the country would be safer in case of war," but their shared obsession with security helps destroy their marriage; Mrs. Flannagan sleeps with a neighbor, Mr. Pastern, to get the key to his bomb shelter. See *The Brigadier and the Golf Widow* (New York: Harper & Row, 1964), 5.

59 Smith, *Virgin Land,* vii.

60 Marx, *The Machine in the Garden,* 6–7.

61 Smith, "The West," 33, 35.

62 Smith, *Virgin Land,* 259.

63 Smith, "The West," 33, 35, 40.

64 C. Vann Woodward, *The Burden of Southern History* (Baton Rouge: Louisiana State University Press, 1960), 172–3. See also Reinhold Niebuhr, *The Irony of American History* (New York: Scribner's, 1952).

65 Marx, *The Machine in the Garden,* 5.

66 Michael Harrington, *The Other America: Poverty in the United States* (New York: Macmillan, 1962), 1, 2, 3, 4, 39, 40.

67 Paul Goodman, *Like a Conquered Province: The Moral Ambiguity of America* (New York: Random House, 1967), 88, 89, 90, 96.

68 Leonard Maltin, ed., *TV Movies,* 1979–80 ed. (New York: New American Library, 1978), 418.

69 Tim Brooks and Earle Marsh, *The Complete Directory to Prime Time Network TV Shows, 1946–Present* (New York: Ballantine, 1979), 805–8.

70 *The Beverly Hillbillies,* prod. Paul Henning, CBS, 1962–71; *Green Acres,* dir. Richard L. Bare, prod. Paul Henning, CBS, 1965–71.

71 Royall Tyler, *The Contrast*, in *The Longman Anthology of American Drama*, ed. Lee A. Jacobus (New York: Longman, 1982), 7–32.
72 Goodman, *Like A Conquered Province*, 94.
73 David Marc discusses *Green Acres* as a "magicom," a situation comedy that "featured violations of the laws of nature as its main attractions." See *Comic Visions: Television Comedy and American Culture* (Boston: Unwin Hyman, 1989), 129–30, 141–3.
74 The desire for "farm living" motivated another urbanite portrayed by Eddie Albert on network television during the 1960s. In a story of alien invasion that aired as a 1964 episode of *The Outer Limits*, Albert plays a man who moves to the country with his wife (June Havoc), only to be trapped in a farmhouse by an extraterrestrial being. The man is taken over, temporarily, by the creature, whose home is "millions of light years" away. See "Cry of Silence," dir. Charles Haas, prod. Ben Brady, episode of *The Outer Limits*, prod. Leslie Stevens, ABC, 1964.
75 Rochelle Owens, *Futz*, in *Futz, and What Came After* (New York: Random House, 1968), 5, 15, 16.
76 Harrington, *The Other America*, 2.
77 As such, Dogpatch provides "a new place to test them atom bombs and guided missiles." According to one of Capp's characters, Senator Jack S. Phogbound (Ted Thurston), the federal government needs "some place we can blow off the face of the earth, some spot that ain't never gonna be missed." Here again, the rural setting becomes the site threatened by nuclear annihilation. Even in a musical satire that marginalizes rural Americans, the pastoral setting retains its imaginative power. Dogpatch, "where our ancestors took their bare hands and built all of this out of the wilderness," is the location for "events of national importance." Li'l Abner (Peter Palmer) goes so far as to call himself a representative man, "a one-hundred-percent red-blooded American," despite his eccentricities. See *Li'l Abner*, dir. Melvin Frank, Paramount, 1959.

The reviews of *Wise Blood* that mentioned the comic strip were "Southern Dissonance," *Time*, 9 June 1952, 110; and Sylvia Stallings, "Young Writer With a Bizarre Tale to Tell," in *Critical Essays*, ed. Friedman and Clark, 21.
78 Woodward, *The Burden of Southern History*, 13, 19–21.
79 Schaub also connects this passage from "The Regional Writer" with passages from *The Burden of Southern History*, in which Woodward "used the experience of the South as a source of directives for United States foreign policy." See *American Fiction*, 125–7.
80 Marc, *Comic Visions*, 80.
81 Owens, *Futz*, 5.

2. The Domesticated Intellectual

1 May, *Homeward Bound*, 16–18, 94, 167–8.
2 Ibid., 208.
3 Ross, *No Respect*, 50–2; Schaub, *American Fiction*, 59–62.
4 "Our Country and Our Culture," *Partisan Review* 19 (1952): 284, 287, 291, 318–19.

5 Guilbaut, *New York*, 4, 177.
6 Ross identifies Mailer and C. Wright Mills as the only symposium contributors who disagreed with the editorial assumptions (*No Respect*, 51).
7 "Our Country and Our Culture," 299.
8 Schaub drew this parallel between the authors in 1991 (*American Fiction*, 59). Thirty years earlier, Hassan noted a similar connection (*Radical Innocence*, 4).
9 "Wanted: An American Novel," *Life*, 12 Sept. 1955, 48.
10 Quoted in Frank A. Ninkovich, "The New Criticism and Cold War America," *Southern Quarterly* 20 (Fall 1981): 18.
11 Schaub, *American Fiction*, 51.
12 "Our Country and Our Culture," 586.
13 James Burkhart Gilbert, *Writers and Partisans: A History of Literary Radicalism in America* (New York: Wiley, 1968), 109, 118–19, 203–4, 251–2, 276–82.
14 See Josephine Hendin, *Vulnerable People: A View of American Fiction Since 1945* (New York: Oxford University Press, 1978), 146–55; Claire Kahane, "Flannery O'Connor's Rage of Vision," in *Critical Essays*, ed. Friedman and Clark, 128; Martha Stephens, *The Question of Flannery O'Connor* (Baton Rouge: Louisiana State University Press, 1973), 150–1; Westling, *Sacred Groves*, 172–4.
15 "Wanted: An American Novel," 48.
16 May, *Homeward Bound*, 3.
17 Fredric Wertham, *Seduction of the Innocent* (New York: Rinehart, 1954), 2, 121, 236, 248, 358, 359, 368.
18 Dwight Macdonald offered one definition of the "impossible alternatives" in his 1963 book, *Memoirs of a Revolutionist* (quoted in Guilbaut, *New York*, 106–7).
19 Guilbaut, *New York*, 36.
20 Marshall McLuhan, "The Southern Quality," in *A Southern Vanguard*, ed. Allen Tate (New York: Prentice-Hall, 1947), 100.
21 Quoted in Kenneth Watson, "The Myth of the 'American Way,'" *Christian Century* 80 (1963): 329.
22 Jackson Lears, "A Matter of Taste: Corporate Cultural Hegemony in a Mass-Consumption Society," in *Recasting America: Culture and Politics in the Age of Cold War*, ed. Lary May (Chicago: University of Chicago Press, 1989), 46.
23 Ibid., 47.
24 Beatrice P. Patt and Martin Nozick, eds., *The Generation of 1898 and After* (New York: Harper & Row, 1960), 182.
25 Ross, *No Respect*, 51.
26 Dwight Macdonald, "A Theory of 'Popular Culture,'" *Politics* 1 (1944): 20. Ross quotes this passage (*No Respect*, 52).
27 Lears, "A Matter of Taste," 46.
28 F. O. Matthiessen, "The Responsibilities of the Critic," in *The Responsibilities of the Critic*, ed. John Rackliffe (New York: Oxford University Press, 1952), 4, 6, 7.
29 William Esty, "In America, Intellectual Bomb Shelters," *Commonweal* 67 (1958): 586, 588.
30 William E. Cain, *F. O. Matthiessen and the Politics of Criticism* (Madison: University of Wisconsin Press, 1988), 106, 111, 112.

31 Cleanth Brooks, Jr., and Robert Penn Warren, eds., *Understanding Fiction* (New York: Appleton-Century-Crofts, 1943), x, xvii, 298, 605.

32 Philip French, *Westerns: Aspects of a Movie Genre* (London: Secker & Warburg, 1973), 35.

33 Whiting, *Antifascism in American Art*, 167–9.

34 "Our Country and Our Culture," 450.

35 Matthiessen, "The Responsibilities of the Critic," 5.

36 David Caute, *The Great Fear: The Anti-Communist Purge Under Truman and Eisenhower* (New York: Simon & Schuster, 1978), 403–30.

37 Matthiessen, "The Responsibilities of the Critic," 10.

38 Richard Hofstadter, *Anti-intellectualism in American Life* (New York: Knopf, 1963), 6.

39 Edward A. Shils, *The Torment of Secrecy: The Background and Consequences of American Security Policies* (Glencoe, Ill.: Free Press, 1956), 13, 14, 134.

40 Leslie A. Fiedler, *An End to Innocence: Essays on Culture and Politics* (Boston: Beacon, 1955), 14, 57.

41 Shils, *The Torment of Secrecy*, 120.

42 Ibid., 77, 78.

43 Ironically, the caption to the photograph that accompanied the wire story on Smedley noted a link between the intellectual "spy" and the pastoral setting. The caption referred to "Agnes Smedley, an American writer, described as a native of a Missouri farm." See MacKinnon and MacKinnon, *Agnes Smedley*.

44 The details of the controversy are provided by Sally Fitzgerald (*HB* 11–12) and Ian Hamilton, *Robert Lowell: A Biography* (New York: Random House, 1982), 143–5. Fitzgerald, unfortunately, perpetuates one of the rumors about Smedley that fueled the controversy. Smedley was not "a Communist Party member in good standing," as Fitzgerald describes her (*HB* 11). According to her biographers, "Smedley's independence from the American Communist Party was a matter of record" (MacKinnon and MacKinnon, *Agnes Smedley*, 302).

45 For a discussion of the moral questions raised by the act of informing, see Victor S. Navasky, *Naming Names* (New York: Viking, 1980), vii–xxiii, 1–69.

46 Quoted in Hamilton, *Robert Lowell*, 152.

47 Alfred Kazin, review of *The Complete Stories*, in *Critical Essays*, ed. Friedman and Clark, 60.

48 Hamilton, *Robert Lowell*, 146, 147, 148.

49 Navasky, *Naming Names*, 5.

50 Cain, *F. O. Matthiessen*, 112.

51 Caute, *The Great Fear*, 51–3; Guilbaut, *New York*, 190.

52 Joseph R. Starobin observes that Henry Wallace, the presidential candidate of the Progressive Party in 1948, "stood almost alone in American life" in his insistence that the U.S. Constitution protected the Communist Party of America (quoted in Cain, *F. O. Matthiessen*, 109).

53 Quoted in Caute, *The Great Fear*, 52.

54 "Our Country and Our Culture," 574.

55 Caute, *The Great Fear*, 406.

56 Fiedler, *An End to Innocence*, 204–5, 207.

57 "Our Country and Our Culture," 299.
58 Ibid., 574.

3. Jesus Fanatics and Communist Foreigners

1 "The American Way of Life," *Fortune*, Feb. 1951, 63, 64–5; Woodward, *The Burden of Southern History*, 184.
2 "The American Way of Life," 194; Watson, "The Myth of the 'American Way,'" 329.
3 Will Herberg, *Protestant – Catholic – Jew: An Essay in American Religious Sociology* (Garden City, N.Y.: Doubleday, 1955), 88, 90–91.
4 "Frustrated Preacher," review of *Wise Blood*, *Newsweek*, 19 May 1952, 115.
5 John H. Marion, "The Christian and Community Conflicts," in *Christians Are Citizens: The Role of the Responsible Christian Citizen in an Era of Crisis*, ed. Malcolm P. Calhoun (Richmond, Va.: John Knox, 1957), 91.
6 In a recent paper, Ragen noted that Hoover Shoats "reassures" his audience. Also, in passing, Ragen likened Shoats to Norman Vincent Peale. See "'And What's Dead Stays That Way': The Soteriology of the Church without Christ," paper delivered at the Modern Language Association Convention, Chicago, 28 Dec. 1990.
7 Norman Vincent Peale, *The Power of Positive Thinking* (New York: Prentice-Hall, 1952), vii, 1, 16.
8 Paul Hutchinson, "Have We a 'New' Religion?" *Life*, 11 Apr. 1955, 143.
9 A. Roy Eckardt, "The New Look in American Piety," *Christian Century* 71 (1954): 1395.
10 Quoted in ibid.
11 Herberg, *Protestant – Catholic – Jew*, 279–80, 284.
12 Quoted in Eckardt, "The New Look in American Piety," 1395.
13 Hutchinson, "Have We a 'New' Religion?" 157.
14 J. Ronald Oakley, *God's Country: America in the Fifties* (New York: Dembner Books, 1986), 321.
15 "President-Elect Says Soviet Demoted Zhukov Because of Their Friendship," *New York Times*, 23 Dec. 1952, late ed., 16.
16 Herberg, *Protestant – Catholic – Jew*, 278.
17 "Parnassus, Coast to Coast," *Time*, 11 June 1956, 66.
18 Charles M. Crowe, *In This Free Land* (New York: Abingdon, 1964), 100, 101, 102.
19 Eckardt, "The New Look in American Piety," 1396.
20 Ralph Lord Roy, *Communism and the Churches* (New York: Harcourt, Brace, 1960), 66, 442.
21 Quoted in William John McCutcheon, "Theology of the Methodist Episcopal Church During the Interwar Period (1919–1939)," Ph.D. diss. (Yale University, 1960), 258.
22 F. Ernest Johnson, "Protestant Social Policy: It's Not Un-American," *Nation* 177 (1953): 67. The Methodist Episcopal Church had merged with two other bodies in 1939 to form the United Methodist Church.

23 Richard H. Rovere, *The American Establishment and Other Reports, Opinions, and Speculations* (New York: Harcourt, Brace and World, 1962), 13.

24 Richard Wightman Fox, *Reinhold Niebuhr: A Biography* (New York: Pantheon, 1985), 121–2, 135, 241–3.

25 Reinhold Niebuhr, "Communism and the Clergy," *Christian Century* 70 (1953): 937.

26 Fox, *Reinhold Niebuhr*, 143, 207–9, 241, 242.

27 "Our Country and Our Culture," 302.

28 Niebuhr, "Communism and the Clergy," 936, 937.

29 Quoted in Harold E. Fey, "Bishop Oxnam's Challenge," *Christian Century* 70 (1953): 885.

30 Bruce Catton, "Witness for Decency: Bishop Oxnam Speaks His Mind," *Nation* 177 (1953): 86.

31 Niebuhr, "Communism and the Clergy," 936.

32 17 Mar. 1953, *Congressional Record*, 83rd Cong., 1st sess., 2024.

33 Malcolm Evans, "Protestants Under Fire: Indignant and Aroused," *Nation* 177 (1953): 108.

34 J. B. Matthews, "Reds and Our Churches," *American Mercury*, July 1953, 3, 5, 13.

35 The information included in this summary comes from the following sources: "'Alien to America,'" *Christian Century* 70 (1953): 838; Crowe, *In This Free Land*, 205; Fey, "Bishop Oxnam's Challenge," 887; "The Matthews Story," *Time*, 10 Aug. 1953, 67; "McCarthy, Matthews, and the Protestant Clergy," *Commonweal* 58 (1953): 383–4. The cartoon, originally published in the *St. Louis Post-Dispatch*, appears in Evans, "Protestants Under Fire," 109.

36 Quoted in "F.B.I. Inspector Defends Protestant Clergy," *Christian Century* 78 (1961): 414.

37 Crowe, *In This Free Land*, 18, 25.

38 Quoted in Fey, "Bishop Oxnam's Challenge," 886.

39 Crowe, *In This Free Land*, 169.

40 The information included in this summary comes from the following sources: Brooks and Marsh, *The Complete Directory*, 350; Caute, *The Great Fear*, 108–10; "McCarthy, Matthews, and the Protestant Clergy," 384; Francis Cardinal Spellman, "Communism Is *Un-American*," *American Magazine*, July 1946, 26.

41 Crowe, *In This Free Land*, 169.

42 Paul Blanshard, *Communism, Democracy, and Catholic Power* (Boston: Beacon, 1951), 3, 4.

43 Vincent F. Holden, "Church and State in America," *Catholic World* 166 (1947): 248.

44 John Cogley, "Catholics and American Democracy," *Commonweal* 58 (1953): 221.

45 Holden, "Church and State in America," 247.

46 Henry James, *The Ambassadors*, ed. S. P. Rosenbaum (New York: Norton, 1964), 38.

47 Cogley, "Catholics and American Democracy," 246.

48 "Is It Bigotry?" *Nation* 166 (1948): 89.

49 Paul Blanshard, "The Catholic Church and Democracy," *Nation* 166 (1948): 601. "A.P.A." stands for the American Protective Association, an anti-Catholic organization that flourished in the 1890s. See Peter J. Rahill, *The Catholic in America: From Colonial Times to the Present Day* (Chicago: Franciscan Herald Press, 1961), 126–31.

50 Robert Fitzgerald, "'My Own Pinch of Salt,'" *Nation* 167 (1948): 64.

51 Paul Blanshard, "Paul Blanshard Replies to Robert Fitzgerald," *Nation* 167 (1948): 110.

52 Blanshard, *Communism, Democracy, and Catholic Power*, 1, 4, 5, 43, 84, 105, 141, 243–4, 263, 285, 286, 287, 292, 296.

53 Charles Clayton Morrison, "Can Protestantism Win America?" *Christian Century* 63 (1946): 425, 458, 490, 586, 619.

54 "From Communist to Catholic," *Christian Century* 62 (1945): 1180.

55 Harold J. Laski, "America – 1947," *Nation* 165 (1947): 643.

56 George La Piana, "The Totalitarian System of Modern Catholicism: Protestantism and Tradition," *Shane Quarterly* 10 (1949): 63. The lecture series that began with this talk provided Blanshard with his "original inspiration" for *Communism, Democracy, and Catholic Power* (ix).

57 Crowe, *In This Free Land*, 169.

58 G. Bromley Oxnam, *I Protest* (New York: Harper, 1954), 5.

59 G. Bromley Oxnam, "Church, State, and Schools," *Nation* 168 (1949): 67.

60 Holden, "Church and State in America," 248.

61 Holden cited Cushing, "the vigorous and forthright Archbishop of Boston" ("Church and State in America," 248). Cogley cited Archbishop John T. McNicholas, chair of the administrative board of the National Catholic Welfare Conference ("Catholics and American Democracy," 224).

62 Spellman, "Communism Is *Un-American*," 26, 124.

63 Holden, "Church and State in America," 252.

64 James M. O'Neill, *Catholicism and American Freedom* (New York: Harper and Brothers, 1952), ix, 3, 17–29.

65 James M. Gillis, "The Catholic Editor Today," *Catholic World* 165 (1947): 350, 352.

66 Robert Fitzgerald, "The Countryside and the True Country," in *Flannery O'Connor*, ed. Harold Bloom (New York: Chelsea House, 1986), 25–6.

67 Leonard M. Olschner, "Annotations on History and Society in Flannery O'Connor's 'The Displaced Person,'" *Flannery O'Connor Bulletin* 16 (1987): 65, 66. Olschner quotes Bishop William T. Mulloy, who spoke for the National Catholic Rural Life Conference when he advocated resettlement "on the land" during congressional hearings in 1947, and U.S. Representative Ed Gossett (D-Texas), who spoke for the opposition that same year. When Gossett turned his attention to the clerical advocates of resettlement, he furnished a preview of the charges that J. B. Matthews would make in the 1953 *American Mercury* article: "Either wittingly or unwittingly," Gossett argued, the religious leaders had aligned themselves "with those who would do this country a great disservice." See "A New Fifth Column or the Refugee Racket," in House Committee on the

Judiciary, Subcommittee on Immigration and Naturalization, *Permitting Admission of 400,000 Displaced Persons into the United States,* 80th Cong., 1st sess., H.R. 2910 (Washington, D.C.: U.S. Government Printing Office, 1947), 408.

68 Blanshard, *Communism, Democracy, and Catholic Power,* 2, 298; idem, *American Freedom and Catholic Power* (Boston: Beacon, 1949), 53.

69 O'Neill, *Catholicism and American Freedom,* 115, 117.

70 Blanshard, *Communism, Democracy, and Catholic Power,* 4.

71 "The Theology of Saucers," *Time,* 18 Aug. 1952, 62. Non-Catholics, too, offered religious interpretations of the UFO phenomenon. Some considered UFOs the means of transport for God's messengers. A California evangelist, O. L. Jaggers, claimed in 1952 that saucers were flying over the United States "as a warning that the judgments of God are about to fall on this unrighteous nation." Several of those who wrote books or booklets on the phenomenon interpreted UFOs as harbingers of the Second Coming of Christ. William Ferguson speculated in 1955 that flying saucers were the spacecraft of "perfected beings" who were "preparing earth" for the divine event; when this event occurred, Kenneth Goff wrote, God would use the saucers to destroy the godless. See Lynn E. Catoe, *UFOs and Related Subjects: An Annotated Bibliography* (Detroit: Gale, 1978), 329, 330; and Richard Michael Rasmussen, *The UFO Literature: A Comprehensive Annotated Bibliography of Works in English* (Jefferson, N.C.: McFarland, 1985), 57, 77, 104–5, 122.

72 The scenario of the fortunate invasion is rare in science fiction films, but one of the first and best-known of the invasion movies, *The Day the Earth Stood Still,* presents the alien as a messenger of peace.

73 Groff Conklin, ed., *Invaders of Earth* (1952; reprint, New York: Pocket Books, 1955), 102.

74 Edgar Pangborn, "Angel's Egg," in *Invaders of Earth,* ed. Conklin, 198, 215.

75 Walter M. Miller, Jr., *A Canticle for Leibowitz* (Philadelphia: Lippincott, 1960), 66, 69; Ray Bradbury, "The Fire Balloons," in *The Illustrated Man* (Toronto: Bantam, 1967), 75–90.

76 C. G. Jung, *Flying Saucers: A Modern Myth of Things Seen in the Skies,* trans. R. F. C. Hull, in *Civilization in Transition,* vol. 10 of *The Collected Works of C. G. Jung* (New York: Bollingen Foundation, 1964), 309, 322, 328, 344, 414.

77 William Tenn, "'Will You Walk a Little Faster?'" in *Invaders of Earth,* ed. Conklin, 225.

78 "The Theology of Saucers," 62.

79 My phrasing here is indebted to Rogin's analysis of political demonology in the United States (*Ronald Reagan,* xiii).

80 Blanshard, *Communism, Democracy, and Catholic Power,* 5, 47.

4. The Segregated Pastoral

1 The information gathered by Olschner is crucial to an understanding of the social context in which O'Connor produced her story; but Olschner limits the scope of historical analysis by presenting the contextual details as "annotations," or "background material," and by treating history itself as "an analogy, in O'Connor's eschatological argument, for humankind's condition on earth." See his "Annotations on History and Society," 75, 76.

2 Lewis P. Simpson, *The Dispossessed Garden: Pastoral and History in Southern Literature* (Athens: University of Georgia Press, 1975), 2, 36, 39.

3 John Bartlow Martin, "The Deep South Says 'Never!'" *Saturday Evening Post,* 22 June 1957, 96.

4 Woodward, *The Burden of Southern History,* 10, 12.

5 Harry S. Ashmore, *An Epitaph for Dixie* (New York: Norton, 1958), 24, 25.

6 "Introduction: A Statement of Principles," in *I'll Take My Stand,* ix, x.

7 Frank Lawrence Owsley, "The Irrepressible Conflict," in *I'll Take My Stand,* 63.

8 Ransom, "Reconstructed but Unregenerate," 18, 23.

9 Robert B. Heilman, "The South Falls In," in *A Southern Vanguard,* ed. Tate, 126, 131.

10 John Gould Fletcher, "Education, Past and Present," in *I'll Take My Stand,* 96.

11 Harry S. Ashmore, "A Southern Challenge and Epitaph for Dixie," *Life,* 4 Nov. 1957, 129.

12 Quoted in Homer Bigart, "Faubus Compares His Stand to Lee's," *New York Times,* 5 Oct. 1957, late ed., 1.

13 Quoted in "Another Tragic Era?" *U.S. News and World Report,* 4 Oct. 1957, 37.

14 Quoted in ibid., 68.

15 Quoted in ibid., 61.

16 Quoted in ibid.

17 Quoted in ibid., 69.

18 Grady McWhiney, "Reconstruction: Index of Americanism," in *The Southerner as American,* ed. Charles Grier Sellers, Jr. (Chapel Hill: University of North Carolina Press, 1960), 92, 93–4; Sellers, "Introduction" and "The Travail of Slavery," in ibid., vi, ix, 42, 67.

19 Howard Zinn, *The Southern Mystique* (New York: Knopf, 1964), 217, 218, 219.

20 Tennant S. McWilliams, *The New South Faces the World: Foreign Affairs and the Southern Sense of Self, 1877–1950* (Baton Rouge: Louisiana State University Press, 1988), 139, 140.

21 John A. Salmond, "'The Great Southern Commie Hunt': Aubrey Williams, the Southern Conference Educational Fund, and the Internal Security Subcommittee," *South Atlantic Quarterly* 77 (1978): 437, 451, 452.

22 Quoted in Martin, "The Deep South Says 'Never!'" *Saturday Evening Post,* 15 June 1957, 23.

23 Ashmore, *An Epitaph for Dixie,* 167.

24 Martin, "The Deep South Says 'Never!'" *Saturday Evening Post,* 15 June 1957, 68.

25 Tom P. Brady, *Black Monday* (Winona, Miss.: Association of Citizens' Councils, 1955), 60–1, 67, 68.

26 Quoted in Martin, "The Deep South Says 'Never!'" *Saturday Evening Post,* 29 June 1957, 58.

27 Quoted in "Another Tragic Era?" 65.

28 Quoted in Martin, "The Deep South Says 'Never!'" *Saturday Evening Post,* 29 June 1957, 58.

29 Robert Penn Warren, "Divided South Searches Its Soul," *Life,* 9 July 1956, 112.

30 L. D. Reddick, "The Negro as Southerner and American," in *The Southerner as American,* ed. Sellers, 145.

31 Arthur M. Schlesinger, Jr., *The Vital Center: The Politics of Freedom* (Boston: Houghton Mifflin, 1949), ix.

32 Louis D. Rubin, Jr., "An Image of the South," in *The Lasting South: Fourteen Southerners Look at Their Home,* ed. Louis D. Rubin, Jr., and James Jackson Kilpatrick (Chicago: Henry Regnery, 1957), 6.

33 Richard M. Weaver, "The South and the American Union," in ibid., 65, 66, 67, 68.

34 "Our Country and Our Culture," 579.

35 "'This Rotted World,'" *Time,* 1 Sept. 1961, 52.

36 Brady, *Black Monday,* 68.

37 Rubin, "An Image of the South," 13–14.

38 Fletcher, "Education, Past and Present," 103, 111, 117, 118, 119, 120, 121.

39 "South Digs in Deeper Behind Its Race Laws," *U.S. News and World Report,* 7 Mar. 1958, 64–5. The term "massive resistance" covered a wide variety of state measures intended to circumvent the *Brown* decision. For detailed accounts of the movement, see Benjamin Muse, *Ten Years of Prelude: The Story of Integration Since the Supreme Court's 1954 Decision* (New York: Viking, 1964), 146–59, 178–200; and Francis M. Wilhoit, *The Politics of Massive Resistance* (New York: George Braziller, 1973), 135–200.

40 Reese Cleghorn, "The Old South Tries Again," *Saturday Review,* 16 May 1970, 76.

41 Muse, *Ten Years of Prelude,* 156–7.

42 Earl Warren, *Oliver Brown et al. v. Board of Education of Topeka,* in *The Public Papers of Chief Justice Earl Warren,* ed. Henry M. Christman, rev. ed. (New York: Capricorn, 1966), 140.

43 Arthur S. Miller, *Racial Discrimination and Private Education: A Legal Analysis* (Chapel Hill: University of North Carolina Press, 1957), 13, 72.

44 Oakley, *God's Country,* 352.

45 William Benton, a former member of the U.S. Senate (D-Connecticut), coined these phrases in early 1956 after his tour of Soviet schools. See "Now the 'Cold War' of the Classrooms," *New York Times Magazine,* 1 Apr. 1956, 15, 46. The second phrase, which Oakley quotes (*God's Country,* 347–8), gained wide currency after the Soviets launched *Sputnik.* Similar phrasing appears, for example, in *Senior Scholastic,* 6 Dec. 1957, 16–18, 26. High school students who read "The Cold War Comes to the Classroom" learned that their scientific education lagged behind the education their counterparts received in the Soviet Union.

46 Thomas D. Clark, "A Decade of Decision," in *We Dissent,* ed. Hoke Norris (New York: St. Martin's, 1962), 47.

47 Alice Walker, "Beyond the Peacock: The Reconstruction of Flannery O'Connor," in *Critical Essays,* ed. Friedman and Clark, 75.

48 Ashmore, *An Epitaph for Dixie,* 19–20.

49 Although she acknowledges the way in which Southern tradition sanctioned certain forms of interracial companionship, Janet Egleson Dunleavy sees "a different, Darwinian set of values" operating in the story. Consequently, she exaggerates the difference between Tanner and his previous incarnation, Old Dudley, in "The Geranium" (1946), the first published version of "Judgement Day." Unlike Old Dudley, she argues, Tanner has abandoned "the code of manners of the Old South." See "A Particular History: Black and White in Flannery O'Connor's Short Fiction," in *Critical Essays,* ed. Friedman and Clark, 191, 192.

50 Eudora Welty, Preface to *The Collected Stories of Eudora Welty* (New York: Harcourt, Brace, Jovanovich, 1980), xi.

51 Walker, "Beyond the Peacock," 75.

52 Crews, "The Power of Flannery O'Connor," 53.

53 Quoted in Reed Sarratt, *The Ordeal of Desegregation: The First Decade* (New York: Harper & Row, 1966), 273.

54 Muse, *Ten Years of Prelude,* 161.

55 Quoted in Sarratt, *The Ordeal of Desegregation,* 267.

56 Ashmore, *An Epitaph for Dixie,* 156, 159.

57 Quoted in Arthur F. Kinney, *Flannery O'Connor's Library: Resources of Being* (Athens: University of Georgia Press, 1985), 145.

58 Ashmore, *An Epitaph for Dixie,* 167.

59 Ibid., 158.

60 Dunleavy provides additional evidence for the idea that "Rayber's liberal position is a pose rather than a conviction." See "A Particular History," 195–6.

61 Crews, "The Power of Flannery O'Connor," 53.

5. The Invisible Country

1 For a discussion of this intellectual trend, see Lears, "A Matter of Taste," 38–48.

2 William H. Whyte, Jr., *The Organization Man* (New York: Simon & Schuster, 1956), 13.

3 Lears, "A Matter of Taste," 44.

4 Whyte, *The Organization Man,* 383, 392.

5 David Riesman, *The Lonely Crowd: A Study of the Changing American Character* (New Haven: Yale University Press, 1950), vii, 60.

6 Lears, "A Matter of Taste," 38, 47.

7 "Our Country and Our Culture," 285, 286, 287, 445.

8 McLuhan, *The Mechanical Bride,* v, 55.

9 Critics of the novel have sometimes oversimplified the question of motivation by arguing that the characters act instinctively. One of the first reviews made this assessment of Enoch and the other characters: "They live, like animals, according

to some anonymous law of the blood." See John W. Simons, "A Case of Possession," *Commonweal* 56 (1952): 298.
10 McLuhan, *The Mechanical Bride*, 48, 58.
11 William Rodney Allen, "The Cage of Matter: The World as Zoo in Flannery
O'Connor's *Wise Blood*," *American Literature* 58 (1986): 259–60, 268; Stuart L.
Burns, "The Evolution of *Wise Blood*," *Modern Fiction Studies* 16 (1970): 160–1.
12 C. Wright Mills, *White Collar: The American Middle Classes* (New York:
Oxford University Press, 1951), 182, 184.
13 Ragen develops this argument at length (*A Wreck on the Road to Damascus*,
107–95). The Hudson Motor Car Company manufactured the Essex line from
1919 to 1932. One advertisement for the Essex at the height of its popularity
promised the "FAST GET-AWAY" that Hazel values so much. See "Essex the Chal-
lenger," *Saturday Evening Post*, 29 Dec. 1928, 36–7; and G. N. Georgano, ed.,
The New Encyclopedia of Motorcars, 1885 to the Present, 3d ed. (New York: Dutton,
1982), 232.
14 Vance Packard, *The Hidden Persuaders* (New York: McKay, 1957), 49, 52–3.
15 Mills, *White Collar*, 161.
16 Whyte, *The Organization Man*, 7.
17 "Our Country and Our Culture," 284, 285.
18 Mills, *White Collar*, 165–6.
19 McLuhan, *The Mechanical Bride*, 58.
20 May, *Homeward Bound*, 18.
21 Lears, "A Matter of Taste," 45–6.
22 McLuhan, *The Mechanical Bride*, 144.
23 Woodward, *The Burden of Southern History*, 6.
24 McLuhan, *The Mechanical Bride*, 58, 59.
25 Television struck many other writers as a sign, or even an instrument, of
national cultural homogenization. In 1958, Jack Kerouac vilified the suburban
home life that featured "television sets in each living room with everybody
looking at the same thing and thinking the same thing at the same time." See *The
Dharma Bums* (New York: Penguin, 1976), 39. Louis Rubin criticized "the enforced conformity of modern industrial life, which measures its days by factory
whistles and its nights by television channel changes." Television antennae, like
"almost identical ranch homes in almost identical housing projects," signified the
loss of regional identity for Rubin. See "An Image of the South," 13, 14.
26 Quoted in Joel Wells, "Off the Cuff," in *Conversations with Flannery O'Connor*, ed. Magee, 90.
27 Quoted in Cyrus Hoy and Walter Sullivan, eds., "An Interview with Flannery O'Connor and Robert Penn Warren," in *Conversations with Flannery O'Connor*, ed. Magee, 30.
28 "The Sun Never Sets on Cacoola," *Time*, 15 May 1950, 28, 29, 32.
29 McLuhan, *The Mechanical Bride*, 144.
30 Paul Blanshard, "The Catholic Church and Education," *Nation* 165 (1947):
525.
31 Blanshard, "The Catholic Church and Democracy," 631.
32 Oxnam, "Church, State, and Schools," 68.

33 "Now Will Protestants Awake?" *Christian Century* 64 (1947): 262.
34 Wilfrid Sheed, "Don't Junk the Parochial Schools," *Saturday Evening Post*, 13 June 1964, 6.
35 Marion, "The Christian and Community Conflicts," 92.
36 Lears, "A Matter of Taste," 48, 50. Lears adopts the concept of "cultural hegemony" from the writings of Antonio Gramsci, the Italian Marxist.
37 Lears, "A Matter of Taste," 49–50.

Epilogue

1 Patrick Cruttwell, "Fiction Chronicle," *Hudson Review* 18 (1965): 444.
2 Robert Martin Adams, "Fiction Chronicle," *Hudson Review* 8 (1956): 630; John W. Aldridge, *In Search of Heresy: American Literature in an Age of Conformity* (New York: McGraw Hill, 1956; Port Washington, N.Y.: Kennikat, 1967), 59.
3 This shift is evident in *Flannery O'Connor and Caroline Gordon: A Reference Guide*, comp. Robert E. Golden and Mary C. Sullivan (Boston: G. K. Hall, 1977), 17–87.
4 Robert Kiely, "The Art of Collision," review of *Everything That Rises Must Converge, Christian Science Monitor*, 17 June 1965, Eastern ed., 7. As a recent anthology illustrates, the link between prophetic characters and "Flannery O'Connor the prophetic poet" has continued to guide interpretations of O'Connor. In their preface to *Realist of Distances* (1987), Westarp and Gretlund explained, "The title of this collection reflects her own definition of a prophet."
5 Joseph Waldmeir, "Quest Without Faith," *Nation* 193 (1961): 396.
6 Robert Drake, "The Harrowing Evangel of Flannery O'Connor," *Christian Century* 81 (1964): 1200.
7 Webster Schott, "Flannery O'Connor: Faith's Stepchild," *Nation* 201 (1965): 146.
8 The most significant, of course, was the voice that the African-American clergy lent to the civil rights movement. The essay known as "Letter from Birmingham Jail" (1963) best illustrates the split between black religious activists like Martin Luther King, Jr., and white ministers who accepted the racial status quo. King rejected the argument, advanced by eight white clergymen from Alabama, that nonviolent resistance should be condemned because it precipitated violence. "Isn't this like condemning Jesus," King asked, "because His unique God-consciousness and never-ceasing devotion to His will precipitated the evil act of crucifixion?" See "The Negro Is Your Brother," *Atlantic*, Aug. 1963, 81.
9 Quoted in James Terence Fisher, *The Catholic Counterculture in America, 1933–1962* (Chapel Hill: University of North Carolina Press, 1989), 237.
10 His first and only novel, *The Foundling* (1951), became a best-seller. Spellman, who also published poetry, donated the royalties to a fund for orphans. See Robert I. Gannon, *The Cardinal Spellman Story* (Garden City, N.Y.: Doubleday, 1962), 260–2.
11 For an excellent overview of the "Catholic counterculture" from the early 1930s to the early 1960s, see Fisher, *The Catholic Counterculture in America*.
12 The information included in this summary comes from the following

sources: Richard Curtis, *The Berrigan Brothers: The Story of Daniel and Philip Berrigan* (New York: Hawthorn Books, 1974), 49, 67–8, 107; Edward Duff, "The Burden of the Berrigans," in *The Berrigans*, ed. William Van Etten Casey and Philip Nobile (New York: Praeger, 1971), 14–15; *Contemporary Authors*, new revision ser. (1984), vol. 11, s.v. "Berrigan, Daniel."

13 Daniel Berrigan, *America Is Hard to Find* (Garden City, N.Y.: Doubleday, 1972), 55, 87–8.

14 Robert McAfee Brown, "The Berrigans: Signs or Models?" in *The Berrigans*, ed. Casey and Nobile, 62.

15 Berrigan, *America Is Hard to Find*, 15, 16, 55, 56.

16 See Brown, "The Berrigans: Signs or Models?" 70; Sidney Cornelia Callahan, "Thank You, Dan. Thank You, Phil," in *Witness of the Berrigans*, ed. Stephen Halpert and Tom Murray (Garden City, N.Y.: Doubleday, 1972), 156; Richard J. Clifford, "The Berrigans: Prophetic?" in *The Berrigans*, ed. Casey and Nobile, 36; David J. O'Brien, "The Berrigans and America," in ibid., 73.

17 Berrigan, *America Is Hard to Find*, 35, 52, 84, 85, 97.

18 Callahan, "Thank You, Dan," 155.

Index

Italic numerals indicate pages on which illustrations appear.

CAMBRIDGE STUDIES IN AMERICAN LITERATURE AND CULTURE

Continued from the front of the book

Printed in the United States
28811LVS00005B/205-207